TRANSCENDENTAL MEDITATION IN AMERICA

IOWA AND THE MIDWEST EXPERIENCE

SERIES EDITOR
William B. Friedricks,
Iowa History Center at Simpson College

The University of Iowa Press gratefully acknowledges Humanities Iowa for its generous support of the Iowa and the Midwest Experience series.

JOSEPH WEBER

Transcendental Meditation in America

How a New Age Movement Remade a Small Town in Iowa

UNIVERSITY OF IOWA PRESS, IOWA CITY

University of Iowa Press, Iowa City 52242
Copyright © 2014 by the
University of Iowa Press
www.uiowapress.org
Printed in the United States of America

Design by Teresa W. Wingfield

The University of Iowa Press is a member of
Green Press Initiative and is committed to
preserving natural resources.

Printed on acid-free paper

ISBN: 978-1-60938-235-3, 1-60938-235-8 (pbk)
ISBN: 978-1-60938-261-2, 1-60938-261-7 (ebk)
LCCN: 2013952706

○　　○　　○

For Donna

who keeps our feet on the ground

CONTENTS

○   ○   ○

Introduction

Who Cares about Fairfield, Anyway?

Remember what people used to say about meditation? Now everyone is doing it.   —SHIRLEY MACLAINE

A LITTLE MORE THAN fifty years ago, a bearded mystic, fond of flowers
and flowing robes, arrived in the United States from India. The giggling guru,
as Maharishi Mahesh Yogi came to be known, soon put a distinctive stamp
on American culture. The country he found was a place of hard-charging
ambition, churchgoing conformity, and extraordinary material success—
the kind of success that emigrants from India had long admired. At first,
many scorned the meditation he espoused as a technique for coping with
stress and for plugging into spiritual realms beyond the workaday world. It
seemed exotic, foreign, and ill-suited to American sensibilities. But the gen-
tle, squeaky-voiced Easterner persisted, and soon rebellious Baby Boomers
—looking for alternatives to the values and ways of life of their parents—
took up his cause. Inspired by celebrity adherents as disparate as the Beatles,
Clint Eastwood, Shirley MacLaine, and Merv Griffin, they lifted his message
and his main product—meditation—into the mainstream.[1]

Since then, the change in attitudes toward meditation has been profound. Nowadays, doctors suggest meditation to patients struggling with ailments ranging from high blood pressure to anxiety. Gyms offer it along with
weightlifting and aerobics. It's even available in the air, via headset on Virgin Atlantic. And supporters urge it on students in violence-plagued urban

schools, along with suggesting it for war veterans, survivors of domestic violence, and others struggling with stressful lives. Even some churches and synagogues encourage members to meditate. And Americans, used to shopping for spirituality just as they choose among toothpastes, today have many choices beyond the practice Maharishi suggested—his mantra-based Transcendental Meditation (TM). The National Center for Complementary and Alternative Medicine, a part of the National Institutes of Health, lists mantra meditation, relaxation response, mindfulness meditation, and Zen Buddhist meditation among the many types on offer. Citing recent studies, it reports that more than 20 million Americans take time out for varied forms of the practice.[2]

To be sure, the little man from central India was not the only advocate of meditation in the United States. Several previous seers and practitioners had brought their own brands of the practice into the country, going back to the late 1800s, and the influence of some still lingers. We can thank some of them for yoga, similarly once mocked and now as commonplace as jogging. Long before that, moreover, some Americans were intimately familiar with meditation and the teachings of Indian visionaries. Early enthusiasts for Indian religious literature include some of the original American Transcendentalists of the mid-nineteenth century, such as Ralph Waldo Emerson and Henry David Thoreau. In *Walden,* Thoreau celebrated the Bhagavad Gita, a core text of Hinduism, for its "stupendous and cosmogonal philosophy . . . in comparison with which our modern world and its literature seem puny and trivial."

But Maharishi was certainly one of meditation's most tireless modern promoters. Like no other guru of his day, he could wow TV talk-show hosts and catch the eye of trend-minded newsmagazine editors alike, garnering extraordinary attention. His message resonated with young Americans hungry for something beyond what they heard in their schools, religious institutions, and homes. When his TM Movement took wing in the late 1960s and early 1970s, these Baby Boomers were weary of war and many were alienated from mainstream institutions. His recipe for spirituality, self-development, and missionary-style outreach couldn't have found a more receptive audience. Soon, there was scarcely a major college campus that didn't sport posters for TM or a sizable city that didn't boast of one or more TM centers. If success is what happens when a compelling product, savvy marketing, and good timing meet, the guru and his TM Movement provide a case study in all three.

With those glory days past, however, the towering question for the movement now is whether it can go on. The guru died in 2008, leaving behind an organization that still boasts a healthy stock of money and property; an accredited university that grants degrees ranging up to and including doctorates; and supporters including respected psychiatrists, a successful radio talk-show host, movie stars and musicians, prominent news anchors on CNN and ABC, and business leaders. More than a million Americans once embraced his meditation technique and some still practice it. With such backing and a rich and colorful history, can the technique and the movement that promotes it outlive the charismatic founder? Or is TM likely to trace the arc so many other American movements—religious and otherwise—have followed, moving from ridiculed obscurity to mainstream prominence before fading into distant memory, a shooting star in the cultural firmament? Moreover, should anyone care if the TM Movement slips away to become a footnote in American history, perhaps not even as well regarded as the Shakers, Amana Colonies, Oneida Community, and other early alternative cultural icons?

In search of the answer, I traveled many times over several years to Fairfield, Iowa, the current U.S. home of the TM Movement. There, I met people who cling to Maharishi's dream that millions around the world will take up meditation. Some hold to the peculiar idea—a product of what we might call the movement's baroque period—that regular practice will usher in unprecedented peace around the world. If only enough people meditate daily—a fraction of the population of each country will do—they will generate vibes that will reduce crime and violence worldwide, these stalwarts believe. Some of these folks run the Maharishi University of Management, a school they created out of the ruins of a bankrupt Presbyterian college in town. Some donate generously to the place.

I also met people who have created a town just outside Fairfield where TM enthusiasts build and sell specially designed homes and run a luxury spa for meditators, offering an array of health-promoting goods that the movement sells. I talked with remarkably successful entrepreneurs who credit their millions to their twice-daily practice of meditation, saying it gives them the focus and energy they need to build their businesses. I met with shop owners who pitch the wares of the movement along with herbal teas, medical treatments, and other goodies that hail from a world seemingly far outside an Iowa farm town. Suited to California, maybe, but Iowa?

On the other hand, I also talked with critics. Some former insiders thundered that the promises of world peace and personal enlightenment proved hollow. Some were turned off by the movement's transformation from an idealistic volunteer-driven effort to teach simple meditation into a global business enterprise with a range of products and services from education and health supplements to architecture. Today's TM Movement even includes a legal arm that prosecutes other proponents of meditation if they threaten movement trademarks.

Some longtime meditators, too, have been turned into pariahs by movement enforcers worried that their visits to other gurus would sully the movement, spiritually polluting it. Some former loyalists have aired complaints about TM publicly in newspapers. One taught in the highest reaches of the university and quit after finding he couldn't make the Eastern-based teachings of the late guru jibe with his religious leanings.

My search for an answer to whether the TM Movement will survive raised a host of questions. Is TM a religion or does its use of explicit religious language merely reflect a linguistic problem, the difficulty of describing the elevated spiritual state of meditation in down-to-earth terms? Setting aside the religion question, is TM-style meditation still a useful tool to help hard-pressed schoolchildren succeed in America's scandalously bad inner-city schools? Can TM be stripped of the tradition and dogma behind it, rather like our culture does with the religious elements behind Halloween and Valentine's Day? Or should it be banned in schools because of its roots in the spiritual ruminations of a foreign culture?

More broadly, does such meditation offer a solution for the anxieties of our age—something that can help Americans cope with the specter of terrorism as they once dealt with the threat of nuclear war? Beyond that, is there more to TM than just a meditation technique? Does it provide a philosophy or way of life? In fact, should the guru's extensive teachings based on ancient Indian texts be promoted far beyond the walls of the university and primary and high schools in the Fairfield community?

Plenty of other questions popped up, too. Are the couple of thousand loyalists who flocked to Fairfield from Chicago, New York, Los Angeles, and elsewhere little more than cultists now, graying idealistic relics cast adrift by the death of their leader? Some non-meditating locals in Fairfield still deride them as "roos," a pejorative abbreviation for guru suggesting they are mindless followers who still don't fit in southeast Iowa some forty years after they arrived. Even as members have made headway politically, taking seats on the town council and sometimes winning higher office, some churches in Fairfield won't welcome meditators as members. TMers insist that there is no conflict between their practices and beliefs and those of various religions; in Fairfield, meditators are active in the houses of worship of Protestants, Catholics, Mormons, Jews, Sufis, and others. But what does the TM Movement's experience say about the limits of tolerance in modern America? Is Fairfield proof that the country has become a bigger tent than ever or is it still resolutely sectarian?

The TM Movement and the Fairfielders associated with it prompted still more questions beyond the group itself. The Baby Boomers who drove the movement put a huge Frye bootprint on the American cultural landscape. As they slip into their dotage, will they leave behind a practice and body of knowledge that can change history, as some loyalists insist (with just a hint, maybe, of the generation's inflated sense of self-worth and its missionary zeal)? Or does the movement die with them?

Indeed, should the Boomers gracefully step aside and let their children blaze their own paths, trails that some second-generation meditators in the Fairfield community say don't include slavish devotion to a dead leader? As their imprint fades, is it time for the Boomers to hang it up, as they might say? Nothing may sting the Boomers in the TM Movement more than irrelevance, should that be their fate. This, after all, was the generation that ended an unpopular war, that gave the world such idealistic efforts as the Peace Corps, that promoted free love for all. Can these folks go quietly into the night? Should they?

For me, like many other Boomers, the TM Movement has long been a curiosity. Like Scientology, the Hare Krishna movement, the Lubavitchers, and fundamentalist Christian groups, it seemed to promise new tools and techniques for spiritual growth and ways to meet the challenges of modern life. Beyond just a drug-free high, it offered the promise of seeing the world in a new and fresh way, even of enlightenment, as Maharishi called it. For some who sampled TM, the appeal proved enduring. For many others, it was a passing fancy.

I, for one, have long been intrigued with countercultural movements and with meditation. But I never joined a commune or an intentional community, the term du jour for like-minded folks who throw in their lot together. Nor did I take up TM and, to preserve my impartiality, did not do so while researching this book. Some movement loyalists look on my independence as a credibility-killing shortcoming—one cannot know the impressive power and ease of the meditative technique without learning it, they say. But I was determined to avoid being labeled a propagandist for or against the movement, instead choosing to report on it fairly, if at times critically, as an outsider. For a fair account of the Shakers, would one look to a follower of Mother Ann Lee or to a disinterested historian?

Finally, the fate of the TM Movement is of special interest in Iowa and the Midwest. Other groups of visionaries have made their marks there; some linger and many are gone. Not far from Fairfield, for instance, tourists visit the Amana Colonies, settlements founded in the mid-1800s by a religious group from Germany that called itself the Community of True Inspiration. Members believed in the gift of prophecy and the influence of the Holy Spirit, terms that to some may echo the ethereal language of TM advocates. The Amana community endured for decades, and its name lives on in the Amana brand name, a moniker affixed to a line of appliances the community churned out to support itself. But the community has dwindled to a few hundred elderly adherents now.[3]

Will this be the fate of the TM community in Fairfield? Will the meditators leave behind dozens of specially designed homes, hotels, and campus buildings, perhaps turning some into museum exhibits? Will the grandchildren of today's Fairfielders lead tours and show videos explaining the group's practices? Or will the community find a way to spread its idiosyncratic philosophy of peace and self-development for decades to come?

Come with me through these pages as we explore these questions and others. Meet some of the good-hearted souls who built this exceptional community, as well as some who are estranged from it. Along the way, you'll come across a few scoundrels, too, just to prove that even the cosmically minded are all too human. You'll meet ordinary people whose tastes for material comforts and whose hopes for their children fit them squarely into the mainstream in the American middle class. You'll meet some whose beliefs fall well outside the norm. Some meditators work fervently to make sure the guru's legacy will endure. Others don't care quite so much anymore. All told, however, they provide a fascinating glimpse into a distinctly American phenomenon, something that is both peculiar to a fractious and tumultuous time and yet also part of the country's long history of yearning for community and for a link to something beyond the ordinary. I hope you enjoy these folks as much as I did.

Classic Americana, with a Twist

AT FIRST BLUSH, the town square in Fairfield, Iowa, seems no different from hundreds like it that grace small communities from New England to California with a pretty gazebo where bands play, a stretch of grass ideal for sunbathing, a monument to historic local events. And all of it surrounded by businesses that offer clothes, medicine, food, and, perhaps, a drink or two. Such town centers are so classically American that Disney and Hollywood have turned them into clichés, timeworn settings for amusement parks, Fourth of July celebrations, political speeches, and romance.[1]

But a closer look at the heart of Fairfield shows how far this place is from ordinary. Hard by a couple of real estate sales offices and kitchenware shops is the Health and Wholeness shop, a retailer of herbal teas, aromatherapy products, and "total health solutions" said to be inspired by ancient Eastern teachings. Nearby, Thymely Solutions offers extracts, homeopathic remedies, and "heaven in a bottle" in planetary gem elixirs that offer "infusions of solar and lunar light with 'blueprints' of rare and superior quality gems." Two vegetarian places serve up savory Indian food on other corners of the square. Across the way you can "feed your head"—to borrow a cherished Baby Boomer phrase—at Revelations, a used books shop and eatery that stocks well-thumbed copies of a dazzling array of spiritual texts along with mysteries, sci-fi, and other fare.

Walk into Café Paradiso, an espresso bar and coffee shop that doubles as a small concert hall for the indie likes of The Roches and Wendy Waldman, and you are apt to overhear conversations a far cry from any found in most of Iowa. Talk of auras, mind-body connections, crystals, and novel health-restoration approaches may ring out, along with less ethereal conversations about music and undergraduate and graduate-student life. A visitor may hear lively chatter about visiting mystics or speakers in town promoting programs such as Brennan Healing Science, something "based on the living dynamics of our Human Energy-Consciousness System and its relationship to the greater world of which we all are intimately a part."[2]

A good number of Fairfield's residents—up to a quarter of the ninety-five hundred or so here, by some estimates—regularly train their minds on realms far beyond this pleasant farm town, which dates back to 1839. Devotees of the late Maharishi Mahesh Yogi and his TM Movement, they gather by the hundreds—more than a thousand at a time on some days—to meditate together twice a day in two sprawling golden-domed buildings at the Maharishi University of Management (MUM), a college a short hop from the town square. Some residents, preferring to "transcend" privately, do so in posh newer homes scattered around town that comply with the guru's architectural principles—with east-facing entrances said to foster enlightenment, affluence, and fulfillment, not the fear, destruction, and quarreling supposedly bred by south-facing entrances. Some such homes carry price tags well above $500,000, far above the reach of most longtime locals. Some can be found in Maharishi Vedic City, a new town created by devotees just outside of Fairfield that is home to the Global Country of World Peace and other TM Movement affiliates. Hundreds more meditators, brought in from India expressly for the purpose, meet to meditate and chant in Maharishi Vedic City each day, for hours at a stretch.[3]

This southeastern corner of Iowa is the unlikely home of TM in the United States. From here the movement that burst onto the global scene when the Beatles took to the giggling guru in the late 1960s has touched several million people worldwide. For many, the touch has been a glancing one, a few sessions that cost as little as a few dollars or more than $2,500, depending on when one signed on. For their investment, the curious learned a simple relaxation-based technique, got a mantra, and were urged to meditate twice a day for twenty minutes at a time. Many fell away when promises of better mental and physical health and expectations of material success bore little fruit, or they moved on to more or less pedestrian pursuits. But for a few thousand people—a constantly shifting group of passionate followers—the exhilaration of meditation and the sense of belonging to a group that promised to usher in world peace meant a far deeper commitment. It meant advanced studies in Europe or India, the pursuit of Yogic Flying—a belief in meditation-induced levitation—or missions to meditate in dangerous places around the world. For some, it meant a move to Fairfield.

Fairfield became a magnet for meditators beginning in 1974, a time when the stars aligned just right for the TM Movement. Flush with contributions, the movement bought the campus of bankrupt Parsons College that year and made it the home of its American university. The lure of Iowa grew for meditators in 1979, when the guru issued a call for them to move to that state so they could gather together daily in the belief that their group practice would spread peace across the United States. The movement built great golden domes on the MUM campus to accommodate the group meditation sessions, one for men and, later, one for women.

While some of the faithful just passed through, as students at MUM or visitors who came for periodic gatherings, others stayed. They built families and careers—in some cases, creating major businesses that employed many non-meditators from Fairfield and beyond. The adherents anchored their lives around TM, studying the Vedic knowledge that their guru espoused and taking advanced training in meditation.

Those who remain today are a diverse lot. Among them are people such as Laura Bordow, who abandoned the affluent suburbs of Chicago's North Shore in 1983 to give her newborn son a less materialistic place—a spiritual place—to grow up. There's Richard Beall, an Ohio farm boy who aspired to a life as a professional baseball player and ended up teaching TM in Ohio, California, and even Bulgaria. Bordow and Beall both took leading roles in the TM community's school. Then there's Eric Schwartz, who was smitten with the TM Movement while in college and ultimately changed schools—moving from tony Amherst College to the less prestigious University of Massachusetts—so he could pursue meditation. With no business training, he built a business that now employs hundreds. Their ranks include Pamela K. Slowick, who found more meaning in TM than in her academic pursuits and so quit Hampshire College to join the movement, a step that led her over time to run for Congress from Arizona for a movement-related political party and to open a homeopathy shop in Fairfield. (More about these folks later.) The group also includes co-authors of the Chicken Soup for the Soul series of inspirational books, about a dozen of whom live or have lived in the Fairfield area.[4]

Now, however, these Baby Boomers and others like them who flooded into Fairfield from Chicago, New York, Los Angeles, and points overseas are graying. Their movement is at a turning point, its fate uncertain. Their guru died in early 2008, leaving behind no successor with anywhere near his charisma. The leaders he installed run a pocket-sized university and a still smaller school for students in preschool to grade 12 in Fairfield, as well as overseeing properties here and in several other spots around the world.

These days, an air of uncertainty afflicts the movement. Supporters, including some serving at high levels in movement institutions, wonder privately about whether their leaders are making the right choices, whether they are adapting to times far different from when they joined as idealistic twentysomethings. Is their movement destined to remain passé, a throwback to the days of bell-bottom jeans and tie-dyed shirts? Or can it adapt and find ways to spread the wisdom and practices that the guru's followers say are timeless?

Maharishi first drew notice from many Americans in the late 1960s, when the Beatles and other pop icons embraced him. Cover stories appeared in such diverse places as *Look* and *MAD* magazines, reflecting the mixed reception he got in the United States—an odd blend of curiosity and derision. Later, in 1975, the guru reached tens of millions—with resulting surges in recruits—when he appeared on the *Merv Griffin Show* and on the cover of *Time* magazine.

But nowadays, the movement garners comparatively few mentions beyond those by Oprah Winfrey, Dr. Mehmet Oz, ABC newsman George Stephanopoulos, a couple CNN journalists, and other enthusiasts who serve smaller audiences in today's fragmented media scene. Even academics who keep track of intentional communities and movements say they rarely hear much about TM anymore.

To be sure, TM still commands attention from a coterie of celebrities, many of them Boomers who came of age with the movement. Paul McCartney, Ringo Starr, and Donovan joined forces, for instance, for a benefit concert in New York in 2009 to raise funds for the David Lynch Foundation for Consciousness-Based Education and World Peace. Lynch, a distinguished filmmaker (*Eraserhead* [1977], *The Elephant Man* [1980], *Mulholland Drive* [2001]) is a devotee who presses for meditation to be taught in schools, and his passion for TM garners ink regularly in such prominent places as the *New York Times*. TM leaders muster praise from such disparate practitioners as comedian Jerry Seinfeld, CNN journalist Candy Crowley and former CNN anchor Soledad O'Brien and ABC's Stephanopoulos, TV talk-show host Ellen DeGeneres, and shock-jock Howard Stern. Wealthy figures such as billionaire hedge fund operator Ray Dalio, founder of the $140 billion Bridgewater Associates, offer encouragement and support. Another supporter, Winfrey, meditated for her Oprah Winfrey Network cable-TV audience in early 2012 in a long, admiring program called "America's Most Unusual Town."[5] Some of the famous stop by Fairfield at times.

But the worry for insiders is whether the movement is on a flight path all too familiar to historians who've studied the lifecycles of intentional communities and religious or cultural movements. Few survive for more than a few years past the retirements, deaths, or disenchantments of their leaders or large number of followers. The Unitarians and free-thinkers who created American Transcendentalism, including such intellectuals as Ralph Waldo Emerson and Walt Whitman, failed to make a go of Brook Farm and the Fruitlands communities in Massachusetts in the early 1800s. A bit later, the Oneida Community in upstate New York—a community of plural marriage practitioners whose unconventional mores infuriated neighbors—dissolved after founder John Humphrey Noyes sought to hand over leadership to his son. And not far from Fairfield, in eastern Iowa, German Pietists of the mid-1800s established the Amana Colonies, which thrived for nearly eighty years—one of the longest runs of any such groups—but the seven towns carry on now only as tourist sites.[6]

Already, signs of strain are showing up in the TM Movement, many involving people in Fairfield. Internal frictions, including an intolerance of dissent, have led to what amounts to excommunication of longtime backers. Some former followers now provide anti-cult therapy to help practitioners pull away. A small but vocal group of critics derides the movement regularly on websites with names such as *TM-Free Blog* and *The Honest Truth about TM*. And ex-devotee Judith Bourque, in her *Robes of Silk, Feet of Clay* (2010), a tell-all book about her secret love affair with Maharishi in the 1970s, alleges other assignations by the supposedly celibate guru at the peak of his prominence.[7]

More troubling for insiders, few second-generation members—including some educated at movement schools from childhood through college—seem interested in taking top leadership roles. Perhaps worse, they lack the opportunity to do so, as sixtysomethings hang on to power. Some of the young people, moreover, reject doctrines that took TM well beyond a once-popular simple meditation technique. They look askance at such beliefs as the idea that practitioners can defy gravity and hover off the ground unaided. Some even bristle at the notion of following a guru at all, preferring to school themselves in esoteric wisdom from many sources.

Furthermore, enrollments have been problematic at MUM and the Maharishi School of the Age of Enlightenment, which serves students from preschool to high school. After peaking at 3,231 in 1989, enrollment at MUM slipped to 1,134 in an official reported count in the fall of 2011, and most were grad students.[8] Just 75 undergraduates earned degrees from the university in the 2012–13 academic year, while 241 students collected master's degrees and three earned doctorates. At the Maharishi School—located on a corner of the MUM campus and designed initially to serve university-affiliated meditators—enrollment has dropped from as many as 700 students in the early 1990s to about 200. Class sizes in some lower grades are now down in single digits, and the 2013 high school class totaled just 19.[9]

Financially, the movement has seen better days, too. Long gone are the times when Maharishi and his followers could jet around the world, drawing tens of thousands of supporters whose payments helped buy property in several spots across the United States as well as in areas such as the TM world headquarters in Vlodrop, Holland. The most recent filings in the United States from several arms of the movement suggest that most of its American assets, net of liabilities, are now worth about $168.4 million, down from $270.9 million as recently as the end of 2008, and much less than the wealth former devotees say the movement once controlled.[10] (Regrettably, no full accounting of the often-secretive movement's fortunes has ever been made public, so comparisons are difficult. But the movement was once awash in cash and real estate, including downtown buildings in major U.S. cities such as Chicago. It appears to be less so now, even though the late guru in the early 2000s was collecting as much as $1 million each for special projects from some wealthy donors.) Reports in publications such as *India Today* suggest that millions of dollars were plowed into twelve thousand acres of land across India, including land in prime areas such as Delhi and Goa, and heirs of the late guru and followers have battled over the legacy ever since the guru's death.[11]

Perhaps as a result of the tumult and the lack of strong central direction, marketing and recruitment efforts are a shadow of what they once were. Where college groups once promoted TM to legions of curious American students from coast to coast, StudentMeditation.org in early 2013 listed outposts on just fifteen campuses in the United States and four abroad. While the Church of Jesus Christ of Latter-day Saints (the Mormons) and the Church of Scientology hawk their wares with well-produced TV commercials, TM has fallen below the radar. For their part, advocates say the movement is working quietly—but effectively—in such areas as persuading corporations to offer TM as a benefit to employees and with such organizations as the Veterans Administration to provide meditation as therapy for traumatized war veterans. It's just less of a retail, storefront operation now, one advocate says, and more of a wholesaler, providing TM teachers in strategic areas where needed.

Decline, of course, could prove troublesome for Fairfield residents, including the seekers who moved to Fairfield to raise families, build businesses, open churches and a synagogue, and put in their daily meditation sessions. Some TMers in town take a cool attitude about it—it doesn't matter if the movement dies, they say, since the knowledge the guru imparted will live on. The guru himself lives on in a bevy of videos. Still others—"townies" long hostile to the "roos"—say the movement can't fade soon enough, even if that means all those odd shops and trendy restaurants shut their doors. As for MUM, the campus might make a nice regional medical complex or some such if the school goes bust, the critics say.

When Parsons College thrived, former residents recall, so did the town—and in far different ways. Katherine L. Walter, who lived in Fairfield in the late 1950s and visited often through the 1960s, remembers pricey clothing stores downtown and Parsons students who drove sporty cars. "They did like to party," says Walter, a professor at the University of Nebraska–Lincoln who chairs the university library's Digital Initiatives & Special Collections Unit. Parsons appealed to the children of the wealthy, and businesses catered to them. When the school faded, Walter says, so did those businesses.

As the New Age businesses now in downtown Fairfield suggest, the tastes of MUM students and meditators are different. Nonetheless, TM's electric effect on Fairfield can't be denied. Largely because of the changes the TMers have wrought, *Smithsonian* magazine ranked it seventh on a list of the twenty best small towns to visit in 2013 (between Petoskey, Michigan, and Los Alamos, New Mexico). The magazine quoted James Moore, manager of the town's all-volunteer, solar-powered radio station, KRUU-FM, and a poet, musician, tennis teacher, and meditator, as saying, "Fairfield is one of the deepest small ponds you'll find anywhere."[12]

The TM Movement shook up the little town's economy, political structure, and entertainment scene. It turned a bankrupt college campus into a busy international place that, over the decades, thousands have called their intellectual home. It spawned businesses that reached into high-tech areas, finance, and telecommunications, as well as into novel creative and artistic realms that local farmers and factory workers could never have imagined. Fairfield, just a short piece down the road from the farmhouse in Eldon that Grant Wood's 1930 painting *American Gothic* made famous, has become a far different place under the movement's influence. The differences—the effects, good and bad, that the TMers have had—are worth meditating on.

2

Going for Baroque

TO GET A SENSE of where the TM Movement is and where it's headed, it helps to know where it's been. Fairfielders such as a movement veteran we'll call Dale offer a special window on TM's past and likely future. (I have withheld Dale's real name because he feared his comments would appear out of context and was uncomfortable about appearing in this book.) Dale took up TM-style meditation in 1971, trained in Europe to teach the technique, and studied its philosophy further at the movement's nascent university in Goleta, California, in 1973. Today, Dale lives in a modest, environmentally sensitive home in an area near the Abundance EcoVillage, a small development of homes about three miles from the center of Fairfield. Residents rely on the sun for heating and cooling, are careful to use renewable resources, and recycle. Their homes are built in accordance with architectural principles laid down by Maharishi.

In 2006 Dale broke with the movement and abandoned TM-style meditation after thirty-five years. For years, he says, TM gave him "better health and dynamism" in his life. But over time, he grew troubled by the message— which he and other TM instructors gave initiates from the outset—that all other meditation techniques were either a "waste of time or dangerous." He now says the approach "set me up to become a narrow-minded true believer."

"Can the TM Movement share this excellent meditation technique and the theoretic knowledge that Maharishi brought out without promising perfection and putting down other self-development programs?" Dale asks. "I hope so. I hope that current TM promoters realize the world is getting tired of partisanship. We see it daily in politics and religion. If TM is promoted as the only way, it will be rejected."

The movement began simply, offering followers a powerful and simple daily meditative technique. Devotees had only to close their eyes, ponder a mantra for twenty minutes, twice each day, and they would feel better. In time, the movement promised much more. It promised to provide the key to solving all problems—mental, physical, even economic—for faithful practitioners. Great life-altering things would flow from TM, teachers told new followers. As the years passed, the movement expanded into offering natural medicines, elixirs, and teas to heal the body and soothe the spirit. Later, it provided an architectural style that claimed to promote good fortune and even good health. It moved far beyond the no-muss, no-fuss, mantra-based meditation one could do alone at home into Yogic Flying, where meditators hopped about on mattresses, aspiring to get to the point when they could defy gravity and levitate. TM, it was said, could give practitioners the power to become invisible and to move through walls. Leaders claimed that if enough meditators practiced in groups regularly, they could move stock markets, reduce crime rates, and spawn world peace. Movement officials even created a political party, running candidates for high office around the country, including the presidency of the United States.

In sheer numbers, the movement's high-water mark came and went in the 1970s. Recruitments swelled in the opening half of the decade as Maharishi became a media darling and the toast of wealthy and influential people. Later, though, as the group's practices and offerings grew more closely tied to their ancient Indian roots, the tide turned. Early on, TM was easy, seemingly nonreligious, and inexpensive. Some devotees, especially those who had begun following the guru in the 1960s, saw meditation and the guru's teachings as spiritual. But for tens of thousands of casual practitioners, TM amounted to little more than a relaxing daily mini-vacation, a psychic timeout from the American rat race. It was also a handy way for rebellious Baby Boomers to set themselves apart from their elders, to blaze a new path of their own.

Many turned away, however, as TM's baroque period unfolded. The period began in the mid-1970s as the group's activities in Fairfield expanded.

It deepened as the town became a center for thousands of devotees who believed they could change history—an estimated seven thousand visited for a "Taste of Utopia" course in 1983–84. Much as a painter might move from splashing simple imagery on a canvas to creating elaborate and detailed works, the movement built on its modest first offerings. As it grew more ornate, however, its annual initiation rates began to dwindle. Its once-thriving chapters on college campuses shrank and disappeared. Mocked by some before, it became even more a butt of jokes and the target of critics who derided the group as a cult given to overblown rhetoric and odd, implausible practices. Dissidents arose in its ranks in Fairfield and elsewhere. To critics and even some long-time loyalists, TM was sowing the seeds of its own decline.

In fact, the forces that would drive both TM's rise and its decline had been in place all along. From his earliest days as the former personal secretary to the Brahmananda Saraswati Jagadguru (also known as Guru Dev), Maharishi took his followers through surprising twists and turns. The path that led to Fairfield offers a fascinating glimpse into how a guru can grab the limelight and marshal followers, only to lose most of them and to leave behind a legacy that may now be well beyond its sell-by date. Other Indian sages who came to the United States traced similar arcs, enjoying their times on the American stage, although none reached the heights Maharishi did.

When Maharishi first came to the United States in 1959, he was one of a string of Indian wise men who saw opportunity here to spread their Eastern philosophies. The line went back to at least 1893, when a swami called Vivekananda made a splash in appearances around New England, at a seventeen-day meeting in Chicago of the World's Parliament of Religions, and in New York City. Hailed by one listener as a "handsome monk in the orange robe" who delivered "human eloquence at its highest pitch," Vivekananda returned a couple of times to the United States over the following seven years. Bestowing mantras on followers to use in meditation, he ordained American adherents who could pass on his spiritual teachings, and in San Francisco, he established a Vedanta Society that thrived for decades, expanding into several U.S. cities. His organization endures, with centers around the United States. The Boston center today is run by a monk who serves as a chaplain at the Massachusetts Institute of Technology and Harvard.[1]

Plenty of other Hindu sages plowed the ground after Vivekananda, many working out of Vedanta Society centers. One, Swami Prabhavananda, established several centers on the West Coast in the 1920s, including the still-operating Vedanta Society of Southern California in Los Angeles. Another, Swami Nikhilananda, had come to New York in 1931 to work in the city's Vedanta Center and eventually went out on his own. He befriended the famous scholar Joseph Campbell.[2] The Vedanta Society found Americans receptive in part because—like Maharishi decades later—its gurus didn't ask Westerners to convert to Hinduism or give up their faiths, according to Philip Goldberg's *American Veda* (2010). The ecumenical approach proved crucial in the Judeo-Christian West. "To this day, virtually every Vedanta temple in the West displays images of Christ (and of Buddha) and holds special services on Easter and Christmas," Goldberg writes.[3] Vivekananda set the tone in a speech in California in which he said, "I accept all religions that were in the past and worship with them all. I worship God with every one of them, in whatever form."[4]

Still other gurus preceded Maharishi. Paramahansa Yogananda's *Autobiography of a Yogi* (1946) influenced generations of Americans smitten by Eastern philosophy. In 1920 in Los Angeles, Yogananda founded the Self-Realization Fellowship, a group that now claims more than five hundred temples and centers around the world. The fellowship's mission was "to disseminate among the nations a knowledge of definite scientific techniques for attaining direct personal experience of God."[5] Goldberg reports that the Self-Realization Fellowship flourished even after its founder's death, in 1952, although its growth slowed through the 1950s and 1960s.[6]

So when Maharishi arrived, stopping first in Hawaii in late 1958 (less than a year before the island group became a state) and then moving to California, the groundwork had been laid. Conformist as much of America was in the 1950s, some independent-minded folks, particularly on the West Coast, were keen to sample Eastern ways. Adherents were drawn to Maharishi's light touch and the easy meditation technique he espoused. A *Honolulu Star-Bulletin* report spoke of the yogi with "puppy eyes" who taught that "meditation leads to blissful peace and happiness."[7] He soon struck upon a persuasive marketing approach for his meditation technique—a sales tack the movement continues to embrace today. The Maharishi in the early 1960s developed his skill for charming celebrities and wealthy and influential people whom he could enlist to become his most committed salespeople. Efrem Zimbalist Jr., a popular TV star, was an early enthusiast. So too was tobacco heiress Doris Duke, who funded an ashram in India that the Beatles later visited.[8]

For the first half of the 1960s, growth for TM came slowly but timing, luck, and careful preparation soon paid off. By 1965, as the counterculture movement grew and a sense of rebellion began to sweep through the country, the guru was developing a solid following among students. Young people at the University of California at Los Angeles, in particular, warmed to him, helping him create the Students' International Meditation Society, a group that soon birthed chapters on campuses all across the country. Academics William Sims Bainbridge and Daniel H. Jackson report that the budding movement began keeping careful records in 1965, and they counted a total of about 1,000 TM initiations as of the end of 1966. By the close of 1967, the pair report, the tally leaped to 5,500, as the word spread about the new guru on the block.[9] The Beatles' infatuation with the guru, beginning in August 1967, kicked the movement into hyperdrive. The Fab Four, along with Mick Jagger of the Rolling Stones, learned to meditate and later visited the guru in India. Other rock stars of the era took to him, too, taking his message to their fans. Among them were members of Jefferson Airplane, the Beach Boys, the Grateful Dead, and the Doors.[10]

Sensitive to shifts in the cultural winds, the press stoked the blaze. The *Village Voice* in November 1967 told readers that "with 2,000 students waiting anxiously in Berkeley for their introductory lectures and initiation, it looks now that Maharishi may become more popular than the Beatles." A month later, the guru landed a cover story in the *New York Times Magazine*. Maharishi drew 3,600 people to the Felt Forum at New York's Madison Square Garden.[11] (Goldberg suggests the movement's gains in the period were sharp: from about 220 Americans who had learned TM by the end of 1965, the total neared 5,000 TM initiates by the start of 1968. His figures for the post-1965 period echo Bainbridge and Jackson's.[12])

As his flock grew and broadened, the guru modulated his message, making it palatable for even the most casual devotee. Before coming to the

United States, Maharishi in 1955 gave a talk in India in which he spoke of connecting with personal deities in the mantras that meditators would use, according to Cynthia Ann Humes in her chapter "Maharishi Mahesh Yogi: Beyond the TM Technique" in *Gurus in America* (2005). By the early 1960s, she writes, he had stopped talking openly about "enlightenment," instead saying the goal was Transcendental Consciousness. He decreed that teachers should not discuss Cosmic Consciousness until after an initiate had meditated and gotten a taste for the realm. While personal deities and terms such as "enlightenment" and "Cosmic Consciousness" seemed freighted with religious overtones, the more neutral term, "Transcendental Consciousness," was free of such baggage, even as it hinted at ethereal notions. "Maharishi discovered people were far more interested in using meditation to reduce stress or for self-improvement—better academic performance, business results, or social life," Humes reports. By 1970, she adds, he had distanced himself from the language of Hinduism or spirituality, even while he laid the groundwork for more advanced Vedic training for key disciples. Soon, he took to using the term "Science of Creative Intelligence" to describe his philosophy and worldview, packaging his Eastern teachings in another term that rational-minded Westerners could accept.[13]

The move was a brilliant stroke. His followers, including well-schooled researchers, developed data that proved the many quantifiable benefits of meditation. As Goldberg reports, the guru "knew that hard data would be as useful in the marketing of meditation as it was for medicines or machines. Decrying the fact that Vedic teachings had been 'shrouded in the garb of mysticism,' he dressed them instead in the language of science, and he urged experts to conduct research on TM." In 1970, UCLA graduate student Robert Keith Wallace published a version of his PhD dissertation in *Science* magazine showing helpful physical effects from meditation. More research followed. "The relaxation message quickly overshadowed the more profound reasons for meditating, but the data armed TM teachers with charts and graphs that impressed not only the public and the press but physicians and scientists as well," Goldberg says.[14]

The ranks of initiates soared. From 15,300 in 1968 the total number of initiates swelled to 436,800 by 1974. Nearly 300,000 new meditators signed on in the peak year of 1975, a time insiders call the Merv Wave because TV talk-show titan Merv Griffin took up meditation. Intoxicated with the technique, Griffin devoted a show to it that spring, welcoming the guru on the air—another example of savvy marketing through celebrities. "By the first commercial, a few million people were probably opening the Yellow Pages to find a TM center," gushes Goldberg. "The show was a virtual infomercial, with personal testimony, name-dropping, and constant references to science." More press followed, and Maharishi appeared a second time with Griffin in the fall of that year. Enthusiasts included Mary Tyler Moore and Clint Eastwood.[15]

Even as he pitched his program in ways that would appeal to secular, overly stressed Westerners, the guru didn't wholly abandon lofty rhetoric and far-reaching claims. When a 1974 study by his followers showed that crime rates declined in cities where at least 1 percent of the population learned TM, the guru said this "Maharishi Effect" had ushered in the dawn of the Age of Enlightenment.[16] The high expectations were understandable, as was the vaulting rhetoric, which suited the "Age of Aquarius," the transformative era some Boomers believed they were living in. For the movement, these were epic times: seeking space to spread their wings, the faithful in 1974 moved their budding Maharishi International University (later renamed Maharishi University of Management) to Fairfield. Young Wallace, the former UCLA graduate student, headed the school.

But the go-go days proved short-lived. "The year 1976 was a shockingly steep fall from grace for the TM movement," writes Humes. That year, a group of parents and clergy sued in New Jersey to shut down TM programs in the public schools, claiming that they were religious in nature. The critics won when a federal judge, in late 1977, stopped the programs. Set back on its heels, the movement's World Plan Executive Council declined at first to appeal, Bainbridge and Jackson report. The council quoted Maharishi as saying, "If the law of the country will demand from us that we teach in the name of religion, then fine, we will abide by the law and feel nearer to God." Ultimately, the movement did appeal and, in 1979, it lost.[17]

The PR cost from the New Jersey case was stiff, as prospective recruits began to look on TM in a harsh light. Its Vedic roots loomed large as critics saw TM as more than just a helpful meditation technique. The movement gave its critics still more ammunition when Maharishi, in 1977, introduced the TM-Sidhi program. This involved hours of meditation daily, going well beyond the simple twice-a-day, twenty-minutes-at-a-time technique. A cornerstone of the new approach was Yogic Flying, the idea that meditators could hover above the ground—a claim based on a classic text of Hindu philosophy, the "Yoga Sutras" of Patanjali. Devotees would have "the ability to know the past and future, knowledge of other minds, the ability to become invisible, passage through the sky," according to a catalog for the Maharishi university in Fairfield cited by Bainbridge and Jackson.[18] Newspaper ads promised "the ability to levitate by mere intention."[19]

The grandiose claims were never demonstrated, of course, even while meditators gathered to hop around foam-covered halls. "All that has been demonstrated is what the TM movement calls the first stage of yogic flying—essentially hopping froglike for a foot or two, looking more like gymnasts than helicopters lifting off," reports Goldberg. "The practice disappointed many practitioners but also satisfied those content with the deepened inner peace and heightened awareness that they said they experienced. In terms of public perception, however, TM sacrificed much of the respectability it had worked to acquire."[20]

Much of the press, once adoring, turned on the movement. *Time* put the movement's changes into business terms: "What is a maharishi to do when sales start to grow sluggish? One answer: announce a shiny new product." The problem was that the product was a turnoff, and initiations slipped sharply. From nearly 300,000 in 1975, initiations plunged to 140,273 in 1976 and to 49,689 in 1977, according to Bainbridge and Jackson.

The claims meditators made about their ability to bring down crime rates and promote world peace soon undercut their credibility even further. The movement suggested that small numbers of meditators, practicing the TM-Sidhi program, could influence the collective consciousness, as the placid brain waves they generated would radiate outward to cast a balm on the larger population. Movement publications over time have suggested various numbers as being needed to create this Maharishi Effect, moving from as high as one-tenth of the adult population to one-hundredth and even one-thousandth.[21] The movement settled on the figure of the square root of 1 percent of a given population, claiming that scores of scientifically rigorous studies demonstrated this Effect.

Then things got stranger—and even dangerous. Believing that the peace-building effects of meditation were real, Maharishi in the late 1970s sent groups of TM teachers into hotspots around the world. At the guru's behest, idealistic young devotees flew into such places as Zimbabwe (then called Rhodesia), Nicaragua, and revolution-bound Iran to meditate for hours daily, in some cases even as shooting went on outside their hotels. Some didn't know until the last minute where they were headed, only that Maharishi had asked them to undertake special missions, and they were determined to heed his call.

"There was a shroud of secrecy about it," recalls Jimmy Caplan, who was twenty-nine at the time, a veteran of training in Fairfield, and a teacher in the busy TM center in Cambridge, Massachusetts. Followers got immunization shots and, in the fall of 1978, climbed aboard buses bound for John F. Kennedy International Airport in New York, not knowing the destination. Some of the organizers didn't know either, it seems—Caplan wound up on a plane headed for Tehran, while his luggage was flown to Rhodesia. Recalls Caplan, "I went to Iran with nothing except the clothes on me."

One group was already established in Tehran when Caplan arrived. His group headed to Isfahan, a city about two hundred miles to the south. The country, recalls Caplan, was afire with riots, strikes, and demonstrations against the ailing Shah. While tumult reigned outside the small hotel where Caplan and his group of twenty or so stayed, the TM practitioners went about their daily meditations in hopes they could generate peaceful vibes. That proved to be a vain hope. After about three weeks, Caplan says, he recalls one night when the noise of guns firing outside awoke him. "I thought it might be the end of me," he says.

Caplan decided it was time to leave when his group moved back to Tehran, but getting out turned out to be far tougher than getting in the country. First, several of his fellow meditators balked at leaving, saying they had gotten no word from Maharishi to move. They felt bound to stay. Then, their hotel keeper back in Isfahan balked at returning passports for some of the meditators because he hadn't been fully paid. Amid all this, Caplan's open-ended return ticket had expired, leaving him to plead with Alitalia officials for an extension. When he finally got the extension and headed to the airport, he learned that some of his friends were delayed; Caplan wound up begging the flight crew on his plane to hold up the takeoff for them. When Caplan saw the Academy Award–winning film *Argo* (2012), about the escape of American embassy staffers from Iran in 1979, he felt like he was watching a replay of his group's harrying misadventure. "It was pandemonium," says Caplan.

Still, Caplan doesn't think it was crazy for Maharishi to send the meditators into the danger zones. Now in his early sixties, living in Austin, Texas, and still meditating daily, he speculates that the Iranian Revolution may have turned out to be less bloody than it could have been because of the meditators. But he also says timing was not on the side of the TMers. "Instability was evident everywhere when we arrived and the pressure kept mounting," he says. "It felt as if the whole country was unwinding." Caplan, fond of quoting Bob Dylan, said the time reminded him of a lyric on *Time Out of Mind*, a 1997 album: "It's not dark yet, but it's getting there."

Meanwhile, throughout the late 1970s and early 1980s, the lofty claims about TM's ability to change history bounced around an echo chamber in Fairfield and in the ranks of TM teachers nationwide. "It really was very much an evangelical movement," says Dale, the ecology-minded Fairfielder. "We were taught that by getting a certain number of people to meditate, we could bring about world peace."

Much of America didn't buy it anymore, though. TM centers closed and student chapters folded. Insiders, puzzled at the guru's shift in course, told themselves that smaller groups of better-trained meditators would make a deeper mark on the world than those who joined out of mere faddishness. "Maharishi added layers of knowledge," recalls Dale. "We just took it all as gospel."

Devotees in Fairfield found great value in what Dale calls the "waves of knowledge that Maharishi brought out in the eighties and early nineties." He, for one, says he "thrived" on the guru's "elaborations." Even if Yogic Flying turned off much of the general public and some meditators, he says it "galvanized the core group."

But he was later turned off by a shift in the movement toward long group meditation programs and a big focus on fundraising that began in the late 1990s. In that period, the movement encouraged wealthy meditators to contribute $1 million or more each to establish a group of ten thousand Yogic flyers in India. The donors in 2003 were treated to a course with Maharishi at his home in Vlodrop, Holland, called "Enlightenment: Total Knowledge and Experience of Higher States of Consciousness." According to a publication by the movement's Institute of Science, Technology and Public Policy, the guru said he would provide intimate sessions during which he would answer "all impossible questions." John Hagelin, who led the institute, told adherents that the ten thousand flyers "would bring to fulfillment Maharishi's lifelong desire to create Permanent Peace on Earth."

TM leaders often made such promises. Dale, like other teachers, had given prospective meditators introductory lectures saying TM would offer the solution to all their problems. Ever since he broke intellectually with the group—"individuated," as he describes his shift from what he labels as "groupthink"—Dale has taken a different view. "The problems aren't all solved. People still die. They still get sick. They still have mental issues," he says. "Obviously TM was oversold, but it wasn't obvious to us at the outset because we wanted to believe it."

While some critics of TM in Fairfield have gotten the cold shoulder from former colleagues in the movement, Dale still counts plenty of friends in it. Several of his relatives continue to meditate and are active in movement-related programs in Fairfield. He is heartened by changes big and small, such as a relaxation of the dress code at the university, a shift from promoting TM to focusing on the well-being of students, and the school's emphasis on such programs as sustainable living. Many students, especially those from abroad, are less interested in meditation than in getting good jobs in the United States, he says, and the university seems to be accommodating them. Dale wants the university to thrive. But he feels the school must free itself of tenets Maharishi held dear, such as the view that TM is the true and exclusive road to enlightenment. "Any adaptation will run up against that initial message," he says. "So I really don't know. I could see over the next ten years the TM Movement becoming more of a history lesson."

The movement's future, like its past, may be bound up in the knotty issue that the New Jersey court wrestled with: the question of religion. Are TM backers advocating a simple, secular practice born of an ancient philosophy, not a religion? Or is the devotion some give to the dead guru and his Eastern teachings proof of the religious nature of TM? Weighed down by myriad issues in religiously traditional America, the argument over TM and religion is anything but simple. Those quick to judge the matter should look at how meditators and non-meditators in Fairfield come to terms—sometimes very differently—with the conundrum.

3

Of God and Man

WHEN WORSHIPPERS at St. Gabriel and All Angels Church gather for Sunday services, some among the couple of dozen or so faithful believe they are in divine company. Angels help out in the services, they say. Indeed, ever since the earliest days of this Liberal Catholic congregation in Fairfield, founded in 1985, members say they enjoyed the blessing of their patron saint, the angel important to Catholics, Jews, and Muslims. As the church proclaims on its website, "We continue to feel the guidance of St. Gabriel to this day."[1]

Such mystical beliefs, while outside the mainstream among fundamentalist Christian churches in Fairfield, suit the meditators who formed St. Gabriel's. The Fairfield church's founders gravitated to the Liberal Catholic Church, set up by English psychics in 1916, in part because it adheres to sacraments and rituals familiar to Roman Catholics but includes a hefty dollop of otherworldly ideas. Its philosophy, for instance, includes the idea of reincarnation, salvation through a series of lives that lead to perfection, and the Kingdom of Heaven.

"The founders went over the liturgy and removed all the references to sin and guilt and being miserable. It's all positive," a longtime St. Gabriel's member tells me as we share snacks after a Sunday service. She adds that the approach echoes the upbeat message about avoiding "negativity" that meditators hear in the TM Movement. She says, "They were psychics and could see the angels and used all the best parts of the liturgies they could find to get the assistance of angels at every service."

Religion is touchy for TM practitioners. Meditators who also are Jews, Catholics, Protestants, and Mormons have affiliated with their various co-religionists in Fairfield while pondering the guru's teachings. Some joined established churches, though they avoided churches that shun meditators; the leaders of such churches see TM as a competing religion that conflicts with Christianity. Meditators often side with the movement's official view that TM is not a religion, but rather that the practice of meditation can "enliven" one's religious practices. At services at St. Gabriel's and at Beth Shalom, a synagogue set up by meditators, speakers may refer occasionally to meditation or Vedic teachings, for instance, but the rituals and practices are distinct from the religions. Jesus Christ is front and center at St. Gabriel's, while Adonai (God) holds pride of place at Beth Shalom.

Critics have stewed about TM and religion for over thirty years. They hold that the movement's dogma, the Science of Creative Intelligence (SCI), is little more than bastardized Hinduism. They point to references to the Divine, to heaven, and to Hindu deities in movement literature, in initiation ceremonies, and in oaths that TM teachers take. The mission of TM teachers, according to an oath one former TM teacher said such teachers sign, is to "spread the Light of God to all those who need it."[2] Some followers warm to a Hindu type of astrology called Jyotish that is said to reveal "the relationship of individual life with cosmic life"; a form of architecture, Sthapatya Veda, said to "connect individual life with Cosmic Life, individual intelligence with Cosmic Intelligence"; and Maharishi Ayurveda, an herbal supplement system said to respect "the intimate connection between the physical, mental, emotional, and spiritual aspects of our being."[3]

To buttress their case, the critics say followers called Maharishi "His Holiness." They note that the honorific "Maharishi" refers to a Hindu teacher of religious and mystical knowledge. Indeed, movement literature is replete with references to the creation of heaven on earth. The Global Country of World Peace, a part of the movement based in Maharishi Vedic City near Fairfield, was chartered "to establish heaven on earth by raising the quality of life of every individual to complete fulfillment and affluence in enlightenment," according to papers it filed for an exemption from federal taxes. And initiation ceremonies seem sacramental, featuring incense, candlelight, and a photo of "His Divinity" Swami Brahmananda Saraswati Jagadguru, who was Maharishi's master.

The stakes are high in the semantic battle. For one thing, if the movement is seen as proselytizing in the same way recruitment-minded religions do, TM might collect fewer adherents. By emphasizing the religion-free technique of meditation—and not the dogma of SCI or Maharishi Vedic Science—the movement can garner followers who continue to observe the religions they hold dear. Even atheists can enjoy meditation, Maharishi taught. Moreover, by carving out the meditation technique—"just twenty minutes, twice a day"—instead of offering the whole package, TM proponents reckon they would be free to bring meditation into public schools without being accused of promoting religion.

Critics, however, see the simple practice of meditating with a mantra as a Trojan horse, a vehicle for seducing the unwary into accepting Maharishi's full package of ideas. Inconveniently for the movement, a federal court in *Malnak v. Yogi* (1977) ruled against even the meditation practice in public schools, holding that SCI/TM and the teaching of it, including such concepts as pure creative intelligence, creative intelligence, and bliss consciousness, "are all religious in nature." The ruling, which was upheld on appeal, barred as unconstitutional the teaching of the system in the New Jersey public schools.[4] That hasn't halted current efforts by movie director Lynch to bring meditation into public schools, especially into violence-prone, inner-city schools where enthusiasts say the practice helps kids. TM teachers, working with the support of Lynch's foundation, strip away the SCI elements and teach just meditation.

Funded by Lynch and other foundations, the Center for Wellness and Achievement in Education (CWAE) has been teaching meditation in some of the toughest schools in the San Francisco Bay Area since 2007. CWAE and school officials point to dramatic downturns in fighting and disciplinary suspensions among hundreds of students and, perhaps surprisingly, a sharp reversal in turnover among teachers as a result of its meditation-based Quiet Time program. Academic performance is also up sharply. The group's website quotes James S. Dierke, a principal at the Visitacion Valley Middle School, as saying, "The Quiet Time program is the most effective program that I have come across in my 40 years as a public school educator for addressing the problem of stress and violence in schools."

Dierke, who joined the CWAE board of directors, says the program produced "remarkable" changes in students. He lists some in an article in the September/October 2012 issue of *Leadership*, a publication of the Association of California School Administrators. Multiday suspensions, the kind usually associated with fighting, dropped 43 percent over four months among Visitacion students taking part in Quiet Time. "Fighting in PE in the sixth and seventh grade dropped by about 60 percent," he says. Students taking part in the Quiet Time program showed much bigger gains in math and language arts test results than a control group—eighth-graders—not taking part, he adds. And teacher absenteeism because of illness fell 30 percent in the year when the program was introduced.

CWAE's program seems crafted to avoid the legal snarls that plagued the TM teachers in New Jersey. Students learn how to meditate with the help of TM-certified teachers, and they get individualized mantras as any TM initiates would. But they don't get instruction in SCI, which landed the earlier program in hot water, or in any philosophy. "There are many philosophies that people associate with meditation," says Jeff Rice, CWAE's director of operations. "We do not teach any philosophy, Vedic or otherwise. One of our goals regarding meditation is to demonstrate that it can be learned successfully without any understanding or reference to philosophy."

Students also can choose to take part or not. They can choose during two fifteen-minute quiet time periods each day to meditate, read, or do other silent activity, as they wish—though most meditate and are glad for it, CWAE officials say. "They can do anything they want to, as long as it's quiet," says Rice, a former Silicon Valley executive who set up the center with a partner, another valley veteran, Laurent Valosek. The pair had previously taught TM to harried valley businesspeople.

"We knew from our own experience working with executives in Silicon Valley and a number of small-scale pilot projects in public schools that meditation could be taught successfully, without any recourse to philosophy, and that if careful and rigorous follow-up was provided, the results could be substantial," Rice adds.

The results have so heartened officials in San Francisco schools that CWAE now provides its program in four schools and has ten on a waiting list. The biggest challenge the CWAE and school officials face is funding: the programs cost up to $800 a year per student to set up and maintain, says Rice. While the school district occasionally fields complaints about whether meditation crosses a religious line, top officials back it enthusiastically. "Quite simply, Quiet Time should be in every school," Carlos Garcia, the recently retired superintendent of schools in San Francisco, says in a testimonial on the CWAE site.

Some parents have disagreed. Religious fundamentalists, arguing that meditation is not appropriate for public schools, blocked an earlier project using TM in a school in nearby Marin County, Rice says. Similar arguments have been raised down the coast in Encinitas, California, about yoga. Attorneys for the National Center for Law and Policy of Escondido, California, sued the Encinitas Union School District in February 2013 to force it to stop teaching Ashtanga yoga. A foundation backed by yoga devotee Sonia Tudor Jones, wife of billionaire Paul Tudor Jones, gave the district $533,000 to teach the discipline. The yoga opponents lost the case in July 2013 but vowed to appeal.

Keeping clear of such fracases, CWAE maintains it is independent. On its website, it explains that it uses TM-style meditation—citing the technique's ease of use and the research backing it up—but it doesn't speak of Maharishi or his philosophy. "We want the emphasis to be on the fact that we are here to address intractable problems," says Rice. TM-style meditation, he adds, is a tool to do that, and it works with all kinds of children, including the academically challenged and those with attention and stress disorders. CWAE also promotes healthy lifestyles, organizing "wellness competitions" where teachers and administrators earn points for such practices as going to bed early and eating a wholesome diet. Winners have gotten Kindles and other prizes.

Stripping meditation down to its basics, however, may not placate critics. TM still remains rooted in an Eastern religious approach that differs markedly from Christian meditation, argues Dean R. Broyles, the lawyer who heads the center that sued to halt yoga instruction in Encinitas. Ashtanga yoga—which includes meditation—is "inherently religious," he holds.

Christian meditation involves filling your mind with scripture, prayer, or thoughts of God, he says, while Eastern-style meditation involves emptying your mind and striving to reach a state of bliss where you see yourself as united with the Divine, as part of God. "For a Christian or Jewish person, it's heresy and blasphemy to say you are God," the lawyer says.

While he says he would have to know more about the details of CWAE's approach to putting TM in the public schools to offer an opinion on it, he does point to the *Malnak v. Yogi* case to support his argument against yoga in Encinitas. No matter what positive effects meditation or yoga may have, he adds, public schools have no business promoting religion in general, much less showcasing specific religions, to students. Even if the approaches are scientifically proven to calm children or otherwise help them, the risk of crossing the line into promoting specific religions is too great, he suggests. "Let's say Jewish or Christian prayer was used to calm kids down," he says. "There would be one complaint and it would be out of there in five minutes." Permitting even stripped-down versions of religiously based yoga or meditation, he warns, puts public schools onto a "slippery slope."

Ironically, the claim to secularity could be the very thing that in the end does in the TM Movement, if it ultimately fades away as so many Utopian movements have. Groups that have survived in the United States—such as Mormons, Seventh-Day Adventists, Christian Scientists, and the Amish— have endured in part because they offer a full and clear dogma to hang on to. Further, they have paying members who do more than just buy a set of lessons in a meditative technique and then go on their way, as most TMers have. For most successful groups, a cash-and-carry approach is a nonstarter. Moreover, they offer a promise of salvation in the life to come, as well as provide a crucial sense of community for everyday life. They are, of course, explicitly religious and don't pretend otherwise.

Some of the groups, those most oriented toward proselytizing, were also very intelligent about preparing for the future, according to Rodney Stark, a professor of social sciences at Baylor University who co-directs the Institute for Studies of Religion there. Brigham Young, who led the Mormons after the death of founder Joseph Smith, took his besieged flock to Utah and then built it up there with recruits his missionaries had converted in Europe. His church fostered a culture of missionary zeal that has been delivering proselytes for over a century and a half and continues to do so. "He was a very smart guy and a very effective leader," says Stark.

For his part, Maharishi was no dummy about marketing, of course. TM thrived as it did because he deftly fused a meditative technique based in Hinduism (or Vedic knowledge, predating Hinduism, as followers maintain) with Western science. Through a raft of studies described as scientific, he persuaded followers that his approach could verifiably improve their lives. He also packaged it well, marketing the simple technique—just twice a day for twenty minutes each time—that wouldn't interfere much with one's life. Finally, the guru was adept at using celebrity adherents to publicize and popularize his technique—an approach TM Movement leaders today continue, tapping such luminaries as comedians Seinfeld and Russell Brand, CNN newswoman Crowley and ex-anchor O'Brien and ABC newsman Stephanopoulos, talk-show hosts DeGeneres and Winfrey, and radio star Stern.

However, if TM were explicit about its religious nature, it would risk alienating more people than it would gain. Stark holds that the problem for TM is that proselytizing groups such as the Mormons and Christian Scientists have been successful in America because of their basis in Judeo-Christianity. "They had a cultural base to build on," Stark says. "You didn't have to tell people to throw away your Bible the way Eastern faiths have to do." Such Eastern creeds, he says, have not found the United States to be fertile ground, at least for developing large and enduring followings. Ultimately, he suggests, that may foil TM, whether it owns up to its religious nature or not.

While publicly maintaining its nonreligious character, the TM Movement in fact gradually deepened its connection with Hinduism over the years. "A hybrid of Eastern and Western sensibilities, the American TM package predating the mid-1970s focused on meditation and its attendant promises of self-fulfillment, shorn of any residue of undue spiritualism," writes Humes in *Gurus in America*. Later, however, Maharishi "incorporated many facets commonly understood as 'Hinduism,' distinguished from the old, unimproved Vedic wisdom by his unique spellings and trademarks," she observes. "In this sense, the TM Movement that evolved into Maharishi's later programs resembles an even more ethnic Hinduism than that which he first exported: Not only is it Hinduism, but it is a specific incorporated brand of Hinduism."[5]

The package of ideas and practices grew to become as fully fleshed out as many religions. "Defying the New Age embrace of sexuality, Maharishi urged favored followers to practice chastity and suggested the preferable path of becoming a celibate monk or nun," Humes writes. "He incorporated Indian cultural habits, 'baggage' ranging from dressing specific colors, speaking in certain ways, reading only accepted books, avoiding certain astrological occurrences, and avoiding inauspicious architectural design. And despite New Age deemphasis of devotionalism, he prohibited free choice in 'guru-shopping,' insisting that followers either love him or leave him."[6] Humes points to a "cognitive dissonance" among followers, noting that Maharishi's initial insistence on TM's nonreligiosity prompted charges of deception and hypocrisy. She asks, "When is a path to enlightenment, which sponsors rituals to deities and is based on meditation that deploys the names of gods, not a religion?"[7] (TM backers argue, however, that the mantras used in TM refer to laws of nature, not gods.)[8]

Perhaps more unsettling to residents of Fairfield—meditators and non-meditators alike—is the question of whether the TM community constitutes a cult. Some meditators in town shrug off the question, saying a religion is nothing more than a cult that has succeeded. To wags, a cult is just a denomination you don't belong to. Stark and William Sims Bainbridge, in *The Future of Religion: Secularization, Revival, and Cult Formation* (1985), define cults as deviant religious bodies that operate in a "state of relatively high tension with their surrounding sociocultural environment" and which generally add a new revelation or insight to justify the claim that they are different, new, or "more advanced."[9] They say TM struggled to avoid the label of religion even though it was based in a religious tradition, and "for a long time, its more religious teachings and practices were revealed only to the inner core of members while ordinary meditators were offered an apparently nonreligious, practical technique." While noting it was in decline, Bainbridge and Jackson call TM "a solidly organized religious cult movement" that, when they wrote of it in 1981 at any rate, was "undoubtedly one of the largest new religions in America."[10]

Whatever it's called, the TM community's practices could alienate non-followers, and they have done that, in varying degrees, both within and outside Fairfield. Battles with outsiders over practices, philosophy, or lifestyles in Utopian communities, though, have been a hallmark of American history. Many such groups have been pilloried for beliefs outsiders deemed heretical or offensive.

The Reverend John Humphrey Noyes, founder of the mid-nineteenth-century Oneida Community in upstate New York, was arrested for adultery stemming from the "complex marriage" system to which his several hundred followers adhered. Later, he ran off to Canada to avoid statutory rape charges, a move that led to the dissolution of the community and its reorganization in 1881 into the corporation that made Oneida cutlery famous.[11] Mormons were persecuted for advocating polygamy and theocracy, and a mob in Illinois killed Joseph Smith in 1844 when he was under arrest for treason. Still battling the Mormons some forty-six years later, the U.S. Congress sought to seize the church's assets, leading church officials to disavow polygamy.[12] Outsiders attacked the New Harmony community in Indiana in 1820, troubled by the group's prosperity, political power, and advocacy of celibacy. One critic, mocking founder George Rapp, urged Indiana officials to outlaw celibacy in the Harmony Society, "as there is many young Girls of Ex[c]elent Conduct and Beheavour in [H]armony And many young men of Good parts . . . it is shurly not Right that those who are man & wife should not Enjoy [each] other as such [just to] please the old gentleman."[13]

By contrast with such extreme examples, splits between the meditators and non-meditators in Fairfield seem like tame stuff, indeed. After nearly forty years, relations now are generally peaceful. Meditators say it is rare to be mocked as "roos" by people shouting from passing cars, as happened in the early days when the movement came to town. "In the first few years, I thought 'fuckin' roo' was one word," joked L. B. Trusty Shriver, a longtime meditator who broke with the TM Movement and who died in mid-2013. Another meditator, Doug Hamilton, added that "both communities have their bigots, but there are fewer of them."

Still, an "us and them" sensibility persists—perhaps not active hostility, but a split based on separate interests and social ties. The cleavage shows up in some churches. Meditators, for instance, are welcome to join one of the oldest churches in town, the First Presbyterian Church, which dates back to 1841 in Fairfield. Several meditators sing in the choir there, and the church has run activities, such as Taize services, that include Christian meditative prayer and singing.

But some members say the friendships end at the church door. "I've never been invited to [a meditator's] house," Robert Rasmussen, a former mayor of Fairfield and member of First Presbyterian, told me on one of my early visits to Fairfield. "Why would I go? What would I do there when I got there?" He says the split is "sad" because "they have just as much to offer." He explains that the separation is mutual, saying, "you have your lifestyle and we have ours and it stops there." Further, he adds, "People would worry about the fact that if the meditator invited you, they would worry about, I suppose, that they're going to try to convert you."

The Reverend Joseph Phipps, pastor at First Presbyterian since August 2008, seconds the idea that "there is a cultural divide between the meditator community and the non-meditators." The meditators in the church choir come to services to sing, for instance, but tend not to attend services when the choir is not on hand and avoid other church functions, such as potluck meals. He says, "Many folks feel, rightly or wrongly, that they have their life and we have ours."

Reverend Phipps suspects the rift is the legacy of a time when there was more open antagonism between the communities. "I don't believe that's the case now, but feelings carry over," he says.

For his part, the Presbyterian minister has reservations about the focus of some meditation, especially if it may involve invoking the names of Hindu deities through mantras—something that TM backers deny as inaccurate anti-TM propaganda—though he doesn't object to meditation per se. "My concerns are what you are meditating on," he says. "The Bible is clear that we're to meditate on God's word, so the issue is not meditation. The issue is, what is the focus of that meditation?" He asks, "Are we focused on seeking God and his word" or the "divinity" of individuals?

Reverend Phipps says he is concerned, too, about the influence of non-Christian ideas on Christians. In a religiously and philosophically diverse community such as Fairfield, "the whole idea is you can pick and choose and take a little from here and a little from there." That, he frets, can very easily seep into one's observance of Christianity.

Not all churches in town, moreover, embrace meditators. Like anyone else, they are welcome to attend services at Immanuel Lutheran Church, for instance, but cannot be accepted as members. "We don't see TM and Christianity as being a compatible mix," says Pastor Mark Brase. TM practitioners, he added, try to "get in touch with Divinity or the Divine nature wherever they can find it," but Lutherans in his denomination, the conservative Missouri Synod, look to Jesus Christ. Says the minister, "We have a God that took on flesh and bone."

The difference is theological, the Reverend Brase says. Meditators, he states, look inward and empty their minds "to be filled by a supreme entity." In a sense, he says, that is making oneself into a god rather than accepting a God who is separate from man. He draws a similar distinction between Christianity and religions that hold that God is found in everything. "God may be the energy behind everything, but I'm not God. The tree outside is not God," he says. God, he maintains, is the Holy Trinity.

Accepting the views espoused by the TM Movement is bound to breed confusion, Reverend Brase argues. This seems especially so in children raised in homes where both TM and conventional religion are observed, he suggests. "There are going to be a certain number of people who see that it somehow fits together and, under an objective view from my perspective, being raised in that would maybe confuse me," he says. "They need the Gospels. We all need Christ."

Much like other non-meditators in Fairfield, Reverend Brase doesn't shun TM practitioners but just has little to do with them. In town since 2002, when he came to Immanuel Lutheran, he doesn't have much occasion to socialize with meditators. He doesn't go to events at MUM and doesn't shop at stores such as Thymely Solutions, a natural remedies store run by a meditator. He does sometime stop by Revelations, the used book store and dining spot frequented by meditators. "The pizza is good, " he says, adding he gets "a kick out of" the offbeat spiritual books there, laughing that visitors can get texts on everything from the spiritual aspects of designing one's house to mowing one's lawn.

Fairfield, Reverend Brase adds, is composed of "two groups that go our separate ways." There is a "certain amount of integration," he says, so meditators and non-meditators may rub shoulders at city government meetings, Chamber of Commerce events, or even meetings of ecumenical groups such as the Fairfield Area Ministerial Association, a pastors' group. But there remains a divide. Meditators and non-meditators don't get together regularly at backyard barbecues, he says. "Within the non-TM group, there really are people who just don't want to have anything to do with them," he says. "I can't speak for them, but I imagine there's a certain group [of TMers] who stay to themselves, too."

The split endures, even though one of the more enthusiastic backers of TM in town hailed from the local Presbyterian church, the longtime pastor John R. Dilley. In a 1975 piece in *The Christian Century* magazine, the minister recalled that church members worried about what the meditators might do with Parsons College, the Presbyterian-affiliated school whose campus the TM Movement bought out of bankruptcy.[14]

"We had visions of flowing robes, burning incense, long hair or shaved heads, prayer beads and sandals (and sandals would be unthinkable inside a pair of overshoes on a cold January morning in Iowa!)," he wrote. But the movement representatives who appeared at a church meeting in May 1974, he said, couldn't have been more at odds with the hippie image. "The two neatly dressed young men with attaché cases who were the university's [Maharishi International University's] emissaries to Fairfield looked as though they had stepped off Madison Avenue into the cornfields of southeast Iowa. Their speech was serene yet assured. Their fiscal and educational knowledge satisfied the business and college contingent present."

The Reverend Dilley pressed state and national officials to help open the way to the movement, even in the face of "the forceful and violent opposition of a vociferous minority group that included a few members of our congregation." Once the meditators agreed to set up shop at Parsons, moving the school then known as Maharishi International University from California to the Parsons campus, apprehension was high among townspeople. "Rumors abounded," Dilley recalled. "Fundamentalist churches drew crowds from 50 and 60 miles away to hear a 'specialist on satanism' who had been called in to disclaim the virtues of TM and the leaders of MIU."

Worries eased, however, when a local paper ran a photo of a dozen or so students getting off a plane in Des Moines, Reverend Dilley recalled. "The fellows all in shirts and ties and jackets and, best of all, short hair; the girls in dresses, not jeans." The Presbyterian church's welcoming service drew more than two hundred students and faculty members, who jammed the parking lot with bicycles and filled the seats, aisles, and balcony at the church. "The electric vibrations which ran through the congregation that morning were fantastic. It was a real spiritual happening, a celebration of the highest order."

Reverend Dilley had a personal reason to be enthusiastic about TM. He had suffered heart attacks in 1970 and 1973 and had his heart catheterized in April 1974. He learned of studies suggesting that meditation could lower one's heart rate and help ease high blood pressure, and his doctors suggested he consider practicing TM. He became a meditator, a move that would require special efforts. "There was only one hang-up: neither a minister nor a psychiatrist may be initiated as a meditator unless special permission is granted by the Maharishi Mahesh Yogi, or unless the person goes through the complete course of 'the Science of Creative Intelligence.' I knew, however, that for a very selfish motivation—namely, concern for my health—I would become a meditator.

"Our entire family have become meditators and we have found no compromise in our commitment to Jesus Christ and to his church," Reverend Dilley recalled. "Indeed, we have found that our entire life style has become more Christian as we both give and receive love with less tension in our lives."

Many TM practitioners, similarly, have no problem pondering Maharishi's teachings and studying ancient Indian sages and, at the same time, practicing Western religions. Like so-called Bu-Jews, who hold that they can practice both Buddhism and Judaism, they just don't see a problem.

Some longtime meditators, moreover, say that adherence to SCI dogma and TM practices in general varies widely in Fairfield. It is akin to Judaism, they say, in that there's a broad range of observance, just as one finds among Orthodox, Conservative, and Reform Jews. Some practitioners go to the sprawling golden domes on MUM's campus to meditate by the hundreds faithfully twice a day; others are not so diligent. Some are vegetarians and avoid alcohol, as Maharishi urged, while others feast on chicken and wine or down hamburgers in local restaurants. Some are celibate, as part of the movement encouraged, and most are not. Some believe it's possible to defy gravity and levitate through Yogic Flying, while others only see practitioners hopping cross-legged across rooms on mattresses. Finally, some draw a line between the simple meditation technique at the core of the movement and the Full Monty of SCI/Maharishi Vedic Science ideas, saying the twenty-minute technique is essentially mechanical and nonreligious.

Los Angeles–based writer Claire Hoffman, in a February 2013 article about moviemaker Lynch in the *New York Times Magazine*, offers a mixed message about the technique and the spirituality it is rooted in. Hoffman grew up in Fairfield and attended the Maharishi School of the Age of Enlightenment, where she got a hefty dose of the guru's philosophy. She seems to have little use for the ideas now but still meditates twice a day. "I use T.M. to deal with anxiety and fatigue and to stave off occasional despair," Hoffman writes. "But that's because, in my head, I've managed to excise the weird flotsam of spirituality that engulfed T.M. for the first part of my life. Now, for me, it is something very simple, like doing yoga or avoiding dairy."[15]

Certainly, there is no question that the ethereal interests of meditators bring a mystical bent to Fairfield. Once home solely to mainstream Christian churches, the town has developed into a spiritual smorgasbord. Seekers can find everything from conventional religious practice to adherence to rival Indian gurus whose heresies—in the view of TM officials—could lead a TM supporter to suffer the equivalent of excommunication. Over two dozen houses of worship operate in Fairfield, some serving just a handful of followers and some drawing hundreds. The faithful can worship Jesus Christ, the Divine Mother, a sole God, or various Hindu deities. Sufis can find their place, along with Quakers. Devotees can send their prayers to the heavens or direct their thoughts deep within, pursuing the Kingdom of Heaven with whom and as they see fit. They can worship for forty-five minutes on a Sunday or a couple hours on a Friday night, or they can meditate privately or in groups for a few minutes twice a day or five hours or more at a time.

The meditators bring a dash of the otherworldly even to otherwise-traditional practices in some of Fairfield's houses of worship. While Beth Shalom, for instance, uses a mainstream prayerbook and follows an order of service on Friday nights that is echoed in conventional synagogues, it is not affiliated with the United Synagogue, the mainstream Conservative organization. It does not have a rabbi, but relies on lay members to lead services. And one is apt in services to hear references to Kabbalah, a mystical strand of Judaism, and "to higher states of consciousness," says Marc Berkowitz, president of Beth Shalom for 2010–11.

"People feel drawn to that concept," Berkowitz says. "In Judaism, the rationalist strain won out hundreds of years ago. The more spiritual and esoteric wing has been enjoying a resurgence. People who are interested in TM tend to identify with that aspect of Judaism."

More traditional concerns led meditators to set up Beth Shalom. The founders moved to Fairfield to help build MUM and to be part of the TM community in the mid-1970s. Nomads, they conducted services in campus dorms, former frat houses, a campus chapel and other campus buildings, or Jewish homes—wherever they could find space. Few, at first, knew how to conduct Jewish traditional worship practices.[16] "Nobody knew how to run services," recalls one early member. "It was the land of the blind."

But they learned, with the help of Chabad Lubavitch rabbis and others who visited, including some meditating rabbis. Fairfield, once believed to house just one Jewish family and one Jewish-Christian mixed marriage, drew more Jews, and they felt they needed a permanent space for High Holiday services. They also needed room to mark the bar mitzvahs and bat mitzvahs of their children, as they came of age religiously at age thirteen (or twelve for girls), and to educate younger kids. In 1984, they learned a Baptist church (once a glove factory) was for sale. They bought and refurbished it, including removing a big tub used as a baptismal font, and created what one writer called The Cosmic Congregation.[17]

Members fondly recall the congregation's heady days. At their peak, Friday night services drew as many as fifty families. The place swarmed with children, the offspring of the Baby Boomers who dominated the TM movement. Religious education classes thrived, drawing some forty youngsters at one point. Potluck dinners drew hungry crowds.

The congregation, however, has grayed. Beth Shalom has drawn as few as a half-dozen worshippers on Friday nights, not enough to make the traditional ten-member minyan required for group prayer. The faithful have had to call around to gather enough members for special prayers at services, such as those recited for the dead. Bar and bat mitzvahs are rare. Berkowitz, on his second tour as president of the congregation, said members in mid-2011 totaled about "seventy-ish," including singles and families. This is perhaps half of what it once was. Financially pinched, too, the synagogue ran out of basic operating money in the 2009–10 fiscal year, falling short some $6,000 and forcing leaders "to scramble and beg for money," according to the synagogue's website.

The decline of Beth Shalom, like that of other shrinking offshoots of the TM Movement in Fairfield, such as the elementary and high schools, shows little sign of reversing. The synagogue, like the movement generally in Fairfield, isn't attracting young families as it once did. A trickle of returning children of members, who've come back to Fairfield after college or jobs in big cities, hardly seems enough to refill the seats.

The same is true of St. Gabriel and All Angels, which once teemed with as many as twenty children in its Sunday school. "We have zero to five these days," one longtime member says. The church still can draw as many as thirty-five worshippers on a given Sunday and twice that on a holiday such as Easter, but it's a far less lively place than it once was. Said the veteran member, "We don't have a lot of young families."

The St. Gabriel congregation began in 1985, when a visiting Liberal Catholic priest attracted one hundred or so people to the MIU chapel. Members in the early 1990s bought their current building, a 1926 structure that formerly housed an Assembly of God church and, originally, a Christian Science church.

Reflecting the meditator membership, worshippers at St. Gabriel's tend to be drawn to lofty matters. As the church describes its Sunday service, a celebration of the Eucharist, it has two parts. "In the first movement, the priest and congregation create a spiritual temple within which to receive a great surge of God's power, by purifying and offering themselves to Christ's service," the church says.

God responds to the offering or sacrifice of individual lives by an offering or sacrifice of his own power to the world. The second movement is concerned with the conservation and distribution of that power. Many things determine how much energy flows down at the consecration: the degree of evolution reached by the priest and the people, the devotion of the celebrant, the number and devotion of people present, the music used, and the nature of the need.

Members are exhorted to "keep in mind the absolute reality of God's energy," which "can be directed just as electricity can be directed." And recipients of "God's offering" may be sitting nearby in a pew or on the other side of the world. "It makes no difference. In the realm of thought, distance does not count. But in this case it is not just the thought vibration that reaches out. The appointed angels gather the allotted spiritual energy, and, instantly finding their appointed recipients, they use it on their behalf in whatever way they see best."

Even death can't stand in the way of this energy, the church teaches.

If the person to be benefited is away from her physical body in sleep or death, then the strong thought of the priest about her draws her into the church so the angels do not need to find her. If the individual is newly dead and still in a state of unconsciousness, the angel will still find him and use the assigned energy as he sees best. He may perhaps bring him out of his stupor, or he may store the energy in the recipient's aura for use when he returns to consciousness.

Discussions of "energy" and "consciousness" at St. Gabriel's may resonate with TM practitioners, since the movement regularly uses such terms. By repeating mantras mentally, meditators are said to enter an altered state of consciousness, a "more profound rest," according to *The TM Book: How to Enjoy the Rest of Your Life* (1991), a popular introductory book by Denise Denniston, a devotee of TM.

During TM the body settles to a state of very deep rest very quickly, in only a few minutes. All the various systems in the body come into a state of balance and deeply rooted stresses that sleep does not dissolve are healed. At the same time, the brain functions in a more orderly, coherent way than it does when you're awake or asleep. During TM the mind is awake and alert while the body is enjoying profound rest.

The meditation experience "is a fourth state of consciousness, different from the three we already experience: deep sleep, dreaming, and waking. It is because the body is rested and the mind is still alert that we call this fourth major state of consciousness 'restful alertness.'"[18]

At St. Gabriel's, Father James Palmer discussed consciousness from a religious point of view in a sermon on the Sunday following Easter 2011. "For Liberal Catholics, the Resurrection is a rich and immediate experience; for the full connection with God in consciousness is always possible in each moment," the priest said. "Resurrect means to bring to attention once again, to awaken or manifest, and to remember That [sic] which we have always been and already are—the Divine Universal Consciousness—which we know as Love. We know the Christ Consciousness as Love because we can appreciate it more clearly and concretely that way in our state of physical manifestation."[19]

As they strike mystical chords in their talks, the church's priests at times also range far afield, dipping into the work of non-Christian thinkers for wisdom. One quoted Rumi, a Sufi poet who refers to "veils," including parents, friends, food, and drink. "When men leave this world and see the King without these veils, then they will know that all were veils and coverings, that the object of their desire as in reality that One Thing. . . . They will see all things face to face." In terms that may sound familiar to meditators, the priest added that one must "let go of the small self, the ego: those things that constantly turn our attention to the things of this world, and find the Kingdom of God, the Christ within our heart."

While addressing such grand thoughts on Sundays, church leaders get involved in more pedestrian matters during the rest of the week. St. Gabriel and All Angels is run by volunteers. Its three priests and one deaconess, as of 2011, were not paid and supported themselves in other jobs; one priest sold auto parts for a living, while the others were involved in computer-related businesses. And earthly concerns may have brought some members their way. About half the members hail from a Catholic background, while the rest had Protestant upbringings, according to a longtime member active in the church leadership. Some were in mixed marriages, which the church tolerates. The church at times also attracted Jews, spiritual seekers who, like the other members, were drawn to TM.

Placid as it may have seemed, the church hasn't been free of dissension. Hewing to the Liberal Catholic church's edicts, it has no use for women priests, though its own priests may marry. When some women members devised a ritual based on Christian women of the Bible, they presented the idea to a bishop in Chicago. "He didn't say a word," one presenter recalls. "He didn't seem to like it." One local member, troubled that women were excluded from the priesthood, set up a competing church in Fairfield.

Despite the grand thoughts they mull over, moreover, some church supporters flash wicked senses of humor about religion and TM. One St. Gabriel's member shares a joke popular in town: "Why are there so many Catholics and Jews in the movement? The Jews know a good thing when they see it and the Catholics will believe anything."

Fairfield is now also home to people who claim a direct connection to the beyond and are happy to share their wisdom, generally for a price. Connie Huebner, who earned a master's degree in the Science of Creative Intelligence at MIU, set up the Divine Mother Church in 1999. "Mother God made her self known to me and offered a great wealth of Divine wisdom," Huebner says in her promotional materials. "It is this Divine Knowledge that I want to bring to as many people as possible. I have developed a personal relationship with Divine Mother. I converse with Her all of the time." In 2013, programs were available online for free or for charges of between $7 and $50, with advanced programming—live and interactive—available for between $200 and $1,500. Huebner accepted Visa, MasterCard, and PayPal.[20]

For its part, the TM movement doesn't exclude members of Western faiths, but it has no use for some rival gurus. It in effect excommunicates meditators—by yanking the badges that give them the right to meditate in the golden domes on campus—if they take up the teachings, for instance, of Sri Sri Ravi Shankar, a once-trusted follower of Maharishi who set up his own movement, and Ammachi, another popular guru. The TM Movement defends such practices in the name of keeping "pure" the knowledge it offered. One longtime TM Movement adherent, however, likens the policy to competition among copier makers, saying a salesperson for IBM copiers could rightly be fired if he or she started selling Xerox machines.

For some adherents who moved to Fairfield to follow Maharishi, this version of shunning has proved to be a long-lasting source of grief. Doug Hamilton, a committed meditator, for instance, was excluded from the domes three times—twice for short stretches in the 1990s for growing a beard and, more recently, for fourteen years, until May 2012. His sin: visiting non-TM spiritual teachers. Hamilton had suffered a stroke in 1998 and visited Ammachi and Karunamayi for help with healing, a violation of the guidelines for TM supporters who want to meditate in the domes.

The shunning unsettled Hamilton because he had been associated with the TM movement for his entire adult life. Like many others, he was drawn to TM in high school, in 1971. Son of a professor in the medical school at the University of Iowa, Hamilton spent a month between his junior and senior years in high school studying with Maharishi in California. At just seventeen, he was one of eleven hundred people, mostly college age, taking the course with the guru. "It was all very large and heady and high-minded," he recalls. "It was very idealistic and yet practical."

When he returned, Hamilton became active in a local meditation center in Iowa City. TM was especially popular on campuses then, and students were drawn, by the dozens, to weekly sessions. "We had easily one hundred people every weekend studying TM," he says.

Hamilton attended Iowa State University and then earned his degree in business administration from the University of Iowa in 1978. He took stretches of time off from school in that period to work full time for the TM Movement, teaching the meditation technique up and down the East Coast, including places such as Washington, D.C., Boston, and Long Island. TM teachers, he recalled, earned little money and so got by with other jobs. "From a practical standpoint, you had to make your life outside the movement," he says.

When a cousin called in late 1978 and tipped him off about a sales position for a textbook-publishing company based in the Chicago area, Hamilton jumped at it. In 1978, he had married a fellow meditator (like many devotees of the movement) and needed steady work. Hamilton stayed with the publishing company, Follett Corporation, working in outside sales until about 1990. He earned enough money to enable him and his wife, Jennifer, to buy sixteen acres in Fairfield in 1986. Over time, they put up a house and set about creating a life raising Icelandic horses on their spread, the Prairie Garden Farm. Meanwhile, he continued meditating, frequenting the men's dome on the university campus.

But Hamilton took up a hobby that got him in trouble with the TM leadership. He indulged an interest in history by becoming a Civil War re-enactor. "I had spectacular nineteenth-century facial hair," he recalls. In the 1990s, the beard was unacceptable in the domes, where decorum counted; perhaps as vestiges of Maharishi's preference for clean-cut looks, women were urged to avoid jeans in their dome and men needed to be clean-shaven. His beard was enough to get his dome badge yanked twice, once for about a year. (The dress code has changed and beards are now acceptable, longtime movement spokesman Bob Roth said.) Later, in 1998, Hamilton's badge was pulled after he consulted the "saints" for help with rehabilitation after his stroke.

Hamilton repeatedly sought reinstatement over the fourteen years prior to mid-2012. He was denied until, he says, "progressive" voices in the movement prevailed over those he calls "preservationists." Finally, in 2012, he was granted an exemption from the guidelines prohibiting devotees from seeing saints. At a meeting where his application was reviewed, he says, he looked around the table at people he had known for years in the movement and said, "'We're all forty-year men here.' Everybody nodded their heads."

Hamilton speculates that he was reinstated in part because the TM leadership wanted to boost the number of meditators in the domes. Further, he says, in the movement there really are few "TM virgins," people who haven't gone to lectures by other spiritual leaders, even those who are rivals to TM.

If he bears a grudge for the long years of being denied entrance to the dome, Hamilton doesn't show it. "It wasn't fun, but it was interesting," he says. He found the tension between the "strict preservationists" and the "progressives" intriguing, for instance.

Hamilton's wife, Jennifer, however, is less charitable. She stopped going to the women's dome after he was kicked out and has built a career teaching a health-promoting form of meditation called Sunpoint. A registered nurse who worked in high-risk obstetrics and later took up Ayurvedic nursing, she studied under several meditation teachers not embraced by the TM Movement. She also taught traditional English and American dance and spent her spare time with a singing group, Prairie Harmony. "She's very, very busy," says Hamilton.

Under the sway of TM practitioners, Fairfield is now a mecca for alternative approaches to health and lots of other things. Far from a parochial little Iowa farm and church-school college town, it has become a cultural cornucopia, offering residents a dazzling array of choices in areas as far-flung as entertainment, education, and self-improvement.

4

Unearthly Delights

WHEN THE CITIZENS of Fairfield wanted to have a good time, their choices were once pretty narrow. A county fair in the summertime, maybe a movie downtown, a football game at the high school, or perhaps a stop at a local watering hole. But those choices have broadened dramatically over the past forty years. Residents in recent times could take in videos such as *The Science of Miracles: The Quantum Language of Healing, Peace, Feeling, and Belief* (2009) at the Fairfield Public Library. They could attend benefit concerts to raise funds for Tanzanian orphanages and efforts to promote sustainable farming in Africa. They could join in on live telecasts with an Ayurvedic physician discussing "Love & Prana II: Karma, Kama, Vajikarna and Kamagani" or spend time with a Hindu priest as he performs predawn sacrificial fire ceremonies to seek blessings from the god Shiva. Such ceremonies, called Yagyas, were aimed at pleading for world peace, neutralizing "negativity," and promoting health or overcoming "planetary afflictions." Participants did need to bring washed fruit and flowers and avoid meat and egg products for the day.

Fairfield, whose glories were once Parsons College and a National Guard detachment, has changed a lot since TMers took over the bankrupt college. Sure, the Thirty-Fourth Army Iowa National Guard Band, based in town, still performs in front of the quaint old gazebo in the town center on Memorial Day. And the Trojans take the field at the high school every fall, facing off against such rivals as the Keokuk Chiefs and the Mount Pleasant Panthers. But Fairfield's small-town character has expanded to embrace the cosmopolitan tastes of people from big cities and both U.S. coasts, as well as newcomers from scores of countries around the world.

Not everyone is happy about the changes. Some non-meditators bristle that the TMers have hijacked the town culture, turning it into a kind of spiritual mecca cum Big City Boomer haven in the Midwest. Certainly, the meditators have had an influence exceeding their numbers, believed to total more than two thousand. "Over the years it has become more pronounced in Fairfield," complains a church secretary who is not a meditator. "It seems to be more a majority thing."

That impression stems from the all-too-visible impact the meditators have had on big swaths of the town's social life. The meditators, many of whom brought money, a sense of rebelliousness, and an appetite for big-city music, art, and entertainment, have made their marks everywhere. Their imprint is apparent in art, with several galleries now showcasing local work, and the chance for residents and visitors to enjoy a monthly 1st Fridays Art Walk, an event set up by a TMer from California in 2002. Their influence turns up in food, too, so vegetarians can feast at several eateries, featuring, among other things, Indian delights, while others could for a time sample high-end Italian food—once exotic to some midwesterners. Retailers responded, opening outlets to pitch Maharishi Ayurvedic medicines that compete with the conventional medications offered at the more familiar Hy-Vee Drugstore.

Popular entertainment, too, has been overhauled. The Fairfield Arts & Convention Center (FACC) now showcases such documentaries as *American Meat* (2013). The film lambastes industrial farming and would likely generate little fan support among Iowa's bigger growers. Visitors can also view exhibits such as *Healthy Pollinators Are Essential for Super Foods and Medicinal Plants* in the FACC's biodiversity learning and activities center.

To be fair, some staple shows at the FACC's Stephen Sondheim Center for the Performing Arts have an appeal to townies. Among recent offerings have been *In the Christmas Mood with the Glenn Miller Orchestra* and *An Evening with Mark Twain*. But East Coast refugees moving up in their Baby Boom years would make for a more likely audience for a *Tribute to Frankie Valli*. And, certainly, few townies would rush to a talk by Mahendra Kumar Trivedi, an Indian mechanical engineer who supporters say can change the molecular structure of cancer cells, radioactive water, viruses, bacteria, fungi, etc. ("More than 4,000 scientific studies have been done to verify his gift to heal," one backer gushed.) And, despite the $100 cost, meditators flock to such programs as a one-day silent meditation retreat at the FACC led in mid-2011 by Amma Sri Karunamayi, a repeat visitor to Fairfield. The program was designed to help participants "realize the truth that you and your Divine Mother are One."

The FACC itself might never have opened if not for meditators, who rallied behind non-meditating locals to get it built. The $7 million cultural center, an ambitious effort for the town, opened in 2007 and promptly went into the red financially, leading to a management shakeup the following year. The "jewel of Fairfield," as boosters call it, featured the 522-seat Sondheim theater, offering a stage for music, comedy, dance, and national touring performances. It provided a venue for local concert and chamber music groups and community theater. The convention portion of the building, with twelve thousand square feet of meeting space, offered full catering and banquet options. Voters in 2010 bailed out the center's finances in a contentious special election, clearing the way for the FACC to tap a city fund so it could pay off its $5 million debt. The city took over the center. In its opening years, the center wasn't able to cover its debt service from revenues and donations alone, and it still depends on donations, some of which come from meditators and their businesses.

For some in town, the FACC's solvency, like just about all other subjects of controversy in Fairfield, became a matter that pitted meditator against non-meditator. Critics among the townies were appalled by what they saw as imprudent management and poor planning in, for one thing, building such a big center. To many it seemed unneeded in Fairfield, which is still a place of modest incomes. (The median household income sits below $35,000, with nearly 22 percent of the population living below the poverty line, according to the U.S. Census Bureau's 2010 count.[1]) For many, Fairfield is also a place of small-town tastes. "When they see a facility of this size, people feel 'that's not us,'" a former FACC business manager tells me. It didn't help that the planners took on a hefty amount of debt and then failed to stage enough money-making events to cover the costs. The idea of having to go to the town for a vote to pay off debt was galling to many, especially to locals who didn't warm to the cultural offerings there. "It was very divisive on many levels," says the former manager, a non-meditator who hadn't used the center herself (until she took a job there) because it didn't offer enough to capture her family's notice.

During much of its early days, some locals refused to come to events at the center because they saw it as a place chiefly serving meditators. That attitude was rooted in misunderstanding, argues one of the cofounders, non-meditator Suzan Kessel. "It is totally a community venture and nonpolitical, although people try to make it political," says Kessel, an artist and a fifth-generation Fairfielder. She and a non-meditator friend, Sally Neff Denney, got the idea to create the center in the mid-1990s, when the Fairfield Art Association lost exhibit space in town.

But Kessel, mindful of the need to have broad support for the FACC, carefully sought out a mix of meditators and non-meditators to back the facility from its earliest days. While she believed a center could have been built without meditator backing, she wanted to rally support from all segments of the town. "Sally and I interviewed certain meditators before we brought them on board," Kessel recalls. "We didn't want the issue to come up and we selected several that were very strong supporters of the project both in their time and their money."

Challenging as it is, the center's managers have striven to offer a mix of events to serve all corners of the community. While some offerings draw only meditators, the managers try to put on productions with broader appeal. For instance, *Ricky Nelson Remembered*, a show by the twin sons of the late singer, packed the house with both meditators and non-meditators. By contrast, a show of country stars, titled *Larry Gatlin & the Gatlin Brothers*, was aimed more at townies, as was a display of mixed martial arts fighting inside a cage. The managers also opened the facility to educational groups, which staged math competitions and history exhibitions, as well as to area entrepreneurs. Looking for financial solid ground, they have sharply boosted the number of events they host.

Indeed, the FACC has become something of a symbolic way to unite the community. Many non-meditators were irked at TMers in 2001 when they knocked down, rather than rehabilitated, the Barhydt Memorial Chapel on the MUM campus. The chapel, a stately stone building on the National Register of Historic Places, had towered over the campus and was its signature image from about 1910 on. It was a place of many weddings and a venue where alums of Parsons College recalled events ranging from convocations and student theatrical productions to required chapel attendance. But the building needed work and didn't suit the administration's plans for the campus. Backers could not rustle up an estimated $1 million to move it. So to preserve the memory of the chapel after it was leveled, backers arranged to install Barhydt's grand organ in the FACC's Sondheim Center. Further, boosters raised funds to install stained-glass windows from the structure in an area of the FACC that serves the Parsons College Alumni Hall, a hall of fame for the school. One exhibit honored performers who had brought their shows to the campus in the 1960s, including Louis Armstrong, Bo Diddley, Gladys Knight and the Pips, and Neil Diamond.

More recently, celebrities who back TM have come to Fairfield from time to time. James McCartney, son of longtime TM supporter and former Beatle Paul McCartney, made his American debut at the Sondheim Center in late 2009, for instance. "The audience, heavily weighted with aging 60s boomers, went wild when the 32-year-old singer/guitarist walked on stage with Light, his band," reported *The Hawk Eye*, an Iowa newspaper.[2] Another TM backer and Baby Boomer favorite, Donovan, joined the younger McCartney. Thanks to the movement, Fairfield also hosted the reconstituted Beach Boys, including original band member and longtime meditator Mike Love, and Moby.

Filmmaker David Lynch, who has emerged as a persuasive front man for the movement in the absence of a charismatic successor to Maharishi, brings out the stars. Some appeared in Fairfield in conjunction with Lynch's "Change Begins Within" weekends at MUM. Stars as disparate as British comic Russell Brand and Paul McCartney, Ringo Starr, Sheryl Crow, Eddie Vedder, and Ben Harper appeared at fundraising events in New York City for the David Lynch Foundation for Consciousness-Based Education and World Peace. Brand, serving as master of ceremonies at a December 2010 fundraiser at the Metropolitan Museum of Art, told the crowd that TM "has been incredibly valuable to me both in my recovery as a drug addict and in my personal life, my marriage, my professional life." Indeed, he said, an idea had just popped into his brain "the other day while I was meditating which I think is worth millions of dollars."[3]

Lynch's foundation, established in 2005, touts TM as a way to address problems that celebrities like to attack. The meditation technique, Lynch maintains, can help people who are homeless as well as veterans, Native Americans, and prisoners, along with students in troubled schools, who are served by the Center for Wellness and Achievement in Education (mentioned in chapter 3). "At-risk populations suffer from epidemic levels of chronic stress and stress-related disorders—fueling violence, crime, soaring health costs, and compromising the effectiveness of education, health, rehabilitation, and vocational programs now in place," the foundation says on its website. Lynch told the *New York Times* that he took up meditation in the early 1970s, when he was having marital problems with the first of his four wives. "I had a whole bunch of personal anger that I would take out on her," he said. "I think I was a weak person. I wasn't self-assured. I was not a happy camper inside. Two weeks after I started, my wife comes to me and said, 'This anger, where did it go?' I felt a freedom and happiness growing inside. It was like—poooft!—I felt a kind of smile from Mother Nature. The world looked better and better. It's an ocean of unbounded love within us, so it's real hard to get a conflict going." (Nonetheless, as the *Times* noted, the couple divorced a year later.)[4]

To promote TM, Lynch developed collaborations with school districts across the country. His foundation has worked with public, charter, and private middle schools and high schools in New York City, Washington, D.C., Atlanta, Detroit, Chicago, Tucson, San Francisco, and Los Angeles to encourage the technique during the school day among students, teachers, and administrators. The foundation website is chockablock with video testimonials from officials who say TM reduced disciplinary problems at inner-city schools that contend with gangs and who say it improved student performance. One student speaks of how the dread she once felt about school has been replaced by enthusiasm about going. Another high school student credits it for his success in sports. "I get disturbing thoughts washed away," says a third. "When you come out of meditating, the problem is just gone."[5]

Lynch, who proselytizes for TM as aggressively as any missionary, provided videos on his site that attack head-on the idea that TM is a religion. The videos quote school officials as saying the practice has nothing to do with religion. Sporting a crucifix on her necklace, one administrator notes she was a "naysayer" about TM because of her religious beliefs but she then praised the practice for making "a great and significant difference." She says, "I'm telling you now I am a believer." Religious questions have come up about TM for years, dogging the movement at least since the 1977 federal court case *Malnak v. Yogi* ruled that the teaching of TM and the Science of Creative Intelligence—the movement's dogma—was "religious in nature." Critics deride TM as "Hinduism Lite," but meditators say the Vedic knowledge that led to the meditation practice predates Hinduism.

Lynch's group rebuts the critics, however, with testimonials that emphasize the practice's success in fostering calmness, reducing stress, and improving focus. The religious elements evident in the movement in Fairfield—mentions of bringing heaven on earth, of "His Holiness" Maharishi, and of the Divine—don't figure into the foundation's approach. Instead, as noted earlier, the Quiet Time program it backs emphasizes the simple twice-a-day meditation technique, saying student participants "score higher on intelligence tests, close the achievement gap, improve test scores, and have higher graduation rates compared to students in control groups. Meditating students also show reduced stress levels, anxiety, depression, violence and substance abuse."

While interested in such outreach efforts, Lynch's foundation has directed much of its largesse into TM operations seemingly distant from American public schools. Legally based in Fairfield but with its main offices in New York and Los Angeles, the foundation reported that in 2011 it took in $8.75 million in contributions and gave away $4.34 million of that. Its largest single grantee, getting $1.83 million, was the Center for Wellness and Achievement in Education, which provides the Quiet Time meditation program in California schools. The foundation also spread some $1.96 million among TM-related entities, including the Maharishi Foundation, the Maharishi School of the Age of Enlightenment, MUM, and the Maharishi Research Institute. It gave lesser amounts to veterans programs, military colleges, and programs to teach meditation to abused women, including Cambodian victims of human trafficking. Expenses gobbled up a good bit of the foundation funds, including $1.15 million in pay and benefits for employees and $441,142 used to produce videos documenting the foundation's successes. A small share of its funds ($227,786) went abroad to programs including "peace-creating initiatives" in Latin America involving teaching Yogic Flying to students in Mexican schools and TM to several hundred soldiers in the military in Ecuador. TM advocates urge that military personnel worldwide be trained in TM as part of what they call "invincible defense technology," arguing that more meditation means less conflict, including less terrorism.

Movement insiders may have had some say over how the money was allocated. The president of Lynch's foundation when the grants went out was John Hagelin, who directs the Institute of Science, Technology and Public Policy at MUM. A Harvard-trained physicist, he also serves as minister of science and technology of another arm of the movement called the Global Country of World Peace. And he ran three times for president of the United States on the Natural Law Party ticket. Hagelin drew $43,000 in pay in 2011 from Lynch's foundation; he drew $37,187 in the prior year and $34,212 in 2009, each time for an average of ten hours of work each week. Hagelin also drew $86,625 from MUM, where he serves as a trustee and institute director. Bob Roth, vice president and executive director of Lynch's foundation, says he and Hagelin plan in time to withdraw from their roles in the foundation to tend more to their work in the TM organization. (Roth drew $112,044 in pay and other compensation from the foundation in 2011.) "That is the plan, but no schedule," Roth says.

Celebrity backers such as Lynch have been integral to the movement for more than forty years. Maharishi labored in the United States to promote the technique and his teachings from the late 1950s on, but his biggest successes came after the Beatles embraced the practice and visited the guru in India in 1968. Images of the flower-bedecked musicians, sitting cross-legged in Indian garb at the guru's ashram, popularized the idea around the world. None had quite the same recruitment power afterwards, although some celebrities continued to talk up the practice. Radio shock-jock Howard Stern, for instance, spoke about how meditation saved his mother's life after she took it up in a battle with depression while he was in college. As Stern told talk-show host David Letterman in February 2011, his mother had seen Maharishi on a talk show and was "transformed" and "elated" by the practice.[6] She took Stern to a TM center when he was age eighteen, and he began what became a lifelong meditation routine, too. "I find it very relaxing," said Stern. He also said he lived with TMers in an Armonk, New York, monastery for a while in his early, poorly paid days in radio. Stern's trademark coarseness was missing in 1985 when he interviewed Maharishi, a session during which he said he felt "reverential" toward the guru.[7]

The stars continue to plump for TM. On June 30, 2012, the David Lynch Foundation staged a comedy night at the Beverly Wilshire Hotel in Beverly Hills, California, to raise funds for its efforts. Talent agent George Shapiro, a longtime meditator, was feted by headliners Jerry Seinfeld, Jay Leno, Russell Brand, Sarah Silverman, and Garry Shandling. Seinfeld, a longtime medi-tator, in a highlights reel praised TM for helping people rid themselves of stress. "It just kind of floats away, instead of finding a home in your mind," he said. "You learn how to just let go of things."

Over the years, the celebrity backers have been a diverse lot that has included Hollywood's Clint Eastwood, Mary Tyler Moore, Gwyneth Pal-trow, Laura Dern, and Hugh Jackman. Backers have also included business leaders such as designer Donna Karan and hedge fund magnate Ray Dalio, who brought in people from Fairfield to train his employees at Bridgewa-ter Associates L.P. in meditation. CNN journalist Candy Crowley, a medita-tor who co-hosted a Lynch foundation gala in 2010, delivered a commence-ment address at MUM in May 2012, exhorting graduates to "be honest and demand honesty in life."[8] Ex-CNN anchor Soledad O'Brien welcomed guests on her morning news show such as hip-hop entrepreneur Russell Simmons, who touted TM. ABC's George Stephanopoulos, who learned about TM from Seinfeld, told the *Good Morning America* audience in late 2012 that TM "can help anybody," as he interviewed Seinfeld and Lynch foundation executive director Bob Roth. Talk-show host Ellen DeGeneres has offered testimonials. Actor Stephen Collins, who served on the board of Lynch's foundation, brought his message to Fairfield in 2010, when he spoke warmly about TM at graduation ceremonies inside one of the golden domes on the MUM campus. Reflecting the split between meditators and non-meditators in Fairfield, Collins's talk appeared to draw few townies. That was so even though the good-hearted minister he played in his famed TV series *7th Heaven* was just the kind of guy churchgoing Fairfielders would warm to.

Along with playing host to celebrity adherents of TM, Fairfield has at times welcomed political stars. Presidential candidate Barack Obama came to town when trolling for votes in 2007, for instance, and he warmed the hearts of meditators by bemoaning a national "empathy deficit." Among his crowd-pleasing lines here, according to politico.com, was "somehow we have lost the capacity to recognize ourselves in each other."[9]

For their part, politicians from Fairfield have not done quite as well in moving much beyond the local stage. But that isn't for want of trying. They aim high, even as high as the White House at times, but their meditating ways may keep them earthbound.

5

Power of the Ballot

CONNIE BOYER SHOULD HAVE been a shoo-in when she ran for an Iowa state house seat. A Republican, she brought an impressive résumé to the 2002 race. She was a sixth-generation resident of Jefferson County in southeast Iowa, had been active in the Chamber of Commerce, Rotary, the Fairfield Strategic Planning Commission, and numerous arts and civic groups. Telegenic and folksy, she also co-hosted a local public cable TV show, helped run a bed and breakfast with her husband, and managed to work full time as chief financial officer at a local bank holding company.

But for some voters, Boyer had a fatal flaw. She was a meditator in a place where praising the Lord—loudly and often or, more conventionally, with the help of old English hymns—is the way some people strive for higher realms. Even though she was homegrown, unlike the out-of-state interlopers who flocked into Fairfield at the urging of their late guru, Boyer carried baggage. At one political meeting, she was challenged about efforts to bring TM into public schools. "One of the questions was, 'we think that because you meditate that you are going to try to force meditation into the schools,'" she recalls, as we chat in her quaint bed and breakfast, the Seven Roses Inn. Boyer said she had no intention to do that, had never been asked by anyone in the movement to do that, and had no plans to press for bills that would do that. The David Lynch Foundation was offering programs to inner-city schools around the country, but Boyer said the effort was simply not on her to-do list.

Meditators have run for all sorts of offices around the country, indeed around the world, over the past few decades. Sometimes they have seemed to be pushing a TM agenda, tilting at windmills in elections they can't win—such as the U.S. presidency—as they try to garner headlines for the practice. On a local level in Fairfield, some may have wanted to make sure that the interests of MUM were considered when such issues as road improvements came up. But several officeholders and would-be elected officials who meditate seem more motivated by the same mix of ego, sense of civic duty, and stances on issues that drive politicians of all stripes.

Still, meditation—like race or religion—can play a big role when voters consider the candidates. Boyer lost her state race by a heartbreaking half a percentage point, with her fifty-two hundred votes falling just fifty-five shy of the tally for her non-meditator opponent. "It was an issue when I ran," she says. Her take on the question she faced: "My guess—it would have been fear, I suppose, of religion. The people that asked me I would consider pretty conservative and traditionally religious."

Years later, however, the ironies in her defeat remain rich. Boyer, a Lutheran who in her late teens and early twenties threw in for a time with a group of born-again Christians, is not a mover and shaker in TM. Rather, she got involved with meditation casually at the time her first marriage was ending, around 1990. That was a time, she recalls, when she was "wanting something deeper" in her life, something she "felt to be more real." She had to overlook a "goofy" TM enthusiast who, she says, smiled too often while introducing the practice to prospective meditators. Eventually, a friend taught her.

Like several thousand other Fairfield residents, Boyer had been surrounded by TM while she was growing up. Back when she was in ninth grade, she recalls, her class debated whether the movement should be allowed into town. Later, when her brother took up meditation for a while, "we teased him about taking his fruit and flowers," she says. (Fruit and flowers play a role in initiation ceremonies into TM.) Still later, Boyer worked as a sales clerk at a local sheepskin clothing shop that was run by a meditator, and she got acquainted with customers who were part of the movement. Some time afterward, she struck up a friendship with a meditator who performed with her as a dancer in a local production of *The Music Man* and who taught her the TM practice.

When she did take up meditation, as a thirty-year-old, Boyer found it felt familiar. The feeling, she says, was much like the experiences she'd had in her fundamentalist Christian group a decade earlier. Of course there were differences. A big one, she said, is that no one involved in TM tells her she'll go to hell if she doesn't believe a certain way. Even today she considers herself a Lutheran, says she knows nothing about the Hinduism to which TM is often compared, and sees no conflict between her mainstream religious affiliation and TM. Indeed, she claims her religious sensitivities have been sharpened by meditation. Boyer says she saw an angel while meditating. "It was outside of myself," she says. "I got a glimpse."

These days, with the crush of activities in her life, Boyer admits she doesn't stick rigorously to the twice-daily meditation ritual that has marked much of the past twenty years for her. "Sometimes I miss," she says. "Life is just a little bit too demanding and busy." She's not as consistent, she says, as her current husband, Robert Boyer. Bob, a clinical psychologist, has master's degrees from Maharishi European Research University and California State University and a doctorate from the University of Oklahoma. He has taught at MUM and abroad.

Certainly, the Boyers have plenty on their plate. Along with running the Seven Roses Inn, they have written a self-published book, *Heart and Mind: A Perfect Union* (2009). In it, they use such movies as *Casablanca* (1942), *The Wizard of Oz* (1939), *Groundhog Day* (1993), and surprisingly, *Mary Poppins* (1964) to discuss how the heart and mind work together. The book draws on material Bob Boyer used in other works, which hit TM themes hard. These books include *Cool Mind, Warm Heart: How to Communicate with Body, Mind, Heart, and Soul* (2007) and such weighty titles as *Think Outside the Bang: Beyond Quantum Theory and Hidden Dimensions to a Holistic Account of Consciousness, Mind and Matter* (2010), as well as *Bridge to Unity: Unified Field-Based Science and Spirituality* (2008). Connie told one interviewer that she's had to "dumb down" some of her husband's scientific style to make his thoughts more suited to a general audience.

Despite her full calendar, Boyer did make time to serve on the city council in Fairfield. She was appointed to fill out a departing council member's term in April 2003 and then won election to a seat in November 2003, serving until 2007, when she opted against another run for the post. Urged by Mayor

Ed Malloy, a fellow meditator, to rejoin the council, Boyer won reelection to a four-year term in the fall of 2011 and took on the job of mayor pro tem. With her on board again, Fairfield in early 2013 had three meditators on the seven-member council.

Acceptance into the local political scene has been a hard-won matter for meditators in Fairfield. It wasn't until 1986 that a meditator, Richard Schneider, was elected to the Fairfield City Council, according to Malloy. Seven have followed since then: Peter Orange, John Revolinski, Ellen Jones, Michael Halley, and Tom Stanley, as well as Boyer and Malloy. Several worked at MUM or the Maharishi School of the Age of Enlightenment.

TM practitioners marked a milestone, after a quarter century in town, with the mayoral election of 2001. Malloy, a genial oil-brokerage-firm president, swept into the mayor's office then and has kept it ever since, winning a new term every two years. Malloy, a former college basketball player from Long Island, New York, with silvery hair and a TV newsman's good looks, had moved to Fairfield in 1980 and served on the city council from 1992 to 1998. During his first council election, he thought he had put to rest the worries about meditators among non-meditating townies. He told an interviewer, "I weathered all of the rumors and concerns that I had a hidden agenda that would serve meditators."

But the worries about the "roos" didn't end for other locals in the 1990s. The non-meditator townies turned out to help incumbent Robert Rasmussen defeat Malloy in his first mayoral run, in 1997. Elections that year were tough in Fairfield for meditators overall. Residents waited in line for up to two hours to oppose a TM practitioner who was running for a school board seat, according to the *Kansas City Star*, which reported that the "specter of the Maharishi running Fairfield" was too great for Malloy to overcome. One Rasmussen ad, which the *Fairfield Ledger* rejected, depicted Maharishi pulling the strings on a mayoral puppet, the paper said.[1]

Among townies, it may not have helped that Malloy was held in high regard by meditators involved in politics through the Natural Law Party (NLP), a quixotic global party based in Fairfield that ran candidates for national and local offices in a slew of countries—almost always unsuccessfully—between 1992 and 2004. Malloy was a member of the national executive committee of the U.S. arm of the group starting in 1992 and co-chaired the national party in 1993. The NLP pushed a platform that pressed for meditation in, among other places, the military. The idea was that a critical mass of meditators would foster peace and a widespread reduction in crime and violence. Malloy was also quoted in 1997 as saying that the profits of his company, Danaher Oil, climbed 20 percent in the first year after moving into a building that Maharishi Global Construction crafted in accord with the movement's architectural principles, Maharishi Sthapatya Veda. Malloy has been a meditator since 1974 and, like many others, met his wife in the movement. Educated in Catholic schools, Malloy inspired five of his seven siblings and his father, a New York policeman, to learn to meditate.

Chastened by Fairfield voters in his first mayoral bid, Malloy bided his time. He stepped down from the city council and served in 1999 on a Strategic Planning Council appointed by then–Iowa governor Tom Vilsack to lay out a blueprint for Iowa's growth through 2010. Another planning council member, writer Chuck Offenburger, gave Malloy high marks for his work with the group. "Malloy became an eloquent voice on the council for a clean environment, organic farming, community building and a big increase in availability of venture capital for entrepreneurial start-up companies," Offenburger wrote. "We kidded him a good bit about being such an environmentalist when he is also president of an oil company."

When Malloy challenged Rasmussen again for the mayoral post in Fairfield, he was better prepared. He beat Rasmussen 1,629 to 1,440 on a platform of strengthening the local economy, revitalizing the town square, and building tourism, as well as beautifying Fairfield. Rasmussen, who at age sixty-nine was twenty years older than Malloy and had served twenty-eight years as mayor, recalls that he hadn't planned to run at first and then didn't put much money into his effort. A touch bitterly, Rasmussen also says Malloy's meditator-dominated ward turned out en masse, delivering 640 of the votes for his challenger. He complains that the TM leaders, who meditate twice a day in the golden domes on the MUM campus, had rolled out the vote for Malloy. "They all get a sheet of paper when they leave the dome telling them who to vote for," Rasmussen says, as we nosh at Revelations, the Fairfield bookstore-cum-restaurant.

Gracious in the way small-town leaders perhaps must be, however, Rasmussen and Malloy publicly papered over any lingering differences when Malloy took over. Rasmussen swore Malloy in, and Malloy in turn declared a "Bob and Martha Rasmussen Day." Malloy also sought to build bridges to the non-meditator community, keeping non-meditators on boards and committees he appointed. Rasmussen told an interviewer that Malloy knew that as mayor he would have to listen to all factions in the community, not just meditators. For his part, Malloy tells me that "the relationship between me and Bob Rasmussen has improved greatly and . . . there is a mutual respect for the long continuous good management of the city."

Given his repeated success at reelection, Malloy appears to have kept most residents happy with his governance. He argued that the gulf between the meditating and non-meditating communities has shrunk as people have gotten to know one another through work, particularly in start-up companies run by meditators, and other areas where people mix, such as Little League or arts events. Malloy says tensions have "dramatically dissipated, dramatically dissipated."

Making a mark at higher levels of government in Iowa, however, has been challenging for meditators. Democrat Becky Schmitz, a meditator, squeaked into the Iowa state senate by a margin of fewer than 200 votes out of 20,500 cast in an election in 2006. She then lost a bid for reelection by more than 1,450 votes in 2010, a year when she said Democrats fared poorly across the state. Her successful opponent was a veteran Republican legislator who came out of retirement to challenge Schmitz. Schmitz, a social worker and mental health therapist, set her sights locally in 2012, aiming to be the first woman elected to a seat on the Jefferson County Board of Supervisors. She won the seat handily, racking up some 4,417 votes—the biggest number in the three-person contest (which produced two new members of the supervisory board). "In my political career, I have not mentioned in any of my materials that I am a meditator because of the biases in this area of the state," Schmitz tells me in an email. Later she adds, "a high majority of the volunteer workers on both local campaigns and the presidential on the Democratic side were meditators." Her intention, she says, is to "represent the entire county."

As we swivel about in the cozy chairs in the Fairfield City Council meeting room, Malloy tells me there's no reason that meditators, if they are solid candidates, can't win state office. He might seek a state office in 2014 or 2016, he says. Boyer lost her race in 2002 in part because some Democratic-leaning meditators declined to vote for a Republican, he maintains. Malloy, who registered as a Democrat in 2004 and built up years of experience in office in Fairfield, believes he can appeal more broadly. "There are a handful of us meditating politicians in Fairfield who, I suppose, could at some time decide to run for state office and test that," says Malloy. "Meditation is mainstream. It's no longer what it was a decade ago, certainly not two, three, four decades ago."

In Fairfield, meditators do make their voices known at times in local affairs. The installation of wireless water meters whose radiation pulses let the city track the use of water, for instance, bubbled up as a major issue in 2012. Maharishi urged his followers to avoid radio waves from such sources as cell phones, and some go to great lengths to heed his warnings, such as by declining to use wireless computers. After the city installed wireless meters in hundreds of homes, some meditators organized a group to demand the right to have them removed, an expensive process that split the city council over the issue of who paid the costs—the homeowner or the city. Meter opponents established a website and collected more than one thousand signatures on an electronic petition against the meters.

Some residents complained of health problems that they blamed on the meters. One resident, cited in a letter to a local paper, said she couldn't sleep. Her energy level had so sharply dropped that she had to give up dancing and horseback riding and could not work. Richard Wolfson, a PhD physicist who has taught at MUM and the Maharishi School, warned in a June 2012 letter to the *Fairfield Ledger* about research linking radiation to reduced fertility, arrhythmia, and impaired mental function.[2]

Like radiation, the question of meditation may linger in the background in elections, but it hasn't always surfaced. It did not arise—publicly at least—when Francis Thicke, a Fairfield-area farmer, ran for Iowa secretary of agriculture in 2010. The PhD agronomist and former soils expert with the U.S. Department of Agriculture had an agenda that had nothing to do with his personal meditation practices of nearly forty years. He ran as a Democrat, attempting to unseat an incumbent Republican on a platform pushing sustainable agricultural practices; promoting greater competition and fewer monopolies in agribusiness; and opposing concentrated animal feeding operations, which are giant, foul-smelling, and polluting operations that are often the target of industrial-farming critics.

Thicke is an organic family farmer who tends to some eighty cows at a time—feeding them grass—at his Radiance Dairy, a spread four miles northwest of Fairfield, and produces milk and yogurt. "Mainly I wanted to bring up issues for discussion that are generally ignored," says Thicke, a former antiwar activist whose only previous electoral experience was as a member of a township board of supervisors in his native Minnesota in 1980–81. "There are a lot of elephants in the living room that nobody will talk about and that is what I wanted to do."

Thicke, a genial but serious scientist who grew up farming and spending his boyhood showing hogs at county fairs in 4-H activities, got into meditation when a roommate at Winona State College took up the practice. After graduating in 1972, Thicke taught meditation part time in the 1970s but admitted in 2011 that he doesn't meditate as much as he'd like. The time pressures of running a farm get in the way, he said. He bought the farm, once called the Super Radiance Dairy after a term used in TM, from a fellow meditator in 1992, when he decided he wanted to leave his government post in Washington, D.C., to get back into farming.

Meditation, Thicke says, was irrelevant in his campaign for agriculture secretary in the state and would have had nothing to do with his agenda had he been elected. Well-known in some Iowa farming circles because he had often spoken about controversial agricultural issues, Thicke believes he had largely settled reservations voters may have had about his meditation practices. He says, "I traveled around Iowa a lot, speaking on agricultural issues over the years. At first, people were a little afraid of me because I was a meditator, but as they learned about my farming successes, I suppose they thought it was no big deal." During his campaign for agriculture secretary, he says, "it never came up—to my surprise."

Thicke, however, did have some help from a few figures in the TM Movement, including moviemaker Lynch and actor Collins, who served as judges on a contest to produce a campaign video. Thicke told one interviewer that

his farm, employing five people, could be a "model for economic development in Iowa," and he criticized his opponent for getting support from big
agribusiness companies such as DuPont and Monsanto. Thicke also had the
backing of alternative farming practices advocates and food industry critic
Michael Pollan, author of *The Omnivore's Dilemma* (2006). But Thicke lost
handily, garnering just 398,428 of the 1.13 million votes cast.

While Thicke ran a serious campaign, TM leaders at times have been
anything but realistic in their electoral hopes. TM honcho Hagelin ran
for president of the United States in the three elections between 1992 and
2000 under the banner of the NLP. The NLP, which has mostly petered out,
seemed to have been aimed at garnering publicity for the TM Movement.
It urged that U.S. military forces train at least 1 percent of military personnel in meditation, saying this would create a "genuine peace-keeping force
that can maintain a powerful, integrated, coherent national consciousness
and thereby prevent the emergence of an enemy." This idea was an extension
of the Maharishi Effect, the TM belief that peace can be brought about if
enough people in every country—the square root of 1 percent of the population—meditate regularly. In the 2000 election, Hagelin was also backed
by part of H. Ross Perot's Reform Party, but in all his races he finished with
minuscule vote tallies.

Hagelin played various roles in the movement, including head of the
Global Union of Scientists for Peace and president of the United States
Peace Government. That's a complementary government composed of doctors, business leaders, university presidents, and others, movement literature
says. Hagelin urged world leaders to create "invincible defense technology"
systems in their countries by supporting advanced meditation by groups big
enough to generate the Maharishi Effect.

What Hagelin and other NLP candidates achieved was getting attention.
The NLP garnered headlines in papers as wide-ranging as the *New York Times*,
Washington Post, *Baltimore Sun*, *Fort Worth Star-Telegram*, *Charlotte Observer*,
and *Washington Times*, as well as in dispatches by Reuters and the Associated
Press. Hagelin appeared on TV networks, including ABC, NBC, and PBS,
sometimes beating the drum for TM and a lofty view of government's role.

"I think government is a spiritual profession or should be because government is the mechanism through which we collectively choose what kind of a world, a country, we wish to create together," Hagelin told PBS interviewer Gwen Ifill.[3]

Winning an election certainly was far from mind for Pamela K. Slowick, a longtime meditator who temporarily decamped from Fairfield in 1992 to run for Congress in Arizona. She had no connection to that state, aside from visiting it on a whim for a short time that year, and she had never run for office. But when the NLP came knocking, Slowick—a ballroom dancer with an easy laugh, quick wit, and big personality—found a place to call home in Prescott, Arizona, and tossed her hat into the ring. "It was clear it was more for the purpose of injecting positivity into the whole political process," Slowick says. "It was amazing."

Slowick, then known by her married name as Pamela Volponi, did a slew of interviews and participated in debates with a Republican incumbent and a Democratic challenger. Though a Democrat herself (although she ran under the NLP banner), she struck up a friendship with the Republican, Representative Robert Stump, who, she said, backed her up in debates. She was invited to Stump's reelection celebration, where he provided a cake for her son's birthday. She drew just 4.1 percent of the vote.

Just as Fairfield's meditating politicians go their own ways, so too do its voters. Fairfield is the county seat and most populous place in Jefferson County, which went heavily for libertarian Ron Paul in the January 2012 Republican Party caucuses. While the libertarian commanded 21.5 percent of the statewide tally, placing third behind former Pennsylvania senator Rick Santorum and former Massachusetts governor Mitt Romney, Paul was the choice of 48.6 percent of Jefferson County residents voting in the GOP caucus. Paul's volunteers in Fairfield pitched their man as the only candidate who could save the country and the world, according to the *Wall Street Journal*.

Meditators warmed to Paul's noninterventionist approach to foreign policy and his stress on personal liberties, the paper reported. "Meditators are for world peace, and Ron Paul would bring world peace," one local resident told the paper. "That is what resonates with this town."[4]

More than politics, though, education matters to the residents of Fairfield. The place is, first and foremost, a college town. The university that drew the TM Movement to town in the first place has long been the community's defining institution. More than any other single institution in Fairfield, it drives the local economy and culture. As it has changed, so has Fairfield's sense of itself—and, thanks to the TMers, the school has changed a lot over the decades.

6

Higher Ed, Higher Realms

EACH MORNING AND EVENING, students, teachers, and other meditators from Fairfield file into a pair of sprawling, golden-domed buildings that
rise above the bucolic Maharishi University of Management north of downtown. Men enter one dome, women the other. Using mantras given to them
by TM teachers, they slip into altered states of consciousness. Some settle
into a state the TM Movement calls "pure awareness" or "restful alertness."
Some have been known to nap. And some soar, mentally at least, above the
mattress-laden dome floors, practicing Yogic Flying.[1]

Between these daily group meditation sessions, students wander off into
gleaming new amber-colored buildings—designed according to architectural principles laid down by Maharishi—for their daily studies. At MUM, an
accredited university that grants bachelor's, master's, and doctoral degrees,
students study mainstream subjects such as business, computer science,
education, art, media and communications, math, literature, and physiology.
Some pursue more specialized areas, such as sustainable living and Maharishi Vedic Science, exploring the guru's teachings in depth.

But for the roughly 625 students on campus—most drawn from outside
the United States and most pursuing master's degrees—classroom studies
and the meditation practices in the domes are seldom far apart, since the curriculum is shot through with the guru's insights. The teachers, most of whom
joined the TM Movement in the belief that the guru's revival of ancient wisdom could change the world, drive home the point in lectures and texts. No
topic, whether the poems of T. S. Eliot, the principles of computer science,

or the practices of business, stands outside the guru's intellectual reach. Classrooms sport posters that link the subjects to the Maharishi's ancient wisdom, or Maharishi Vedic Science. This is no ordinary university.

Take computer science, as taught by Gregory Guthrie, a Purdue-educated PhD who also serves as dean of MUM's College of Computer Science and Mathematics. In his class, computer science and the guru's teachings are like strands of DNA, inextricably bound together.

As twenty-four students from across the globe enter Guthrie's classroom on one spring morning in 2012, for instance, they see on one wall a colorful poster that spells out the connections. Detailed columns and rows link terms from computer science with ancient Indian thought. Such wall charts reflect attempts by Maharishi and his followers to unify all knowledge under common principles.

If students want to pursue the connections further, they can explore them in depth in *Consciousness-Based Education and Computer Science* (2011), a text published by the Maharishi University of Management Press that features Guthrie as a contributor. Guthrie aims in his section of the book to redefine computer science in the light of the guru's teachings. He includes a grid—titled "Veda—The Unmanifest Structure of Natural Law"—that lists the terms Algorithms, Software, and Machines in a box with Computing Systems. This sits above boxes labeled Symbolic Computation, Symbolic Mathematics, and then Vedic Computation and Vedic Mathematics. Off to the side are the terms Concrete Relative, Abstract Relative, and Absolute. The point is that the guru's teachings unify "traditional objective science and a new subjective science."[2]

Guthrie, a tweedy sort who sports a jacket and tie in the formal style common at MUM, underscores the idea in a slideshow presentation. Amid descriptions of proxies and chains of responsibility and objects—terms computer science students everywhere might know—appear messages such as this: "All desires (requests) that are in accord with Nature find immediate fulfillment in higher states of consciousness because they get the support of all the Laws of Nature."

To drive the idea home, Guthrie elaborates in the slideshow: "The level of support of Nature we experience depends on the level of consciousness,

Nature can handle any request. The more we are in tune with Nature, the more fulfillment we will experience."

Balding and bespectacled, Guthrie brings to his classroom both a scientist's gimlet eye and the eye of someone focused on other realms. Guthrie's science background includes working at Bell Laboratories in processor development before he joined MUM in 1983. He helped set up the computer science program that he directs at the school. He also runs his own consulting firm, working for such outfits as IBM and AT&T, even as he does research that his school biography describes as "connecting the descriptions of the mechanics of consciousness as presented in Maharishi Vedic Science to the theoretical descriptions of information and computational systems in Computer Science."

Guthrie linked the areas in a 2011 interview published by the website Master Degree Online.com. "I really cherish the opportunity to be here at MUM, to be with the very bright students in our program, and to explore and share with them the most advanced knowledge of Computer Science, and at the same time the most advanced knowledge of full human potential," he said. "It is very beautiful and interesting to see how these two very important, powerful, and abstract ideas have such parallel basic principles and dynamics."[3]

All across the curriculum at MUM, students are taught how subjects as far-flung as history, English, and assorted sciences can be better understood when set in the worldview espoused by TM. Everything relates to consciousness and perception, they learn. Consider the poetry of T. S. Eliot, famous for *The Waste Land* (1922) (hardly an upbeat work, with such lines as "April is the cruelest month"). Terrance Fairchild, who chairs MUM's literature and writing department, casts the poet's work in the light of TM. In *Consciousness-Based Education and Literature* (2011), another text published by the university press, Fairchild takes up Eliot's *Four Quartets* (1943), a series of poems that deals with time. Fairchild argues that

> because Maharishi Vedic Science is the most comprehensive discussion
> on the relationship between life in time and life in eternity, between
> ignorance and enlightenment, and because its practical methodolo-
> gies—the Maharishi Transcendental Meditation technique and the

Transcendental Meditation–Sidhi program—provide the means for living life in eternity, it exists as the most appropriate body of knowledge for elucidating the full scope of Eliot's masterpiece.[4]

Another contributor to the text, former MUM associate professor Susan Andersen, casts Walt Whitman as a precursor to Vedic Science. She argues that the writer predicted that a science would someday emerge that included the subtler forces of nature, including God, and would be the "true foundation of America." Her contention was that "the science Whitman imagined is a science of nature, a science of life that anticipates Maharishi Vedic Science, a science of natural law. The science Maharishi has founded is both theoretical and empirical, a science that aims to unfold the fullness of both individual and society, a science to complete Whitman's prophetic vision of a whole nation engaged in self-culture."[5]

Still another contributor, Douglas A. Mackey, examines psychologist C. G. Jung, film director Ingmar Bergman, and writer Thomas Pynchon in the light of TM. They all "have pointed very strongly towards the transcendental state in their work," Mackey writes. "They use the metaphor of the Quest to dramatize the innate human need to go beyond the ever-changing field of the relative world and discover the absolute, pure nature of the Self."[6]

Certainly, MUM's educational style is a far cry from the training that students got at Parsons College, the defunct school whose campus the TM Movement took over, ending ninety-nine years of Presbyterian influence at the place—albeit a waning influence in the final days. Parsons, established in 1875 by Presbyterian church leaders, trained the occasional minister and often was run by members of the clergy, but it had strayed far from its religious roots by the time it closed. Once a straitlaced place—where alcohol, cardplaying, smoking, pool, and profanity were banned; chapel attendance was mandatory; and students studied Greek or Latin—Parsons had devolved into a party campus known for rambunctious fraternities and fast cars.

By the 1960s, Parsons had become notorious as a "second chance" college for the "academically average" who got by on dubious academic offerings. Marking the beginning of the end for Parsons, *Life* magazine in 1966 profiled the school's partying ways in a detailed look at its controversial leader, the

Reverend Millard Roberts, calling him "The Wizard of Flunk-Out U." Soon after, Parsons lost its accreditation and its leader, and even after it won reaccreditation in 1970, declining enrollments and financial strains pushed it into bankruptcy in 1973. Parsons marked its "gallant death," in the words of writer Susan Fulton Welty, with the commencement ceremonies for the graduating class—its ninety-fourth—in June that year.[7]

While Parsons was going through its death throes, TM was surging nationwide. It was drawing adherents by the thousands, and leaders of the TM Movement were making ambitious plans for their educational offerings. Propelled by support from celebrities such as the Beatles and catering to the hungers of a Baby Boom generation unsettled by violence at home and war overseas, the movement thrived in the late 1960s and early 1970s. According to the school's account of its history, in 1971 Maharishi began developing what he regarded as a new science, the Science of Creative Intelligence (SCI), based on his understanding of consciousness. At first, his notion was to teach SCI as a supplementary course at universities around the world, and his followers introduced it at schools such as Yale and Stanford. Soon, however, he zeroed in on the idea of establishing his own university with a curriculum that would incorporate SCI in various subjects.

Movement officials put together a founding faculty, including PhDs from Ivy League schools where meditation had established footholds. They crafted a curriculum and in 1973 opened the doors of Maharishi International University—as it was first called—in a rented complex in Goleta, California, near Santa Barbara and the University of California. Soon the facilities were jammed with devotees, and TM leaders began looking for a real campus. When Parsons put its facilities on the market, the movement jumped at the idea, snapping up the campus for $2.5 million. And the TM Movement was determined to make a good impression on locals in Fairfield with its debut class of students.[8]

Clean cut and well dressed, some five hundred of the young newcomers impressed the midwestern farmers as they poured out of a long line of yellow school buses that summer. "In an era of 'hippies' with torn and patched jeans, scraggly hair and bare feet, the newcomers were neat in dresses and suits; their hair was trim and their feet were shod," author Welty puts it in *A*

Fair Field, her history of the town, published first in 1968 and updated in 1975. "Better still, they were well-mannered, friendly and anxious to refurbish the campus."[9]

Indeed, if locals worried about getting students more troublesome than the frat boys who had gone to Parsons, the movement soon gave them reason to relax. "They established a school free of problems from drugs and alcoholic drinks, and devoted themselves to their studies. To the community they offered courses in Transcendental Meditation which attracted about two hundred townspeople in the first year," Welty reports. "They shared the campus and their own talents with the community in concerts, in a public May Day Festival, and by sharing [the campus's] Barhydt Chapel with churches needing a meeting place."

But the TM leaders had aims far grander than endearing themselves to Fairfield locals, some of whom the movement soon riled by rebuilding parts of the campus. MIU aimed to develop the full potential of the individual, realize the highest ideal of education, improve governmental achievements, solve the age-old problems of crime and all behavior that brings unhappiness to the family of man, bring fulfillment to the economic aspirations of individuals and society, maximize the intelligent use of the environment, and achieve the spiritual goals of mankind in this generation.[10] (Since then, officials have rewritten the goals to be gender-neutral, substituting "our world family" for "family of man" and "goals of humanity" for "goals of mankind." In some publications, too, the movement has reordered the goals, putting education first, moving environmental concerns higher, and listing drug abuse as one of the problem behaviors.[11])

The school got going with a missionary fervor and purpose. It was a key part of a World Plan, as it was called, to eliminate the eternal difficulties "of mankind in this generation by training one teacher of the Science of Creative Intelligence for every one thousand people in all parts of the globe." The university's inaugural catalog says it was founded "to disseminate this knowledge in all countries by training teachers of the Science of Creative Intelligence in every community in the world. This is the World Plan."

The World Plan aimed "to establish 3600 centers of self-sufficiency in this knowledge everywhere in order to train teachers of SCI in all areas and infuse

SCI into every nation's educational systems," the catalog explains. "Mahari-shi International University will implement the World Plan and stand as an international guardian of the purity—and therefore the effectiveness—of this essential new field of knowledge."

Much has changed since that founding class entered. Not far from where Parsons students once played football, the movement built the two gleam-ing domes for up to sixteen hundred meditators combined, opening them in the early 1980s. MIU changed its name in 1995 to Maharishi University of Management, aiming to stress what it calls the practical value of deep knowl-edge and experience and to enable "every student to fully manage his or her life." Six years after that, it obliterated one of the last symbols of Parsons and its Presbyterianism, leveling the deteriorating church building on campus—the Barhydt Chapel—that Parsons alumni had venerated and some of whom still mourn. Built in about 1910, the chapel was listed in the National Register of Historic Places. But MUM had no use for it and was eager to embark on its own building plans.

Indeed, MUM has rebuilt much of the campus. It knocked down at least forty-three buildings between 2000 and 2008, according to its promo-tional materials, and built seventy new ones. New buildings were designed to incorporate the principles of Maharishi Vedic Architecture, or Mahari-shi Sthapatya Veda, which include facing east, crafting the structures to cer-tain proportions, and placing rooms strategically by function. "Because the individual is cosmic, everything about individual life should be in full har-mony with Cosmic Life," the movement quotes its guru as saying. Maharishi Sthapatya Veda design gives dimensions, formulas, and orientations to the buildings said to "provide cosmic harmony and support to the individual for his peace, prosperity, and good health—daily life in accord with natural law, daily life in the evolutionary direction."

Along with the physical layout, the school's curriculum hews to the guid-ance of the dead leader. The "consciousness-based, unified field–based edu-cation" MUM provides is all-encompassing. MUM President Bevan Morris, in a school publication inviting students to visit, puts it this way: "students study the totality of the laws of nature through different disciplines of sci-ence, arts and commerce, but also through their common basis in the unified field—which can be experienced by anyone in the self-referral field of their own consciousness."[12]

Such descriptions, commonplace in TM circles, send outsiders into bouts of head-scratching. But teachers repeatedly draw connections between the various disciplines and the wisdom of the ancients in India, as interpreted by the guru. The elaborate wall charts suggest that modern knowledge all flows from the ancient Vedic insights or, at least, can be better understood by applying them. To cite Morris again, "Through special charts the faculty have prepared, students understand the parts of each field of knowledge they study in relation to the total knowledge of the field, the total field in terms of the source of all laws of nature in the unified field, and the reality of that unified level of intelligence as their own consciousness in its self-referral state."[13]

Unified field? Self-referral? Such notions may stump mere mortals. And some meditators argue it's impossible to understand these ideas unless one "transcends" into a meditative state where, over time, linkages difficult to see in the workaday world seem to become apparent. Nonetheless, TM honcho Hagelin, a physics professor at MUM, takes a whack at spelling it out in the same MUM publication:

Modern science has systematically probed deeper levels of nature's functioning—from the surface, macroscopic level of nature's diversity to the molecular, atomic, nuclear, and subnuclear levels—culminating in the discovery of the unified field, the unified source of all the laws of nature, at the foundation of the universe. Through its purely self-interacting dynamics, the unified field creates from within itself all the particles and forces that compose the universe, and all the diversified streams of natural law governing the universe.[14]

If anyone doubts the significance of the notion, Hagelin underlines its importance. "The discovery of the unified field is the culmination of 50 years of advanced research in quantum gravity theory—and the fulfillment of Einstein's lifelong dream of finding a single unified source for all the diversified laws of nature governing the universe." Indeed, the unified field–based education provided at MUM, he writes, is "the most important, most advanced, and most scientifically significant system of education in the world."

Such highfalutin rhetoric is common in the movement. Understatement is not its strong suit. Guthrie points to how personal and educational goals are both addressed uniquely at MUM. "I welcome all new students," he says,

> and would encourage you to consider the fundamental importance of an educational system that includes providing you with the highest values of your own intellectual and personal experience, at the same time that you learn your advanced Computer Science; this integration, and holistic approach, is so enriching, fulfilling, and important to success, that you will wonder how any other educational system could still not take this advanced approach![15]

Putting aside the self-promotional puffery, MUM offers an alternative in higher education that, to its credit, removes major hurdles to learning with which most conventional colleges and universities struggle. Drinking, stress, and fatigue are rampant in most such institutions, for instance, but not at MUM. Alcohol remains a no-no on campus and there is no Greek life or big sports program to foster a boozing culture off campus or drinking on the sly in the dorms. Meditation takes care of stress and fatigue. And a block system in the curriculum—where students focus on a single subject at a time for several weeks instead of juggling a half-dozen at once—levers down the academic pressure and focuses student minds. In the dorms, the sexes are segregated, curbing other distractions.

"We know the three or four things that work most at odds with learning," says Craig Pearson, a scholarly, Duke-educated TM teacher who developed a writing program and university press at MUM and, since 1998, has served as the school's executive vice president. He stated that

> if there were some devious force that wanted to come in and interfere with learning, here's what they would do: they would make sure that there's plenty of alcohol around because when you're under the influence of alcohol, learning is very difficult. They would make sure that people are under a lot of stress because when you're under stress,

learning doesn't happen. And they would make sure that people are sleep-deprived.

"And what characterizes American college life other than alcohol and sleep-deprivation and stress?," asks Pearson, exasperated at the benighted state of most university education. "The locus of those three things in America is college campuses and these are the places that are supposed to be about learning."

By contrast, the culture and offerings at MUM are nothing short of a new paradigm in education, he says. And it is not just a matter of the convent-like abstemiousness of the place, which curiously echoes the earliest alcohol-free and prayer-filled approaches at Parsons. Through the twice-a-day meditation sessions—in the domes, in group meditation rooms, in the dorms, or sometimes just before the end of a class in a classroom—the school seeks to sharpen the minds of students as it educates them. Often, they learn by doing, not just by ingesting information, according to Pearson.

Students find kindred souls, as Pearson finds when he talks to prospective students at monthly visitors' weekends. The administrator says, "So many people talk about how they want to take care of themselves, eat healthy food, develop their creative potential and their innate spirituality—and how they feel like they are strangers even among their friends, because no one else shares these values—and how they are amazed to find so many like-minded people here."

Meditation is the key. MUM teachers encourage students through meditation—or "transcending," in TM parlance—to see how the material they learn fits together and how it connects to the students themselves. It is no mere intellectual or analytical exercise, says Pearson, who describes the experience as unifying one's consciousness. "When the mind settles inward, it transcends (goes beyond) thought," he says. "Consciousness is left silent and awake in itself, in a state of pure wakefulness. . . . Through their meditation, people shed their stress and anxiety, and their natural inner ease and radiance shines through."

Officials aim to take students beyond merely absorbing facts and acquiring skills by helping them develop their inner selves. "That experience of transcending literally expands what you might call the container of knowledge, expands their consciousness, cultivates their intelligence," Pearson says. "So when they walk into my classroom in March, they are more intelligent, they're more awake, their consciousness is more developed, their moral maturity is greater, their creativity is greater than it was when they enrolled in September, the previous fall."

The meditation program is integral, MUM officials maintain. And they suggest that the change in students in their first year is not just a matter of their maturing and getting a handle on college life and mastering subjects. Says Pearson, "What happens in our classroom is not just the imparting of knowledge the way it happens elsewhere, but the connecting of those parts of knowledge to each other and that wholeness of knowledge to the student's own self."

Certainly, the opportunity for such inner growth is a draw for some students who thrive on the healthy atmosphere. Not all toe the movement line, however. The policies of providing only vegetarian food and no alcohol on campus leave some students cold, for instance, and send them off in search of hamburger restaurants and bars in Fairfield. "I see the benefits of being a vegetarian, but I'm not a vegetarian," says graduate student Damian Finol, who was twenty-nine years old when we met in early 2012 and who came to Fairfield from Venezuela. "Whenever I get a chance, I eat out."

Some students, too, have bridled at the limited Wi-Fi. Wireless computer connections were long discouraged on campus because the late guru was suspicious of electromagnetic radiation from devices such as cell phones. In the fall of 2012, officials relaxed the rules as a concession to student demand, but they still bar Wi-Fi networks in such areas as the meditation domes, other meditation areas, some dorms and areas within dorms, and spots where students are required to be for more than a half hour or so. A campuswide ban on smoking, too, is tough for students from cultures where tobacco use remains common, so some students wander public trails near campus to light up. As for the segregation of the sexes, students find plenty of opportunity to mingle, on and off campus. Classes, of course, are coeducational. Certainly, many of the movement's Baby Boomer couples met as TM teachers.

The school has turned off plenty of students, moreover. One website of online reviews of colleges and universities warns prospective students to avoid the school, and its review section is filled with sharp critics. One critic calls MUM "all brainwash and hypnosis." Another, who moved from India, ridicules the devotion adherents pay to Maharishi, saying, "That guy did some real mind games on these folks." A third, who grew up in Fairfield, calls MUM a "cult disguised as a college" and bemoans its "worthless" degree. Yet another says he left the school after a year and half, noting, "All they care about is you becoming part of the TM cult, and adding to the false scientific idea of the 'Maharishi Effect' and 'Super Radiancy'; all pseudoscience with biased statistics." But MUM's defenders also posted comments on the site. One lambastes the critics as a "small but noisy group of anti-meditation activists [who] have most likely splattered this MUM review page with their usual strange and distorted comments." Another calls his time at the university "the best experience of my life," labeling MUM "an oasis of friendly, happy people and an awesome school." Yet another slams the critics for comments that "are mostly so extreme and obviously unbalanced" and praises MUM for its "supportive and open student culture," even while acknowledging that "some academic programs are not as strong as others."[16]

Yet the university has an appeal for some students who don't fancy fraternities and sororities, don't need a football team to root for, and don't have a need for alcohol. It draws older students, especially those from other countries who see an American university degree as a step to the good life, and maybe a step to a good American job. The two dozen students pursuing master's degrees in Guthrie's computer science class, for instance, came from places as far-flung as China, Ethiopia, Egypt, and Nepal.

MUM's appeal to foreign students is striking. About three-fourths of the students come from outside the United States, according to Pearson, who adds that the campus is a "world family." The students in 2011–12 hailed from eighty-seven countries, drawn particularly by computer science and an accounting-MBA program. The relatively low cost—with tuition and fees estimated at about $26,430 for an academic year for a graduate student in 2012–13—is a big draw, as are the opportunities for placements in American companies that can lead to full-time jobs.[17]

Finol, a computer science student, found schools such as Johns Hopkins and MIT far tougher to get into and much pricier. MUM, by contrast, required a down payment of only $5,000 and was flexible about the terms for repayment. Students who take a so-called practical option can stretch their schooling over thirty months, including about eight months on campus and the rest working at a company and finishing courses through distance education. Students, placed in jobs around the country, typically take out a bank loan to pay the balance of their tuition, then repay the loan from their earnings at work, Pearson says.

"They work out a payment plan with you," Finol adds. "If you have a great job and it pays really well, you can pay your loan before it's due. But if you don't find a really good job, they can accommodate your needs."

Finol, planning a career in cybersecurity, was drawn to MUM because a friend had attended. His friend wound up with a job working for a Microsoft contractor. Microsoft has employed 158 of the 972 students who, as of mid-2012, had graduated from MUM's master's degree program for computer professionals, according to Pearson. He adds that the university has developed relationships with about one thousand companies interested in its graduates. Microsoft declined to comment on its relationship with the school.

Most international students know nothing about meditation before they come, according to Pearson. Some, indeed, are suspicious about it at first. Finol shared the skepticism of fellow Venezuelans, for instance. "A lot of people in Latin America see meditation in a weird way," says Finol, who is Roman Catholic. "They think it's a religious thing, which it is not. I did my research and talked to my friend—he's also very Catholic—and really it has nothing to do with religion. It's a technique and an exercise that can help you concentrate and be more relaxed and see the world in a different way, but it has nothing to do with religion."

Now, Finol says, he meditates the usual twice a day. For students who can't find the time in their dorms, some classrooms come equipped with low-lying chairs in the back of the room suited to meditation. "I find it quite comforting," he reports. "When I was in school in Venezuela, in college, it was quite hectic. [Meditation] gives me a little bit of time to look inwards and helps me relax and focus more. It's great for getting your thoughts in order and relieving stress. It's a godsend."

MUM appeals most to graduate students who often come with a few years of work experience in their fields. According to the National Center for Education Statistics, in the fall of 2011 the school reported total enrollment of 1,134, down from the prior fall's tally of 1,180 and from the recent peak of 1,206 in the fall of 2008.[18] In the fall 2011 count, 784 were graduate students, and 372 of them were attending only part time. Some 626 students were in Fairfield, school officials said, with others studying off-site.

Such programs as those offering master's degrees in computer science and business are popular, especially with foreign students. On the undergraduate level, especially, such trendy interdisciplinary programs as a sustainable living program draw students.

Despite successive modest declines in total enrollment in the fall of 2010 and 2011, MUM officials take heart from the recent growth of the student body, noting that the school typically enrolled between 500 and 750 degree-seeking students each year between 1975 and 2005. MUM's latest tallies have fallen far short of the peak figure of 3,231 students that the school reported in 1989, but that count was inflated by a program that gave college credit to meditators in Fairfield who attended group meditation sessions in the domes on campus for from two to four hours a day. Enrollment gradually slid back as locals lost interest in the credit, according to Jim Karpen, who edits the campus newsletter. He says, "People apparently eventually lost interest in filling out the forms." The latest figures also fell short of the 1,422 total enrollment reported in the fall of 1997.[19]

MUM continues to face challenges, especially in its undergraduate component. Keeping students is a big one at MUM, as it is at many colleges nationwide. MUM enrolled thirty-seven new students in 2008, for instance, but only nineteen of them returned in 2009, according to Pearson. That retention rate—perhaps the all-time lowest, according to the administrator—has since improved, with 80 percent of all new undergrads admitted in the fall of 2010 returning the following fall. Between the fall of 2011 and the spring of 2012, some 90 percent of the new undergraduate students stayed on, as did 88.6 percent of all the MUM undergrads, MUM registrar Tom

Rowe says. (Small numbers can skew the rates, of course. MUM admits tiny classes each year.) In 2012, Pearson said MUM's retention rate is on par with private four-year colleges nationwide.

Graduation rates at MUM, as at other schools, pose another challenge. Only 50 percent of those who entered MUM in the fall of 2005 to pursue bachelor's degrees graduated in either four or six years. By comparison, some 54.7 percent of students on average at private four-year schools nationwide graduated in four years, while 68 percent graduated in six years, as reported in 2010 by ACT Inc., the nonprofit educational research and testing organization.[20]

In the 2012–13 academic year, counting both the winter and spring graduations, MUM awarded undergraduate degrees to 75 students, master's degrees to 241, and doctorates to three students, according to registrar Rowe. Officials said the undergraduate class was the largest in more than twenty years. The graduates, at all levels, came from fifty countries, including more than 100, combined, from Ethiopia and China. Only one-quarter of the group, 78, hailed from the United States.

When students quit MUM, they leave for lots of different reasons, Pearson suggests. The school may not offer majors the students decide they want. Finances may be challenging, or they may want to be closer to home. Some join a program connected to the university called the Invincible America Assembly, where they meditate for prolonged periods daily in exchange for a stipend of about $800 a month. Occasionally, he says, students are suspended for drug or alcohol use. "Some may have a creative awakening (which they will often attribute to their Transcendental Meditation practice) and decide that what they really want to do is start a business or travel," he adds.

The university is dealing with retention challenges, Pearson says. It is adding staff to tend to student life issues, restructuring its academic advising program, renovating dormitories, and encouraging students to learn TM at home before they come to campus. The university reimburses most of the TM costs if students decide to enroll.

The school needs to keep more of the students it loses and hike enrollment substantially if it is to stay on the pace laid down in its updated strategic plan, available in 2013. It aims to boost enrollment in Fairfield to 1,196 by 2017–18, nearly double the 2012–13 tally. However, as enrollment totals have slipped, MUM has downshifted its projections for Fairfield enrollment (in 2011, it optimistically projected 1,507 students in Fairfield by 2015–16 and more recently scaled the figure down to just 954 by then). Counting on more gains, including in overseas sites affiliated with the school, it hopes to hike overall enrollment to 2,572 by 2017–18. It also has lofty financial aims, planning to hike the school's endowment from $9.9 million in 2013 to $20 million in cash and $60 million in pledges by 2017–18.[21]

The university may also be feeling some pressure from faculty and staff to hike their pay. Traditionally, personnel have been paid meager salaries—as little as $300 a month in the 1980s, a base stipend that has since climbed to $700 for instructors—and accepted modest housing, insurance, and the chance to take TM classes as a trade-off. "Compensation at Maharishi University of Management has been unique since the University's inception," the MUM strategic plan says. "Long-term staff and faculty have been mostly volunteers, receiving only a modest cash stipend. Many have continued with low stipends for 25–30 years."

More recently, the school stepped up pay for newer faculty, particularly in popular growth programs such as those that target computer professionals. This has spawned a double standard where new hires were earning more than people who had been teaching at MUM for twenty-five years. Even in the placid groves of MUM, the disparity "caused some growing pains and needs to be addressed," the plan says. The Higher Learning Commission, the body associated with the North Central Association of Colleges and Schools that accredits MUM and other universities in the region, flagged a need to "focus on equitability" in pay, according to the plan.[22]

Raises may be on the way, although they are likely to give MUM faculty little to brag about. Instructors earning $700 a month would get a boost to $1,500 a month in five years or less under the strategic plan. Professors' earnings would rise from $850 to $2,500, and deans' would grow from $1,000 to $3,000, the plan suggests. In addition, they would get benefits, such as room and board, valued at between $3,000 a month and $4,500, up from the recent range of between $2,100 and $2,400. MUM professors, on average, earned just $18,052 in the 2011 academic year, and associate professors just $13,249, as reported by the National Center for Education Statistics.

Still, the faculty, staff, and leaders at MUM haven't been drawn to the school by the money. "They have been inspired by helping pioneer a new approach to education, and many (myself included) have found this tremendously fulfilling," Pearson says.

The school's strategic planners still focus on higher aims. They plan to reduce campuswide carbon emissions, reduce water use, and increase the amount of locally sourced food on campus—all of which are now trendy causes at many campuses. But they also list world peace as one of their supporting priorities and objectives. To propagate peace, they intend to "create national invincibility and contribute to a more peaceful world through the application of the Maharishi Effect," the claimed reduction in violence and crime that takes place when enough people in an area meditate. At MUM, officials plan to boost the size of the group practicing TM "to reduce tension and negative trends in the US and the world," as well as to inspire more students to take up the TM-Sidhi program—an advanced approach that can involve hours a day of meditation—and to support schools that train Vedic scholars.

Credit the people who built and run MUM with boundless optimism— or with a blinding and unrealistic sense of mission. Despite the enrollment challenges they face in Iowa, movement leaders in recent years took steps to build yet another university—aiming to enroll forty thousand students there. They bought some 1,148 acres of land a few miles from the eighteen-hundred-resident town of Smith Center, Kansas, at first with the idea that their tract would be home to a new city, a world capital of peace. "Peace palaces" were envisioned that would house several hundred people, part of a string of such facilities in Indiana, Ohio, and Nebraska that the Global Country of World Peace planned.[23] Because Smith County is the geographic center of the United States, TM leaders saw it as "a natural seat of power and a unifying point for the whole country," as one movement website says. Then the idea shifted to creating Maharishi Central University, a place the movement says would serve "as a powerful generator of peace and invincibility for the U.S. and for the entire world."[24]

At the moment, however, the new university consists of about a dozen empty buildings or building sites in various stages of construction. Work on them halted around 2008 when the guru died, and the project has been on hold since.[25] The group has sold off land, too, paring its holdings to about seven hundred acres as of early 2013. Some locals doubt any student will ever set foot there. "I don't think they'll ever have any," says Al Frieling, a broker who sold some of the land to the group. "We're out in the middle of nowhere."

Many folks in Smith County would be happy if the university proves to be just a departed guru's fantasy. The TMers were so unpopular—with ministers deriding them as cult members—that the county commission refused to support a $38 million bond issue the movement was seeking. "People think they're going to kidnap their kids and brainwash them," says Frieling. He adds, nonetheless, that he got on fine with the meditators, who he says were always true to their word in his dealings with them.

The schools the movement has tried to foster have far different purposes than most. But idiosyncratic as a university such as MUM may seem, it fits into a long line of alternative schools that have popped up in American educational history, according to Miles T. Bryant, a professor of educational administration at the University of Nebraska–Lincoln. He includes in the list the defunct Windham College, as well as such tiny colleges as Goddard and Marlboro. Such schools, he says, were often launched by charismatic educators who espoused ideas outside the educational mainstream and usually demanded conformity to their ideas. Over time, Bryant adds, such schools have had to reinvent themselves to attract students whose priorities and tastes change. They become "shape-shifters," he says.

Bryant is impressed that MUM has endured. "It is remarkable that this place has survived for so long," he says. "It occupies a niche market, I guess. And [it] creates its own niche too."

MUM has weathered a few storms, but none prepared it for the tragic events of 2004. A fatal stabbing on campus raised practical questions about safety and admissions policies. It also put a spotlight on the limits of meditation in promoting well-being and on Maharishi's notion that group meditation can spread peace across a campus, a country, and even the world.

7

Death in Paradise

LEVI ANDELIN BUTLER was the kind of student that MUM craved. By all accounts, he was a good-hearted soul who wanted to make the world a better place. Butler volunteered for several years in a program to help students with problems in La Quinta, California, where he went to high school. When he was shopping around for colleges in 2003, the lofty spiritual and social aims at MUM drew him like a faithful pilgrim rushing toward a shining city on a hill. His first six months at the school, however, proved to be his last.

Butler was stabbed to death on March 1, 2004, two weeks shy of his nineteenth birthday, in a bustling dining hall on the normally tranquil campus in Fairfield. A fellow student and passing acquaintance, a twenty-four-year-old with a history of mental problems, slipped away from a group enjoying a vegetarian dinner and pulled out a knife that he had stolen from an administrator's apartment. As that administrator sat thirty feet away, the assailant, Shuvender Sem, plunged the knife into Butler's chest repeatedly, once so hard that the knife broke, leaving the tip to be recovered in an autopsy.

For Butler's family, the young man's death was tragic. For the TM Movement, it was a searing event that raised questions about the limits of the usefulness of meditation. Could the practice really help people with problems ranging from mild depression to advanced mental illness? Further, the idealistic young man's death challenged a core tenet for adherents of TM, the claim that group meditation could reduce violence in a town, a country, even the world. This claim—for the so-called Maharishi Effect—had emerged as a central organizing principle for the movement. The guru had sent groups of meditators—psychic shock troops, some called them—to trouble spots around the world to put the Effect into play. It was partly why the movement set up shop in Fairfield, a placid place where hundreds could gather for twice-daily meditations that the faithful believed would promote peace nationwide.

For MUM, Butler's death posed still more problems. It led to troublesome litigation and embarrassing questions about promises the school made about safety at MUM. It could hurt enrollment by driving away students from a program already struggling with high attrition rates and also by dissuading prospective students from attending. Further, the university's circle-the-wagons approach—its failure to notify police about an earlier attack that day by Sem—raised questions about the movement's insularity and fear of bad publicity.

Butler's death, finally, marked a sorry milestone for the meditating community in Fairfield. It was bracketed by a pair of high-profile suicides in town—one in 1990 and the other in 2008—where troubled young people put themselves in front of trains. A couple of other suicides have followed since 2008.

By all accounts, Butler was a rising star who could have emerged as a leader in the TM Movement. Described on a MySpace page set up to memorialize him as a fencer, martial artist, and philosopher, Butler was also an accomplished ballroom dancer who won national competitions.[1] Regarded as a high achiever by teachers at La Quinta High School, from which he graduated in 2002, he founded the school's philosophy club and was a standout on its debate team. For all his interest in competition, he was also known for his gentleness. "He was a bright young man with immense potential and was not a confrontational person," a former English teacher of his, Donna Salazar, told the *Desert Sun*, a local newspaper, at the time of his death.[2]

Even today, friends get choked up when they recall him. "I really miss him," says Jan Ryan, former coordinator of the Desert Sands Student Assistance Program. "It's still really hard to have him gone. He was so young. The world lost somebody here." Originally a participant in the program, which offers counseling and a broad array of services to students and their families, Butler so warmed to its work that he served as a volunteer during high school. Later, when he graduated, officials there fibbed about his age (then seventeen years, just short of the required minimum age) to hire him.[3]

"He was a seeker. He was interested in social justice," Ryan recalls, noting that Butler was undergoing an "existential crisis" of his own when she first met him. Talented and weighing many options in his life, he was troubled by the idea that others struggled with myriad problems. "He had it good and other people didn't, and that puzzled him and confused him," she says. "It also inspired him."

As Butler grew through his high school years, leaders of the student assistance program enlisted his help in training others, especially in promoting conflict mediation. He once spoke to a crowd of five hundred people at a countywide conference, telling them about how useful their work could be. "I would say the crowd was seriously electrified," Ryan recalls. Butler had carte blanche to leave school when needed to help with the Desert Sands program.

Butler's charisma was so striking that another former official in the Desert Sands program called his ability to rivet a crowd "magical." Jim Rothblatt, a retired counselor and program specialist, even compares him to President John F. Kennedy. Rothblatt saw Kennedy during a long-ago campaign and got a chance to shake his hand. "At that moment, I could have followed that guy anywhere," he says. "Levi had that same sort of impact on the people he came in contact with." Whatever his career choice ultimately would have been, Butler's "potential was limitless," Rothblatt adds.

A promising catch for MUM, Butler was heavily wooed by the school. He had attended a community college near home, the College of the Desert, in the 2002–3 school year and was intrigued by MUM after visiting its website in early 2003. Butler's brother, Joshua, had suggested that Butler consider the school because of its emphasis on spreading peace, resolving conflict, and living sustainably, according to a lawsuit Joshua later brought against MUM.[4] Once MUM learned of Butler's interest, legal papers say, it launched recruitment efforts that included mailings and phone calls to the young man and his parents, Khaldun and Evelyn Butler.

Butler seemed happy with the MUM program, his friends and family recalled, and MUM was glad to have him. At a memorial service on campus after his death, Khaldun Butler told his son's fellow students, "He truly loved you and was inspired by you. . . . Levi also told me on the phone the other day that there was no place on earth he would rather be right now than right here." For their part, MUM officials spoke glowingly of him: one noted his "incredible creativity and multiple talents," another his "clear insight and intellect, along with a wonderful artistic ability." He quickly developed a reputation as one of the brightest and most likely to succeed.

While at the school, Butler developed a passing acquaintance with Shuvender Sem, a troubled young man from Landisville, Pennsylvania, who had graduated from the tony Lancaster Country Day School in 1997 and had enrolled at MUM in January 2004, bringing with him a history of mental problems. Sem had been hospitalized repeatedly in the prior two years, diagnosed as paranoid schizophrenic. He had not been taking his medications for several months.

For critics of TM, Sem's abandonment of medication is troubling and telling, reflecting a preference among some practitioners for meditation and herbs over Western medicine as treatments for mental illness. Movement advocates have long contended that meditation can reduce dependence on drugs in the mentally ill. In his blog *The Honest Truth about TM*, David Orme-Johnson, a former professor of psychology at MUM, pointed to studies that suggest it reduces psychiatric illness, decreases depression, and can spawn "improvements in schizophrenia."[5] Author Denise Denniston, a MUM faculty member, wrote in *The TM Book* that "regular practice of the TM technique is excellent insurance against all diseases, including mental illness."[6] Indeed, lawyers for Butler's family argued in their complaint that Sem "came to the Maharishi University of Management because he had been led to believe the TM techniques taught at the school, combined with TM-related 'Vedic Medicine,' could free him from dependency on anti-psychotic medications." (The university, in its answer to the complaint, denied this claim and many others. Both the denials and the assertions by Butler's lawyers were never tested in court.)

On the day he stabbed Butler, Sem had previously attacked another student. Sem and the student, John Killian, were watching a Maharishi video shortly before 2:30 in the afternoon in an "Education for Enlightenment" class. Sem grew agitated, rose, and began making strange gestures, according to the Butler complaint. "Suddenly and without provocation, Sem began screaming obscenities and stabbed John Killian in the face and throat with a pen," the complaint says. "Fortunately, John Killian was able to deflect the pen slightly with his hand, possibly saving his own life. The pen punctured his hand, chin and throat and left a red ink scratch across his throat."

Another student, Akbar Nazary, grabbed Sem and stopped the attack. Teachers took Killian to a restroom, gave him a bandage, and encouraged him to return to class, telling him he probably didn't need stitches. A teacher suggested Sem apologize to Killian, which he did "with a flat expression in a monotone voice, and with no indication of genuine remorse," the complaint says. Killian, asked to return to class, did so to find some students in shock and crying. Nonetheless, a teacher continued to run the guru's video "and attempted to act as though nothing had happened." Other teachers "represented that the reason Sem had attacked Killian was that Sem had been meditating improperly." (The university denied these descriptions of the events.)

Using a nickname for Shuvender, one student in the class, who blogged anonymously about the assault, said students were "quick to dismiss Schube's action as some kind of massive stress release."[7] The student said it "looked like a massive emotional outburst leading to emotional unstressing via punching John in the face." When meditators have bad reactions— even getting into fistfights—TM teachers may blame them on "unstressing," where the release of deep-set stress is said to spur strong emotional or physical reactions.

Killian drove himself to a hospital, where he received multiple stitches. The Butlers' lawyers contended that when Killian described how he had been injured and reported the excuse given by MUM staff that Sem had simply been meditating improperly, the treating doctor responded, "In the real world, we call that assault and battery, and people go to jail for it."

Students later said Sem had acted in a bizarre and aggressive manner on previous occasions and had demonstrated clear signs of schizophrenia, including his claim that he was being followed by a black cat.

Even as Killian was being treated, MUM officials opted not to call police or even campus security. One professor contacted a MUM adjunct faculty member at the time, clinical psychologist Robert Boyer, who advised that Sem was dangerous, should be kept off campus, and needed to be evaluated by a psychiatrist immediately. The university officials opted to return Sem to his home in Pennsylvania and made flight arrangements that afternoon, the university said. Until Sem could leave, he was turned over to the school's dean of men, Joel Wysong, who took him to his on-campus apartment, a move that had tragic consequences.

In a statement to the press Pearson, the university's executive vice president, played down the first attack as a "10-second scuffle" that resulted in a bruise and a little blood.[8] But Sem's behavior after the assault was worrisome. He stood in Wysong's kitchen, "turning in circles, waving his arms, clapping his hands, and muttering to himself as he looked toward the ceiling," acting so bizarrely that Wysong feared for his safety, the Butlers' lawyers contend. Nonetheless, when Wysong moved to another room to meditate, he heard Sem rummaging through drawers in the kitchen—grabbing a knife, apparently unbeknownst to Wysong. After he finished his meditation, Wysong found that Sem was missing and headed out to search for him. It was close to 7 p.m., and he found Sem in the Annapurna Dining Hall, where he chose to let Sem mingle with the other students as he sat some distance away.

At first, there was no problem, although Nazary—the student who had subdued Sem earlier in the classroom attack—was alarmed that Sem had showed up in the dining hall. He moved closer in case Sem grew violent again. Shuvender sat with several students from the Enlightenment class.

"We were talking, laughing, generally having a good time," the student who blogged about the event wrote.

> I mentioned to Schube that fistfights had broken out in dome before, that one person had even been knocked unconscious in a fight over a simple square of foam. At this Schube completely zoned out. He left the table and we heard swearing behind us. I don't remember the exact words. It was something along the lines of "what the fuck did you just

say to me?" "What the hell is going on?" I saw Levi stand up, his shirt looked like something had been spilled on it. Schube seemed to punch him, and then I saw Schube pull away from Levi, pull his hand back, and Akbar grabbed Schube's wrist from behind, and wrenched it behind his back. . . . Levi was clutching his chest, and looked shocked. There was chatter, screams, and generally, "He stabbed him!" . . . Levi turned purple, then collapsed into someone's arms.

Students called 911, and police and an ambulance rushed to the scene. Paramedics removed a three-inch knife blade from Butler's chest and shocked him with a defibrillator to restore his heart's natural rhythm. At 7:29 p.m., nearly a half-hour after the assault, the paramedics put him into the ambulance, still breathing but with a weak pulse, and raced to the emergency room at Jefferson County Hospital. He died there.

Meanwhile, Wysong had taken Sem off to the side, and police took the assailant away. If MUM officials had "followed their own stated policy of reporting all serious crime to local authorities, Shuvender Sem would have been arrested after the attack on John Killian, and Levi Butler would be alive today," the Butler family lawyers argue in their complaint.

Indeed, the Butlers' lawyers held that MUM should have screened Sem for psychological problems when they considered admitting him and taken precautions to protect other students if they still chose to enroll him. Further, they should have noted red flags that he was mentally ill, such as odd answers he gave in a sentence-completion test he took about five weeks before the stabbing. Among them: If my mother "were a guy I would not have been born" and education is "the root of all evil." Worse, his belligerent behavior included threatening to kill a fellow student by bashing the student's head into a sink and then stomping on him when he was on the ground, according to the Butler complaint.

Three days after the stabbing, a psychiatrist evaluated Sem. The psychiatrist, Dr. James Brooks, noted that Sem had a history of chronic paranoid schizophrenia and had been treated with medication but had stopped taking it several weeks before coming to MUM. A court order handed down in federal court in 2008 recounted that Sem had visited Dr. David Sands in the MUM health clinic that January but had not been treated for psychosis at the time.[9]

The order, issued by U.S. District Court judge James E. Gritzner, suggests that the visit was another lost opportunity for noting Sem's problems. "MUM argues that Dr. Sands found no indication of mental health issues," Gritzner writes. "The health center admissions form suggests otherwise. Sem went to see Dr. Sands complaining of an upset stomach, a tense neck, pressure in his head, lack of focus, and spots on his nails. In the personal history section of the admission form requesting previous illnesses, Sem circled 'yes' for both chicken pox and nervous breakdown."

In June 2005, some fifteenth months after he stabbed Butler to death and attacked Killian, Sem was found not guilty of first-degree murder and assault with intent to commit serious injury by reason of insanity. In Jefferson County Court at Fairfield, prosecutors agreed with the defense lawyers that Sem was insane and needed to be institutionalized, but not jailed. He was committed for psychiatric care and spent six years in treatment, sometimes in a prison hospital and sometimes at the Independence Mental Health Institute, a state psychiatric hospital. He is still getting treatment.

Released in March 2010, Sem now lives with his parents in Pennsylvania and speaks to law enforcement and medical groups about mental illness, particularly schizophrenia. The year 2012 saw the publication of a book about his battles with the illness, called *Murder and Misunderstanding: One Man's Escape from Insanity.* "There's no cure for this disease," he tells me in a conversation from his home. "You can only control the illness through medication and therapy. I don't have any symptoms, but there is no cure. You have to keep up with your therapist and you have to keep taking your medicine like a religion. Those things will help."

Sem, who regularly sees a psychiatrist, a therapist, and a social worker, says MUM was exactly the wrong place for him to go as his mental struggles deepened. "I was trying to heal my life," he says. "I'm Indian, so I figured it would be a good fit. The people were very nice when I first visited and I thought I could heal myself. It was a big mistake, a big mistake."

Meditation, he says, was not a healthy treatment for his psychosis. And the university's response to his problems fell tragically short. After his first eruption in the classroom, he says, officials should have called the police and subdued him. "That was a flag. They could have called the cops, but they didn't," he says. "I do accept responsibility. At the end of the day, it was my fault. But, at the same time, things could have been done differently. The second one didn't have to happen."

He says MUM officials were unrealistic about handling his problems and are unrealistic in their teachings. "They want to live in a Utopia," Sem says. "I don't have much respect for that university. I don't think that what they were doing in general was science; I think it was hocus-pocus. Teaching people about enlightenment—I don't think that's true. They're brainwashing the kids."

As horrors such as the December 2012 attack on elementary-school children in Connecticut make clear, he says, society in general falls short in dealing with mental illness. "I wish there was more our society could do for the mentally ill to help them recover," he says. "I want people to have a serious debate about mental illness. There should be more healing in our society for people like me who suffer from the disease. You can't heal in prison. You regress. We need better places."

At the time he stabbed Butler, he says, he was paranoid and delusional. He was hallucinating and believed stabbing the boy was "the right thing." It was only months later, after a lot of medication, that he understood how terribly wrong it was. "I do a lot of reflection about what happened in the past and I'm very remorseful about it," he says. "I'm sorry for what happened. There's nothing I can do to take away the pain—my own pain or the pain for the other family involved."

Years afterward, the court system continues to wrestle with the results of Butler's murder. Lawyers for the Butler family sued MUM in both Iowa and California. In Iowa, the parents sued on behalf of the estate of Levi Butler. However, Iowa did not permit Levi's parents to sue for the personal loss they suffered in his death because he was eighteen years old, so they turned to their home state of California to bring a suit on their own behalf. Meanwhile, Levi's brother, Joshua, brought a suit in Iowa on behalf of Levi's estate, and it was headed toward trial in that state when MUM settled. In California, Levi's parents haven't gotten far. The family's lawyers lost a lower-court battle in California over whether it was appropriate to bring a case in California—a jurisdictional matter—but as of early 2013 were awaiting an appeal.

The legal tussles have proved to be anything but peaceful. MUM's lawyers may have felt compelled to settle the Iowa case after Judge Gritzner handed Butler's family several victories in a December 2008 order that could have set the stage for a battle royal at trial. The university asked that critical statements by a MUM graduate and a former MUM physics professor not be allowed into evidence and that the case be dismissed. The judge shot the university down on all those fronts, ruling that the statements were admissible and that trial could proceed on Joshua Butler's claims of fraudulent misrepresentation, negligent misrepresentation, and negligent screening or admission of students. A jury would have had to decide whether the university was wrong—fraudulently so in light of its claims of safety—to expose Levi Butler and others to danger by admitting Sem and, allegedly, by not handling him appropriately after his assault on Killian.

MUM settled the case in early January 2009, only days before trial. Whether MUM would have ultimately prevailed or not, the trial might have featured embarrassing testimony by 2004 MUM graduate Charles Knoles and by Kai Druhl, a former physics teacher at MUM. Knoles, who knew both Butler and Sem, said in an affidavit in the Butler case that he personally knew of breaches of MUM's stated safety policies. Among them was the case of a MUM student claiming in 2001 that an instructor was harassing her. Knoles claimed that MUM administrators routed the complaint to student government, of which he was a member, but took no further action. Knoles said he was so troubled by Butler's death and the negligence that he believed led to it that he chose to teach meditation outside the TM organization. He now teaches "Vedic Meditation" with his father, Thom Knoles, a former student of Maharishi. Their organization, the Veda Center of Flagstaff, Arizona, serves a different niche of the market than does the TM Movement, Charles Knoles said. Nonetheless, it has had legal difficulties with a TM organization educational arm, the Maharishi Foundation, which aggressively protects such TM-trademarked or service-marked terms as "Vedic Science."

For his part, Druhl quit TM and stopped teaching at MUM in 2000, after being associated with the movement for twenty years, because he felt it didn't deliver the benefits it promised. Soon, he embraced Christianity, which he felt was incompatible with TM. In his affidavit, he said that during his tenure at MUM, "given the corporate culture [there], it would have been inconceivable to me to call police onto campus except through campus security, the Dean's office and in the most extreme circumstance." *The Observer*, a British newspaper that took an interest in the case, quoted Druhl as saying, "There was a definite understanding between staff members that you must not allow any bad news to leak out. You were required to keep up this image of a perfect campus at all costs."[10] Indeed, in their complaint, the Butler family lawyers point to the university's request to reporters shortly after the stabbing to refrain from interviewing students.

The judge might also have compelled the school to bring in for testimony Bevan Morris, the university president who works only a few weeks a year in Iowa. An Australian, Morris spends much of his time in Holland, where the TM Movement has its global headquarters. Morris was deposed in the case earlier and was asked whether the attacks were inconsistent with the Maharishi Effect—the idea that meditators could spread peace in a place simply by gathering to meditate in sufficient numbers. His answer was that

the Maharishi effect research shows a trend of declining crime and other negativity when there are large groups. It's a trend. It's not the elimination of all crime. And [MUM] like any university, like any school, like any business, like any church, any organization, is not an island. [MUM is] completely in the midst of the country that [it is] in. And in this country there are 16,000 murders a year and 18 million people who are seriously mentally ill. So the likelihood that [MUM] can be completely free from that influence is—is just not likely. It couldn't be.[11]

Some meditators in Fairfield worked up novel explanations for the violence that took Butler's life. Some blamed the alignment of the planets, according to *The Observer*, while others faulted declining numbers of people meditating in the golden domes on campus. The Maharishi Effect, they said, thus couldn't take effect. (The phenomenon requires a group of meditators equaling the square root of 1 percent of the population in a given place, meditators say. That would have meant fewer than 175 were required to spread peacefulness across all of Iowa.) Indeed, according to Druhl, to prop up its numbers, the TM Movement has since begun paying meditators as much as $800 a month to come to the domes twice a day for prolonged meditation sessions.

Whatever the reason, Judge Gritzner in his order points devastatingly to Morris's comments and those of other MUM administrators as undercutting claims about safety on the campus. "The testimonies of current MUM administrators contradict MUM's claims that MUM enjoyed a 'crime-free' campus because of MUM's curricula and practice," he writes.

By its own reports to the National Center for Education Statistics, MUM does seem like an oasis of safety—comparatively. It reported only six arrests on campus for drug law violations and seven for liquor law violations for the years 2008 through 2010, for instance. It reported only ten burglaries on campus in those years, along with one motor vehicle theft. No sex offenses, robberies, or arsons.[12] The far bigger University of Iowa in Iowa City, by contrast, logged 310 arrests on campus for drug law violations and 344 for liquor violations, as well as 19 forcible sex offenses and plenty of other crimes (including 13 aggravated assaults) in the same three-year period.[13] The Butler and Killian stabbings made it obvious, however, that MUM wasn't crime-free. Troublingly, the litigation that followed raised questions about whether the handful of crime reports since then provided the full picture.

As for Fairfield overall, it seems to be about as safe as many other small towns, but it isn't free of crime, the Maharishi Effect notwithstanding. For 2010, for instance, the FBI's uniform crime reports logged fifteen incidents of violent crime in town, including two forcible rapes, two robberies, and eleven aggravated assaults. The agency reported 263 incidents of property crime in Fairfield that year. By comparison, similarly sized Grinnell, Iowa, recorded 20 incidents of violent crime and 172 property crimes, while another like-sized town, Norwalk, Iowa, logged just 7 violent crimes and 104 property crimes.[14] Such reports undercut claims that the campus and Fairfield both have no crime. "We have it, just like any other place," says Fairfield police chief Julie Harvey.

Indeed, some local law enforcers cast doubt on research the TM Movement generated to prove the Maharishi Effect, research that includes some fifty empirical studies and field experience worldwide, according to Pearson. Gregg Morton, a former Fairfield police officer who was elected to the job of Jefferson County sheriff in late 2012, says crime rates ebb and flow. So the timing of studies could influence their results. Lately, in Fairfield and across the county, he says, crime has been rising. In the early 2000s, he says, police were busting meth labs around the county. More recently, scrap metal thefts have risen. And police routinely deal with complaints of domestic violence, some of it among meditators. "They get burglaries. They get domestic abuse and assault," Morton says. "They're not different from anybody else."

The Butler case, moreover, raises questions about the effect meditation can have on mental illness. "Individuals with certain types of psychiatric illnesses may actually have their illness exacerbated through meditation," says Richard J. Davidson, a professor of psychology and psychiatry who directs the University of Wisconsin's Laboratory for Affective Neuroscience. For schizophrenics, Davidson adds, the practice "may further blur the distinction between what's out there in terms of reality and what may exist in a person's head." No one undergoing traditional medical treatment for mental problems, including depression, should give up the treatment in favor of meditation, adds Davidson, who is an expert on a broad array of meditation styles.

Regrettably, just such troubled people may be inclined to look to the practice for help when it appears traditional treatments fail them. Druhl, the former MUM professor, says at least one other schizophrenic student at the school quit taking drugs in favor of meditation and an herbal remedy. The switch didn't help, and the student eventually suffered a breakdown. "There were certainly initial benefits for some of the students, but the promise of complete enlightenment is just not true," Druhl told *The Observer*. "It just doesn't happen and I saw how this intense meditation can damage some students, particularly if they have mental problems."

Officially, teachers are likely to tell devotees being treated by physicians to follow their medical advice, according to Druhl. However, he says, "the actual message . . . is that modern medicine is a fraud, and that 'Vedic medicine' (which includes meditation) is superior." It is, he argues, "a case of double-talk."

Bob Roth, a longtime spokesman for the TM organization, says each meditator should "do whatever your doctor tells you. If they want to come off medicine, we say, 'do whatever your doctor advises.' We don't advise medically." However, Roth also notes that antidepressants and antianxiety drugs may help as few as one-third of users, generate poor reactions in others, or provide no benefit to still others. Organizations such as the Veterans Administration, as a result, are looking for alternatives when their clients aren't helped by drugs, and meditation may be a useful alternative.

Aside from the strong legal defense MUM mounted against the Butler lawsuits, school officials appeared to respond with sensitivity to the young man's family. But a memorial service held in honor of Levi Butler shortly after his death seemed curiously infused, as well, with movement doctrine. While officials praised Butler warmly, parts of the service dwelled on recounting Maharishi's teachings and praising the school.

Pearson, the university official, opened the Butler service, for instance, by explaining how the young man waited until August to apply and so didn't think he could get in until February. Butler called the admissions office just a week before school was to start. Pearson said that "to his [Butler's] surprise, he was told that, in fact, it was still possible to enroll. That's one of many distinctive features of Maharishi University of Management."

In moving to MUM, Pearson went on to say, Butler was making a big change in his life. It was, he said, the most "significant direction possible, and that's the direction within." Further, Pearson noted that TM taught Butler "to dive deeply inward," and he quoted an ancient Chinese text that said, "What the undeveloped man seeks is outside. What the advanced man seeks is within himself." He alluded to this change in direction as "Maharishi's great gift to Levi. This is Maharishi's great gift to the whole human race."

Pearson then paired his praise for young Butler with an extraordinary nod to TM-style meditation, saying:

had Levi, with his incredible creativity and multiple talents, gone on to write the modern equivalent of Shakespeare's plays or compose the modern equivalent of Brahms' symphonies or had he gone on to discover the equivalent of Newton's laws or Einstein's theory of relativity, had he become a world famous dancer, one of his loves, he would not have achieved anything nearly as great as what he achieved in these last six and a half months of his life. The true achievement in life, the goal of the wise throughout the centuries, lies within.

Joel Wysong, the MUM administrator who had taken Butler's assailant to his apartment before the stabbing, also spoke of meditation at the memorial service. He said Butler was asked about his experience practicing TM just a week or two into his time on campus. "When my thoughts fall away and I move into a new consciousness of total awareness of my being in relation to the rest of the universe, a great feeling of joy arises in my chest and a wholeness is felt," the young man responded, according to Wysong. "All thought is gone and all thought becomes irrelevant. Nothing is required of me. I'm in a state of pure being."

Maharishi's teachings—about life, death, and so-called natural law— were much on the minds of the speakers. John Hagelin, the professor of physics at MUM, called Butler "the sort of student we dream about . . . an enlightened student." Then Hagelin quoted the guru's comments about leaving the "physical body" and one's "inner divinity." Further, he said of Butler, "We will certainly miss him, and we wish Levi tremendous Godspeed and great bliss in support of the infinite nourishing power of natural law in his blissful tremendous journey ahead."

Finally, the university's president, Bevan Morris, quoted Maharishi as saying, "Only those who have the light . . . can show the light to others." Morris called upon everyone to be a "champion of peace in the world created from the level of the infinite peace of consciousness itself." And he suggested that the dead young man was enjoying "his evolution to the highest level."

For his part, Maharishi had spoken briefly about Butler's death earlier, putting it into an impersonal but global, critical, and enigmatic context— even tying it to U.S. foreign military actions far from Fairfield. Two months after Butler's death, *The Observer* quoted Pearson saying, "Maharishi Mahesh Yogi has made one comment regarding this event. He said that this is an aspect of the violence we see throughout society, including the violence that our country is perpetrating in other countries."[15]

MUM set up a safety review committee to see whether the campus could be made safer. The group included two outsiders—an official of a local mental health service and a Fairfield police officer—and six people associated with the university. Recommendations in the committee's July 26, 2004, report included stepping up security efforts on campus, improving screening of applicants to the school, providing professional counseling off campus for troubled students, and requiring prompt reports of criminal or dangerous activity to campus security officials and police.

Still, the report points to features at MUM that it said shielded the university from many of the problems with drugs, alcohol, and mental health concerns that afflict other colleges. These features include recommended 9:30 p.m. bedtimes, zero tolerance of alcohol, and fresh food. "The practice of the Transcendental Meditation program by all students (and faculty and staff) does much to systematically reduce stress, anxiety, depression, and neuroticism while promoting self-confidence, self-esteem, and balanced personality development and helping create a peaceful and harmonious campus climate," the report says. Further, it notes that all students are required to attend group meditation sessions each morning and afternoon and that this "offers an additional indicator of student well-being—lapses in attendance in this program tend to be a red flag that a student needs attention."

Troublingly, though, the MUM campus is no stranger to people struggling with personal issues. Nearly fourteen years before the Butler stabbing, a depressed MUM kitchen worker put himself in front of a train in Fairfield only a couple of hours after his twenty-seventh birthday. Mark A. Totten's death, shortly after 2 a.m. on November 29, 1990, came as a shock to people who knew him as a pleasant, if reserved, man who had become a strict vegetarian and committed meditator. Totten was a "nice guy, quiet, intelligent," recalls Michael H. Jackson, a South Carolina man who had worked at MUM as a baker in the mid-1980s." If Mark was depressed for the year or so that I knew him, it certainly did not show."

Totten, the bright son of a Bentley College professor, had a normal childhood in the Boston area, according to his family. He enjoyed stamp collecting, puzzles, running, and funny movies, recalls his younger sister, Julie Totten. He had achieved an almost perfect score on standardized math tests and was admitted to Carnegie Mellon University, which he attended for a year and a half before dropping out.

But he had been chronically depressed since high school, Julie Totten says. "I don't think he was ever happy," she says. "He was in a lot of pain. He was looking for a solution and Transcendental Meditation did help him feel better in some ways. It helped him feel calmer and helped him have some kind of hope."

Meditation—even several years of practicing it—wasn't enough for him, however. Totten took classes in TM and lived on campus at MUM, accepting a paltry amount of pay along with room and board so he could develop his meditation technique. During the year before his death, Julie visited him in Fairfield and told him that his family was troubled by his involvement with the TM Movement. "He didn't want to hear that," she says. "I went to some classes and I said, 'Mark, this doesn't make any sense, I think it's all gibberish.' And he said, 'Yeah, a lot of it I take with a grain of salt.'"

Before his death, there were telltale signs of depression. Totten had gone to a doctor on campus, for example, but complained only of a stomachache, headache, and lack of appetite. The doctor, who Julie said was a meditator, did not pick up on the hints that there was more going awry. Julie, however, saw his sadness as she visited with him in the fall of 1989, and she later found that some others on campus noticed problems, too.

After Mark's death, Julie and her parents visited MUM to try to understand what had happened. The administrators were gracious to them, she said, although she felt they were wary that the family planned to sue—which the Tottens had no plans to do. "We talked to some students," she says. "They said Mark was introverted and didn't say much. They didn't know him well—nobody seemed to know him well. But they said he didn't seem 'enlightened' ... they could tell he wasn't a happy-go-lucky person."

Julie Totten today doesn't fault the TM organization or MUM for her brother's suicide. Depression wasn't as well-recognized back then as it is now, she says. Indeed, it still needs to be better understood, says Totten, who set up a nonprofit organization, Families for Depression Awareness, to educate families and caregivers about depression and bipolar disorder.[16] But she also believes that meditation by itself is not a cure for clinical depression. "It's a medical condition and it needs to be treated with a medical model," she says.

Of course, medicine doesn't always work in preventing suicidal depression, and proponents of TM say their technique can be helpful. The David Lynch Foundation, in its efforts to promote TM as a technique to help homeless people, prisoners, Native Americans, and veterans, posted a video in mid-2012 on YouTube in which an army combat veteran credits meditation for saving him from suicide. "For the first time in I don't know how long, I felt hope. It's helped me out tremendously with my depression and blood pressure. I don't take anxiety medicine at all anymore," said the Afghanistan war veteran, Luke Jensen, who learned the TM technique in 2011 after finding no success with an array of antidepressants and antianxiety drugs. "I had consistently thought about suicide before I learned TM. It was the first thing to kinda get that away and get that off my mind. It changed everything."[17]

It hasn't always been as effective, however, for troubled people in Fairfield and Jefferson County, of which the town is part. Eleven people killed themselves in the county between January 1, 2008, and mid-2012, according to the medical examiner investigator, Mark Hagist. Three of the suicides appeared to involve meditators or the families of meditators, he says. One, which shook the meditating community, was that of Nicole M. Rowe. Like Totten, Rowe put herself in front of a train in town. On September 13, 2008, she dressed in dark clothing and made her way to a bend in the rail line between 9 p.m. and midnight.[18] She was just twenty years old.

A relative who shared information about Rowe with me describes Rowe as having been a "very troubled soul," afflicted by bipolar and borderline personality disorders. She was not a practicing meditator, although she had learned the technique. "I don't think it would have helped her with her very challenging emotional difficulties," the relative says.

The young woman had attempted suicide several times before, after developing emotional problems as far back as middle school. She had attended a now-defunct Maharishi school in Silver Spring, Maryland, for first and second grade and then public schools in the prestigious Montgomery County system. She had been hospitalized a few times as her psychiatric condition deteriorated.

Before her problems took over her life, Rowe had become an accomplished athlete, earning letters in track and cross-country in school. Hospitalized, however, she couldn't finish high school and so didn't get a diploma. She later breezed through an equivalency exam and attended community college classes, including at Indian Hills Community College near Fairfield. Her father, Kenneth Rowe, told Gazette.Net, "She had a beautiful voice and she wrote beautifully."[19]

A dark-haired young woman with striking blue-gray eyes, she appears in a photo on the news website with an endearing hint of a smile. She showed a taste for style, sporting a couple of necklaces; colorful earrings; a small, diamond-shaped forehead ornament between well-manicured eyebrows; and an appealing headband. Her appearance belied the emotional challenges she was wrestling with. "She would take things, have public outbursts, break things," the relative says. "It was unpredictable what she would do. She had an uncontrollable temper sometimes, but she also had a very sweet side."

Rowe had moved from Maryland to live in an apartment near her mother, who had gotten involved in the meditator community in Fairfield. While she was in Fairfield, Rowe "tried to live as an adult, but self-control was beyond her reach and she could not really hold down a job," the relative says.

Rowe got into scrapes with police, so ultimately a local court tried to supervise her care. When her emotional difficulties flared up, the young woman was hospitalized anew, but a lack of suitable psychiatric facilities proved to be a problem. "Being in Fairfield did not really help and likely harmed her condition," according to the relative.

Indeed, authorities—as well as TM—appeared to have failed Rowe. "The week before her death, Nicole had gone to the local psychiatric clinic and explained that she was having self-destructive thoughts," the relative says. "They looked for a hospital for her treatment and informed the Fairfield judge of her situation. The judge brought her into his chambers and made Nicole promise that she would not kill herself. Nicole agreed but, of course, this was not the way to handle the situation."

Rowe's mother was out of town, and no one was available to take her to an appropriate hospital, perhaps one in Cedar Rapids, the relative says. On several other occasions when she was in a manic phase, police had taken her to a hospital. This time, however, they declined because "she was not manic, but depressed."

"It is a sad story," Rowe's relative says. "She was under the care of many doctors but was irregular with her medications. She was also in and out of many psychiatric hospitals for sometimes many days at a time. . . . TM can be helpful with milder cases of emotional problems, but not much use in these difficult cases."

Psychiatrist Norman E. Rosenthal, a clinical professor at Georgetown Medical School and an enthusiastic practitioner of TM, suggests the meditation technique be used as a supplement after conventional methods have been tried in treating depression. Professionals rely on antidepressant drugs to treat such a condition but often see their limitations, he says. "I suggest that TM be considered as a nondrug therapy when a person has not fully responded to conventional treatment—*not as a standalone therapy*," Dr. Rosenthal says in *Transcendence: Healing and Transformation through Transcendental Meditation* (2012). But he also argues that it can help people who just have the blues: "It may work as a stand-alone treatment for people who are simply down in the dumps."[20]

Deaths, including those of young people, are part of life in every college town, of course. Suicide is a sad reality even in rural communities. And with high-profile shooting incidents on several campuses around the country, safety issues and mental illness have become major concerns in college life. Handling such matters is especially delicate at MUM, where peacefulness is far more than just a necessary backdrop for academics. Spreading peace is the raison d'être at both the university and at the Maharishi School of the Age of Enlightenment, the college prep tucked into a leafy corner of the MUM campus.

LOOK

50 CENTS · FEBRUARY 6, 1968

WHITE COP, BLACK REBEL
A searching report on our crisis in
law and order, and a possible solution

WHY I'M BATTLING LBJ
Senator Eugene McCarthy's own story
of his decision to run

AND NOW—
MEDITATION
HITS THE CAMPUS
How Hindu monk Maharishi
turns the students on
—without drugs

MEDITATORS
AT YALE

1. Editors at *LOOK* magazine were entranced by TM's appeal to young people.
Photo of meditators by Paul Fusco, Magnum Photos. Photo of Maharishi by Michael Alexander. Courtesy Magnum Photos.

2. The editors at *MAD* magazine took a more bemused view. © *E. C. Publications, Inc. All Rights Reserved. Used with Permission.*

3. Levi Butler's murder on campus at the Maharishi University of Management in 2004 shook up the TM community. *Photo provided by his mother, Evelyn Butler.*

4. Fairfield's town square has become a home to businesses that would fit in Harry Potter's Hogsmeade.

5. Café Paradiso, home to music, coffee, treats, and otherworldly conversation.

6. Mayor Ed Malloy, the first meditator to win the mayor's seat, aspires to higher office.

7. Connie Boyer, a Fairfield City Council member and mayor pro tem, lost a bid for Iowa's House of Representatives in part because she meditates.

8. Pamela K. Slowick, who founded the Thymely Solutions shop in downtown Fairfield, credits meditation for her entrepreneurial success. It did not, however, help her in a bid for Congress in Arizona in 1992.

9. Eric Schwartz says meditation helps him run a thriving investment advisory, management, and brokerage firm, Cambridge Investments.

10. Meditators gather by the hundreds at least twice a day in a pair of golden domes on the campus of Maharishi University of Management.

11. Students find food, books, and recreation in the student center on the MUM campus.

12. To build anew, MUM tore down many of the old facilities on what once was Parsons College.

13. The Maharishi School of the Age of Enlightenment educates students from preschool through grade 12 in reading, writing, arithmetic, and meditation. It occupies a corner of the university campus.

14. Richard Beall, the head of MSAE, once aspired to a career in professional baseball. Now he oversees a school that routinely produces winning athletes, especially in tennis.

15. The $7 million Fairfield Arts and Convention Center offers programming that appeals to both meditators and non-meditators, but sometimes the groups don't mix.

16. Meditators built a neighborhood of homes according to Maharishi-inspired architectural principles in a new city they created near Fairfield, Maharishi Vedic City.

17. Wealthy meditators have built some of the costliest homes in the Fairfield area.

18. The Raj, a spa in Maharishi Vedic City, offers pricey health treatments to visitors from around the world.

19. Visitors to Maharishi Vedic City can see the capitol of the Global Country of World Peace, though they can't go in.

20. Douglas and Jennifer Hamilton, longtime meditators, have battled TM authorities over their fondness for rival gurus.

8

Enlightenment for All Ages

CHILDREN THE WORLD OVER power up laptop computers every school day to link wirelessly to the Internet. Such connections, indispensable for such trendy devices as iPads, are as common as blackboards in many countries. But that's not the way for a couple of hundred students at the Maharishi School of the Age of Enlightenment (MSAE) in Fairfield. "We know we're often bathing in other people's Wi-Fi, but we've decided not to contribute to it in our learning environment," says Richard Beall, head of school at MSAE. The worry is that the unseen electromagnetic waves could interfere with clear thinking and sleep as well as pose health risks, including cancer.

For MSAE, the issue goes deep. Maharishi, the school's founder, was wary of electromagnetic radiation. He urged people to avoid cellphones and wireless Internet connections, telling followers in 2007, "I don't want to have it in the room." Taking his counsel to heart, followers since then have cited health worries, pointing to studies on cellphones around the world. They've shielded electric wires, urged people to unplug devices and shut them off when not in use, and they avoid Wi-Fi.

MSAE's students and staff do use computers, but they link them to the Internet by cable. Officials at MUM are similarly wary. Wireless computer networks are barred in some gathering places on campus, such as the meditation domes and in some dorms, although MUM has reluctantly loosened its once more severe stricture on Wi-Fi. At MSAE, officials only grudgingly tolerate cellphones, and MSAE and the university campus are—in Beall's words—"swimming against the stream" among educational institutions in the United States in curbing Wi-Fi in computer uses.

That's not the only way that MSAE hews to its own course. The students at MSAE meditate daily. From age ten through their senior year in high school, they practice the essential TM technique a couple of times a day. Sporting white polo shirts, khaki pants, or uniform green plain jumpers, they meet on the fourth floor of the well-lighted, modern, and airy school building—built in accord with the late Maharishi's architectural principles—for yoga, breathing, and meditation. Middle- and upper-school students begin their day with a group program promptly at 8:33 a.m. (or five minutes earlier for older students). Then they break for breakfast, followed by class at 9:25 a.m. After classes end at 3 p.m., they meet for another group meditation. Lest younger kids feel left out, they begin their days with a Maharishi Word of Wisdom session, an eyes-open meditation technique that backers say kids as young as four years old can do while walking.

School officials call it "consciousness-based education," which Beall says boils down to a matter of "how awake we are, how alert we are." To sharpen their young minds, the students meditate for periods roughly equal to their age—ten minutes for ten-year-olds, fifteen minutes for fifteen-year-olds. "The student that walks into the classroom is not the same one that got out of the car," adds Beall. "They've downloaded some of the fatigue and stress or whatever and they go into the classroom wide awake. And our teachers better be ready for them."

Meditation and the insights of Maharishi are a big part of what students at MSAE learn, but not everything. They get lots of reading, writing, and arithmetic as well. Indeed, they get such good educations that some graduates have gone on to Harvard, Stanford, MIT, and the like, and the school routinely produces National Merit Scholars and wins academic and athletic competitions. "We call it 200 percent of life," says Beall, a tall, square-jawed, former semipro baseball player who grew up on an Ohio farm and earned an undergraduate degree at Wittenberg University in 1974. He later earned his master's degree and doctorate at Maharishi University. "We're a college-prep school and so we're trying to prepare our kids for the best college experience that they can have. And we have that obligation to them, so we're giving them a conventional education. But the other 100 percent of that is the idea of inner development."

MSAE's aim, to provide "consciousness-based education," is loftier than cultivating Ivy Leaguers. The school's mission is "to enliven the total brain physiology of every student, and thereby create successful individuals who radiate an influence of peace and harmony in the world."[1]

To that end the curriculum, from literature to science, is shot through with the late guru's insights. The MSAE program is infused with discernments from the study of the Science of Creative Intelligence (SCI), the intellectual framework for TM that students study as a discrete subject in later years. All students pick up SCI all along the way, every day.

"They learn the sixteen principles of SCI. These are the universal principles like 'the nature of life is to grow,' 'life is found in layers,' 'every action has a reaction,'" says Laura Bordow, director of MSAE's lower school (preschool to sixth grade) and a former preschool head. The principles, officials say, were developed by Maharishi in consultation with educational experts.

Teachers will draw attention to these principles—say, the idea that life is found in layers—as the ideas pop up across subject areas. Students will study the layers in trees and in skin, and observe the idea in the layers of clothing people wear during winter. As they take up meditation, students will experience layers of consciousness, Bordow adds, exploring "finer and finer layers of our thought process."

As the students advance, the principle may be discussed in seventh- or eighth-grade biology—in, say, sessions on cells and layers of cells. Still later, in ninth or tenth grade, as they study physics, students will explore layers in quarks and photons. SCI principles, she says, offer insights for the entire science curriculum. "The main thing is that we want to connect what we experience inside to nature and to what's around us," Bordow says. "That we are not isolated from this world around us, that we are a part of it."

The subjects come first, Beall says, and the principles follow. Teachers "teach their subject matter and then step back from that to see what deeper principle might underlie that learning objective," the school chief says. As they unify the subjects, these principles form a "big ideas" approach, one that Beall says is being echoed by the Iowa Department of Education. In schools all across the state, experts encourage teachers to ask what the "big ideas" are, "rather than focus exclusively and intensely on specific content," Beall says. Consultants for the state have been impressed, he says, "that we had been doing that for thirty years."

Of course, the principles might not fly in all schools, even if the idea of looking for the big picture is appealing to educators. The big picture, as the guru saw it, may differ from the way others see the world. Beall says the guru's sixteen principles reflect an understanding of how nature is structured and functions. Sometimes called "natural law," he says they are attempts to foster "higher-ordering thinking" in students, bids to get them to see connections in the world and to understand how such ideas connect to them.

Mantra-like, the ideas suffuse the curriculum. Students discussing Huckleberry Finn, for instance, might try to understand his personality by applying SCI principles about energy, intelligence, and creativity. "They begin to understand very basic laws of nature in the light of his personality," Bordow says. "What if Huckleberry Finn were to meditate, maybe? What would he be like then? What were the qualities of his own consciousness that made him who he is? They begin to see a relationship between who they are and Huckleberry Finn and his environment."

To the irreverent Samuel Clemens or to modern outsiders, the idea of Huckleberry Finn sitting in a lotus position and repeating a mantra might seem, well, odd. But Maharishi's followers embrace their guru's vision that areas as far-flung as science and history can be fitted into a single system of understanding. They call it a "unified field" and espouse it throughout the curriculum. Posters hang in classrooms that sketch out historical epochs and ancient civilizations in terms of the principles of SCI. Ancient Greece, for instance, is related to the qualities of gentleness and strength, as well as the principle that "wholeness is captured in every part." Athens and Sparta are related to insightfulness and foresight. Mesopotamia and Egypt are linked to the idea that "the nature of life is to grow."

The teachers rely on the principles as a handy way to organize their material, though the idea can seem forced. Retired history teacher Lawrence Eyre, who doubled as tennis coach and an SCI instructor, points to the Pony Express. "The reason it was successful, until it was supplanted by the telegraph, was that it built upon a principle of rest as the basis of activity, 'rest and activity are the steps of progress,'" he says. "If they wanted to ride a horse to exhaustion and a rider as well, [they were] not going to make any money or get the mail delivered anywhere. But, by stationing those horses and resting points at manageable distances, they could get communication across the entire country incredibly fast. . . . They took advantage of that natural law."

Students come to see events great and small under the rubric of this natural law. To an outsider, the guru's wisdom can seem at times pat, maybe even loopy. Eyre taught, for instance, that war is "really a collective sigh of stress" and a "purification that eventually can lead to progress." Not that the guru or Eyre advocate war; indeed, a core teaching of TM is that meditation removes stress and so can prevent conflict. But war occurs, Eyre says, when "stress reaches a breaking point, when it cannot be absorbed and saturates the atmosphere."

The late guru held, further, that war arose when conditions violated basic principles of natural law, such as the idea that the nature of life is to grow, Eyre says. When nations feel confined or hemmed in—or are literally or economically enslaved, he said—they cannot grow and so sometimes react with violence.

By teaching students to apply the core principles to all that they learn, Eyre says, the subjects become "more accessible" to them. History is not just "one blasted thing after another" but part of a pattern that fits into or, to its peril, falls out of sync with, such natural law. And by applying the same set of principles to all subjects, he says, students see how they all are related. He argues that this view solves a long-standing challenge of helping students see connections among disparate fields of knowledge.

Eyre, who graduated from Yale in 1970, points to biology and electronics as other examples. Blinking is necessary, for instance, for the human eye to work well—another illustration of the principle of rest and activity. Radio waves, which fluctuate rather than run in a straight line, also illustrate the idea, he says. "Those underlying proverbs, or principles of how nature functions, are shared by every subject and make each subject the students study accessible," Eyre says.

As students absorb these maxims, they look at all subjects in relation to Maharishi's teachings. A movement publication that discussed TM schools worldwide singled out this approach as one of the novel features of the movement's educational institutions. "Students take the usual subjects—mathematics, science, language, social sciences, sports, the arts, writing, computer skills, etc.," reports the *Introduction to Invincibility Schools: Total Knowledge for Every Student, Invincibility for the Nation,* a 2007 publication. "The unique feature is that the main topics of each course and the main points of each lesson are related to the knowledge of the full potential of human development, the knowledge of consciousness, which gives each field deeper meaning for the students and greater relevance to their daily life." Further, the publication notes, "All courses are taught in light of the knowledge of the full development of human consciousness."[2]

This proclivity for packaging ideas and folding them under a single umbrella, a view laid out by the guru, is common in the movement. In a 1987 academic paper titled "The Maharishi Technology of the Unified Field in Education: Principles, Practice and Research," MUM professors Susan L. Dillbeck and Michael Dillbeck discuss a classroom chart that connects "the parts of the knowledge with the wholeness of the Self." They refer to Vedic Science, which they say "describes the unified field as the unmanifest, unchanging basis of all subjective and objective existence, a field of infinite creativity and intelligence containing all the laws of nature in 'seed' form."[3]

The movement is fond of sketching out the ideas in heavily worded posters, packed with columns and connections. Picture a sprawling wall chart that is split vertically into two sections, for instance. On the left, the writer lays out the objective approach to knowledge through modern science and other disciplines. On the right lies the subjective approach through Vedic Science. Students and teachers are meant to link the two.

"The left side of the chart diagrams the whole discipline being studied, from its most abstract foundational areas (at the bottom) to its most applied areas that serve society (at the top), and depicts how the whole discipline emerges from a unified basis of natural law," the Dillbecks say. "Each level gives rise to the next more expressed and diversified level according to an ordering principle. For example, the unified field chart for physiology is organized hierarchically: DNA gives rise to RNA, proteins, cells, tissues, and organs."

"On the right side of the chart is a cone-shaped diagram representing the experience of the Transcendental Meditation and TM-Sidhi programs, during which the mind settles down from its more excited levels to the least excited state of awareness, transcendental consciousness," the Dillbecks continue. "This subjective approach to knowledge gives the direct experience of the unified field. Both sides of the chart are visually unified by the band across the bottom of the whole chart, illustrating that the unified field of natural law is the common source of both approaches of knowledge."

Movement publications are rife with such connections and charts, as the TM leaders look on widely differing subjects through the lens of the guru's worldview and teachings. Authors link knowledge of all sorts to an ancient Indian system of thought that influenced Maharishi, called the Veda and Vedic Literature.

Such teachings, said to predate Hinduism, are spelled out in a text called *Human Physiology: Expression of Veda and the Vedic Literature* (2001), by Tony Nader. Readers learn how, in the words of the book cover, "Modern Science and Ancient Vedic Science discover the fabrics of immortality in the human physiology," and Nader's publisher says the author "compared every aspect of human physiology, at all its stages—the DNA, cell, embryo, up to the adult human physiology and found that at every level, there is a precise one-to-one correspondence between the structure and functions of human physiology and the 40 aspects of the Veda and Vedic Literature, which are the fundamental structures of Natural Law, as brought to light by Maharishi in his Vedic Science."

Nader, a Beirut-trained neuroscientist who is Maharishi's successor in the movement, leads the Maharishi University in Holland. In 2000, the guru anointed Nader as king of the Global Country of World Peace, a part of the movement set up as a nonprofit organization in Vedic City, near Fairfield. He is known as Maharaja Adhiraj Raja Raam or His Majesty King Nader Raam, and no fewer than four photographs of him—three with him sporting a crown—adorn the cover of his $450 physiology text. The book, which Beall says is not used in the curriculum at MSAE but which in early 2012 was on display in one of the classrooms, is saluted on its cover as "a textbook of life for everyone."

Charts such as those that fill the Nader book and adorn the classrooms in Fairfield are aimed at putting academic disciplines and each day's studies into a single context for students. This approach "connects them to the holistic basis of the subject they are studying and reminds them of their personal, directly experienced connection with the knowledge," the Dillbecks contend. "When combined with the practice of the Maharishi Technology of the Unified Field, unified field charts develop in the students a more intimate relationship with the disciplines and a greater interest in understanding them more deeply."

Teachers have been driving home such lessons to students at MSAE since 1975, when it was set up as an elementary school for the children of faculty and staff at the university. As the enrollment grew and students aged, the organizers added a high school in 1981. This, proponents say, completed "the world's first seamless system of 'Consciousness-Based' education," giving supporters the ability to study the guru's insights from preschool through a PhD, all in the same leafy setting in southeast Iowa.

Such "consciousness-based" schooling refers to "how awake and alert we are, to our environment and ourselves," MSAE's website says.

> What if we could optimize consciousness? What if we could give students a tool so they are wide awake throughout the day, every day? Every part of the educational experience would be enhanced: their ability to learn and express their creativity, the quality of their social relationships, even their reaction time in athletic competition. . . . That is what happens with Consciousness-Based Education. We invest in a unique type of rest that pays dividends in all the other activities of the day. The tool we use to achieve this at Maharishi School—and in hundreds of Consciousness-Based Education schools around the world—is the Transcendental Meditation technique. We don't just fill students heads with information, we systematically expand the container of knowledge, the student's own consciousness.[4]

Maharishi, who fancied himself an educator in the broadest sense of the term, was certainly sweeping—if at times inscrutable—in defining the school's technique. "As a result of this educational approach, students grow in the awareness that all streams of knowledge are but modes of their own intelligence," he said. "They come to feel at home with everyone and everything. Their creative genius blossoms with increasing confidence and self-sufficiency. They cease to violate Natural Law and grow in the ability to accomplish anything and spontaneously to think and act free from mistakes—the fruit of all knowledge."[5]

The school does, however, also fill the students' heads with plenty of practical information. Its offerings are meaty enough that MSAE has been accredited by the Independent Schools Association of the Central States since 1986 and is regarded by the state of Iowa as a college preparatory school. And for all its transcendent ambitions, MSAE markets itself by hailing the very worldly successes of its students. Given its cost—which ranges upward by grade from about $1,700 to $14,000 a year, not counting room and board—it may have to in order to win over parents.

Over the past three decades, school officials say, more than 90 percent of MSAE grads went on to universities. A number of them, perhaps half of the classes in some years, went to MUM, but others went to the nation's top-ranked schools. MSAE has generated seventeen National Merit Scholars and more than one hundred finalists, semifinalists, and commended scholars. Its students have covered themselves in glory at state science and engineering fairs, competitions including the International Intel Science and Engineering Fair and the International Sustainable World Energy Engineering Environment Project Olympiad. They have shone in math competitions, problem-solving contests, drama, photography, art, and poetry. In tennis, the school has produced a bevy of state champions (seven singles, five doubles, and four team champions), and in 2009 their coach, history teacher Eyre, was recognized as the U.S. Professional Tennis Association National High School Coach of the Year. Students have also excelled at competitions in golf, track and field, and soccer.

Perhaps surprisingly, considering how passive meditation is, nothing about TM runs counter to competition. Students and teachers at MSAE revel in their achievements in the classroom and on the playing fields. Eyre, who says he taught some fifteen thousand people to play tennis in a career dating back to 1966, credited meditation with boosting the performances of his athletes. He took up the practice and in 1973 began encouraging it among his players. Through 2011–12, Eyre's final year as coach, his athletes at MSAE had meditated their way to sixteen state championship titles and an overall record of 240–67 over twenty-five seasons.

The players succeed because they show "composure under fire," the coach says. Emotions run high in a match, he added, and players whose nervous systems are free of stress, fatigue, and strain have an edge. An hour of tennis may involve just fifteen minutes of hitting balls, with the rest providing far too much time for tensing up, getting distracted, or feeling strained. A player who is focused and calm can avoid such problems, which are especially common in young players. "There are a lot of short fuses in high school tennis," says Eyre.

While making their marks in such realms, however, the students also learn some decidedly unusual things. They study Sanskrit, the language of the Vedic tradition, for instance, because Maharishi held that the "perfect orderliness of the Sanskrit language creates orderliness and balance in the brain physiology, expands the memory, and purifies the physiology."[6]

The language may be far less useful than, say, Spanish—which MSAE recently added—but head of school Beall believes its effects are far-reaching. "Your Kindergarten student will begin by learning the Sanskrit alphabet," the school's website says. "During the Lower and Middle School years, he or she will progress to read the classical texts of Vedic Literature, such as the Bhagavad-Gita, in the original Devanagri script. . . . He or she will read Sanskrit aloud for ten minutes at the beginning of the school day and enjoy the settling effect of the rhythms and sounds of this ancient language."[7]

School officials claim the effects are profound. They claim that scientific research has shown that during the reading or recitation of Sanskrit, the functioning of the brain "becomes highly orderly and coherent, enhancing the overall development of the student, the basis of effective and enjoyable learning." MSAE officials say that pronouncing the sounds of the Vedic Literature "enlivens balance and integration in the mind and body of the students."

Students also get a hefty dose of education in Ayurveda, the science of natural medicine that Maharishi encouraged. This approach to health care is said to handle health "from the deepest level—the knowledge of the inseparable connection between consciousness and its expression, the physiology." Students learn about meditation, yoga, herbal formulas, diet, organic agriculture, and the putative effects of Vedic architecture.

Until recently, students in the high school learned Vedic astrology. This field, called Jyotish, was said to help a student avert future dangers and capitalize on good times. Jyotish, the school once said on its website, is a "science and technology to know past, present and future." But MSAE recently stopped teaching the field. Beall says, "It's a very subtle skill and can lead to misinterpretations and confusion in amateur practitioners—including students."

The MSAE students do still learn architecture according to Vedic principles. They are taught that buildings designed in accord with the "Sthapatya Veda" approach promote health, happiness, and fortune. They learn that main entrances should face east, for instance, to orient the structures to be "in harmony with the solar, lunar and planetary influences on the earth." Buildings need to be designed, they learn, so different energies of the sun correspond to specific activities of each room. Measurements and proportions matter, too, as does proximity to bodies of water and an unobstructed view of the sun.

Students at MSAE excel in math competitions and may credit their performance to the Vedic math approach. In the elementary grades, this includes arithmetic based on Vedic sutras or aphorisms. Such aphorisms include "by one more than the one before," "all from 9 and last from 10," and "vertically and cross-wise." MSAE officials say such sayings are algorithms for computation. "On a deeper level, each sutra produces a high degree of orderliness in the brain that promotes rapid and precise solutions," the school's website adds. "Vedic Math helps culture each student's ability to function from the level of silent wakefulness while solving specific mathematical problems, thus supporting harmony with natural law."

Much like MUM, MSAE fits into a pattern of private schools that have popped up over time in the United States—particularly in the 1960s and 1970s. This was a banner time for independent, often countercultural schools. Bryant, the University of Nebraska–Lincoln education professor, hears echoes of the classic East Coast prep school in MSAE. "It is the country away from the evils of urban life," he says. Further, it is what educational theorists have called a "total institution," a "people-changing organization that controls or manages all aspects of its clients' lives." It falls into a pattern that hearkens back even to great British prep schools. "Fairfield has both that preferred setting and a set of lofty values," Bryant says. "That progressive attribute for which Iowans are known must have played a role in the '70s, when the place was created."

Bryant is struck by the aim in the curriculum on higher-order thinking and learning objectives. It's reminiscent, he says, of Bloom's Taxonomy, a highly structured approach toward education that was developed in the mid-1950s by educational psychologist Benjamin S. Bloom. Bloom broadly espoused the idea of developing the skills of evaluation, analysis, and synthesis in students, an approach that public education often struggles with, Bryant says. "Maharishi's principles of life must constantly require students to draw comparisons and to arrive at some form of evaluation in much of their classwork," he adds. "It would be quite attractive to a well-educated population of parents."

Given the immersion in TM and the teachings of the late guru, however, the school tends to attract the children of meditators but few others. This, in part, may account for the steep declines in enrollment that the school has experienced in recent years. Bordow fondly recalls the early 1990s, when more than 700 students packed the classrooms. The tally has dropped to about 220 in preschool through twelfth grade. The high school graduating class in 2013 totaled just 19, drawn from nine countries.

Why the slide? "Demographics," says Bordow. Baby Boomers, who flocked into the TM Movement and moved to Fairfield or sent their children to MSAE from afar, have aged. And, for much of the time since the decline began, the school labored without aggressive outreach efforts. "There wasn't a lot of marketing or recruitment," the administrator says. "It was like we were the best-kept little secret in these cornfields of Iowa. We had great success and a lot of things going on but . . . there just was no reaching out."

Now that's changed. The school is hoping to boost its numbers by tapping into parents' fears about the pressures—and dangers—of urban schools. They hope to build enrollments thanks to widespread popular acceptance of meditation, as well as such trends as the emphasis on sustainability, yoga, and organic vegetarian food. (That's the fare served in the cafeteria.) They also see the separation of the sexes in the classroom and the use of uniforms as appealing to parents worried about the distractions their children face in conventional schools. Many parents, Bordow adds, are also looking for a connection to spirituality. At the same time, the school pitches the idea that it offers "Academic Excellence without Stress."

The school now has a marketing committee working on outreach techniques. It is wooing students from countries all over the world where TM has a presence, offering boarding options in Fairfield such as living with local families. At a 2012 celebration of the school's international diversity, students offered greetings in twenty-four languages. About twenty students come from overseas now, hailing from as far away as China. Beall points to a student whose father was drawn to the school, by way of its website, because of meditation. He believed the practice would calm the girl, a high schooler who plans to go on to the Wharton School and to return to China to run her family's hat factory.

Administrators travel the globe to talk up the school to parents who are eager to send their students to the United States and who would see MSAE as a launching pad for a U.S. college education. Indeed, Bordow sketches out a future that could include houses, similar to British public-school houses, where students from all across the globe could share quarters. "We'd like to have them live in groups," she says. "It would be wonderful to have a little Chinese house with a mother who is Chinese and a little African house with a mother who is African and can cook their food."

The administrators hope, too, to draw second-generation meditators who have returned to Fairfield to raise their children. They want to reach meditators across the country to drive home the message that their children can thrive in a small-town alternative lifestyle. "We're repackaging," she says, pointing to the new MSAE website. "It's a new paradigm."

Backing away from such esoteric areas as Vedic astrology and Sanskrit grammar—both of which the school recently dropped—may also improve the school's ability to market itself to a broader audience. Beall denies that marketing played a role in such moves, but he notes that school officials are also reassessing Sanskrit reading instruction "to determine how to maintain quality control going forward."

Families that choose to send their children to the school or to move to Fairfield themselves to become more involved in TM are likely to have different feelings than the Baby Boomers who flocked there in answer to the guru's call. Maharishi, of course, is dead. But Bordow expects other forces will prove as alluring. "People coming here now are not looking for the same thing that I was looking for," she says. "They're not going to be devoted to Maharishi or they're not going to be committed to this as a lifestyle. What they're looking for is a strong, solid community to live in that is safe, that is small-town and is going to give a good education to their children."

MSAE cannot promise that its students will always be angels. Children do misbehave, such as a preschooler who bit another child. While that's a far cry from students who may tote guns and knives into classrooms in some inner-city schools, it nonetheless merited aggressive intervention by the teachers, administrators, and parents. "We've got our issues," Bordow says. "There's very minimal, minimal drugs and alcohol. But when we have it, it's something we take very seriously. . . . We're not isolated from our culture, and as the society begins to change, there's collective stress in the environment. The world is a mess out there."

Still, graduates say that the school is a far better place to grow up than high-stress public or private schools. There's no bullying, they say. Students tend to be welcoming toward newcomers.

Certainly, Bordow feels committed to pulling the school out of its enrollment tailspin. She got involved with MSAE by way of TM. Bordow, who hails from Skokie, Illinois, and earned her undergraduate degree in education at Barat College in Lake Forest, Illinois, in 1974, taught kindergarten for a year in Lake Forest and then decided to deepen her knowledge of TM. She trained to become a TM teacher in 1976, studying in Fairfield for three months and France for three months. She taught meditation in the Chicago area from 1976 to 1980, married a fellow meditator, and helped to start the

Banner Preschool at Beth Hillel, a synagogue in Wilmette, Illinois. She visited Fairfield often.

Her life changed in 1983, when she had a son, Adam. She found the north Chicago suburbs too materialistic and worried about the effects this would have on her boy. "It was not the environment I wanted to raise my son in," she recalls. "We knew that there was something else. We knew that there was a place where we could help our child grow spiritually. . . . I wanted him to have this understanding that there's something more to life than what we see around us through the senses. I wanted him to have a connection to that inner core, to that deep foundation."

Meditators in Fairfield got hold of her résumé, visited her for a whirlwind tour of Chicago-area preschools, and offered her the chance to run a new Maharishi preschool. She did so from 1985 to 1991, a period when enrollment typically totaled about 150 per year. Bordow, who earned her master's degree in SCI at MUM in 1986, then took over leadership of the lower school at MSAE.

Likewise, Beall took a circuitous path to the school. After earning a bachelor's degree in interdisciplinary studies at Wittenberg in 1974, he played semipro baseball in Florida. A center fielder, he tried out for the St. Louis Cardinals but didn't make the big leagues. He had discovered TM a couple of weeks before graduating from college and took up the practice in earnest, training to become a TM teacher, which he did for several years in Ohio in the 1970s. He taught TM in Berkeley, California, for a while and, after marrying in 1981, started teaching at MSAE. He earned a master's degree in education at the Maharishi University in 1982. Beall left to teach TM in Bulgaria for a time in the 1990s and returned to earn his doctorate at MUM in 1996.

Beall, who has an entrepreneurial streak like many in the TM Movement, ran his own school for a while. After working as an educational consultant in North Carolina, he helped found the Carolina International School in Charlotte, a publicly funded charter school. He and other founders planned to offer meditation at the school until a local citizens group raised a row, arguing that the practice was religious and so had no place in a state-funded school. It opened, without meditation offerings, and Beall ran it from 2004 to 2008. He left after another administrator was convicted of embezzlement and jailed. His experience there, he says, "was a time of extreme highs and lows: the acclaim the school received and the lives it changed, along with the financial problems caused by a dishonest employee." He was happy to return to Fairfield.

Beall, Bordow, and Eyre all remember when the classrooms were fuller at MSAE. The school is evolving, they say, from a convenience for faculty members at MUM into what they hope will be a global magnet. If the school survives over time, bringing in students from afar may be its ticket.

Like many private schools, MSAE will also likely depend on the generosity of business leaders who feel they have a stake in its health. Some of those business leaders say they owe their fortunes to TM. The guru, who cultivated the wealthy and powerful to help spread his message, never suggested there was a contradiction between pursuing the ethereal and commercial realms. And some of his most passionate followers took his word on this to heart.

9

Just Business

FOR PAMELA K. SLOWICK, meditation is more than a pleasant daily pastime. She credits her livelihood to a recurring month-long vision she had while meditating in 1994. "Every single day, I closed my eyes and after thinking of the mantra a couple times, bingo, there was the store," the effervescent Slowick recalls.

> Every day there was a new aspect—the flower essences for emotions, the homeopathic remedies to heal the body. I saw the different companies and the couch where we would have the mamas sit and research remedies. Every day, for twenty-eight days, this was happening. On the twenty-eighth day, I had a thought—talk about thick—"what if these thoughts are only happening in my head?" This was the first inkling I had that this might be my baby.

The result: a year later, she opened Thymely Solutions, a shop that might seem more at home in San Francisco or in Harry Potter's Hogsmeade than just off the main square in a southeastern Iowa farm town. Slowick and her half-dozen staffers offer bulk herbs, natural vitamins, supplements and tinctures, aromatherapy oils, and homeopathic remedies in the shop and online. They comb through the "bewildering array of natural products" available to stock some three thousand of what her website calls the "purest, organic, non-genetically engineered health products available."[1]

Retail outlets such as Slowick's are among the visible signs of the economic shot in the arm that adherents of the TM Movement have given Fairfield. Since the mid-1970s, the town has been a hotbed of entrepreneurialism as followers of the guru developed businesses that catered to one another and to markets well beyond Iowa. Restaurants now serve Indian and vegetarian food. Revelations, the used bookstore chock-full of spiritual-development texts, doubles as a popular breakfast and lunch spot. Café Paradiso, a coffee shop, provides snacks and cutting-edge music. Outside downtown, Cambridge Investment Research, a fast-growing independent broker-dealer, employs hundreds who serve financial planners and their customers nationwide. Real estate developers in Fairfield have thrived by building homes that comply with the movement's architectural principles. Several charming bed-and-breakfast inns welcome visitors from around the world, as does a luxury hotel-spa just outside town in Maharishi Vedic City.

This commercial upsurge, which has remade parts of town, has been recognized by groups outside Fairfield. The National Center for Small Communities in 2003 gave the city a Grass Roots Entrepreneurship Award for cities with populations of less than ten thousand. A year later, the town was named the Most Entrepreneurial City in Iowa by the Iowa Community Vitality Center. The Fairfield Entrepreneurs Association claims that one-third of all venture capital raised in the state in the twenty years beginning in 1990 was invested in Fairfield-based companies. The area brags about being labeled "Silicorn Valley" because of a concentration of high-tech and Internet-based companies. Every bit as industrious as the Amana Colonies with their famed refrigerator enterprise or the Oneida Community's cutlery operation, Fairfield's TM community entrepreneurs created hundreds of jobs for movement supporters and outsiders alike.

But do the group's teachings have anything to do with the commercial successes? Some TM backers insist that meditation is the secret weapon for successful businesspeople. It focuses their minds, clearing them of the clutter that most people struggle with and giving them the power—and inner calm—needed to make smart decisions, they contend. Others, including some who have broken with the group, scoff at this. Success in business would have come to these entrepreneurs anyway, they say. It's all a matter of personality, timing, and luck, and meditation is irrelevant. People on both sides of the argument admit that Fairfield's entrepreneurs had no choice but to launch their ventures; much like the earlier Utopians, they moved into a place where there were too few jobs for all the people needing them. If they wanted to keep body and soul together, they had to create their own opportunities.

Maharishi certainly had no trouble with the idea of his followers making money. While more of those who flocked to Fairfield were spiritually minded rather than business oriented, they did warm to the guru's idea that life was a "200 percent" affair—with 100 percent focused on inner consciousness and 100 percent focused on enjoying the outside world, according to Eric Schwartz, one of Fairfield's most successful entrepreneurs. "He encouraged them to go out and make a lot of money, so they could have a good, high quality of life and then focus on meditation," says Schwartz. "They could make money so they would have more time to commit to spirituality, not make money because money was more important than anything else."

For some Fairfield entrepreneurs, money and spirituality have gone hand in hand. Maharishi referred to "wealth and wisdom squared" when he urged followers, at a three-thousand-person gathering in 1979 at Amherst, Massachusetts, to move to Fairfield, recalls another adherent, Fred Gratzon. For most of the business leaders, though, success in the material world came by circuitous and surprising routes.

Slowick is a good example. Before opening her shop in August 1995, she had some slight experience in retailing—as a saleswoman and then manager for a couple of mall clothing stores in Michigan and Maryland and as the health-section manager for a market her husband ran in Fairfield. She had schooled herself in homeopathy, mainly to raise her two boys in a healthy way, and had held workshops in Fairfield for people interested in alternative medicine. But she had no conscious desire to run her own place. In fact, after the images of a shop came up persistently as she meditated at home, Slowick shelved the notion because she didn't know how to handle the risk of being accused of practicing medicine without a license by selling homeopathic treatments.

Soon after, however, as she visited her ailing father in the Baltimore area, she stopped into a pharmacy that stocked alternative remedies. When a customer asked about flu treatments, the pharmacist checked his computer and printed out a suggested remedy. Seeing a way that she could guide customers to consult an independent source for advice themselves, by computer, she then felt free to open a shop. When space opened up in Fairfield, she jumped at it, converting a former tire storage center into a cozy retailing spot. She figured out how much business she would need to do to make it work. "The first week, we met our minimum and we've been thriving ever since," Slowick says.

Slowick seems to have a similar knack for real estate, a business in which her late father had worked. After attending a seminar in Fairfield about techniques for becoming an "enlightened millionaire," she moved into buying apartments and condos. At the time, in 2001, she was $32,000 in debt for private-school costs for her sons. But she managed to clear away the debt and build up holdings of forty-four housing units, including six condos in Hawaii that she finds time to visit regularly.

Beyond the initial visions that led to the Thymely Solutions store, Slowick credits meditation for much of her success. She meditates morning and evening, for forty minutes each time. Often, she says, her mind at first buzzes with thought before settling down with the help of a mantra. "It gives you two times a day where you transcend, which means you go beyond all the chatter in your brain," says Slowick, who taught TM for years before settling in Fairfield in 1982. "In that silence is where the power resides, where the good ideas reside, the connection to the source." Meditation, she adds, gets her in touch with her inner intelligence.

Meditation and the TM Movement, indeed, shaped much of her life. Like many other Baby Boomers drawn to the movement in its peak years, she started the practice in 1972. She was sixteen years old and attending a private high school in Baltimore. "I was considered the weird one, the spiritually weird one," she jokes. After attending Hampshire College for two years, Slowick traveled to Italy for a training session for TM teachers, where she met her first husband. She married, quit school, and taught TM at a few places in the United States before settling in Fairfield in response to the 1979 call by Maharishi for meditators to move to the town.

During the 1980s and 1990s, Slowick sent her sons to the Maharishi

School in Fairfield. In 1992 she moved temporarily to Arizona as her first marriage was ending. TM's Natural Law Party had asked her to run for Congress there and she obliged. Shortly after losing the election, she returned to Fairfield and met her current husband, a graphic artist, at a dance on the MUM campus. "My current husband was my gift for having run for the NLP," she says. "It took a lot of guts to pick up and run for politics. Public speaking is not my forte. I uprooted my kids. But once I did it, I knew I must have done something right when two months later I fell in love with Wayne. And twenty years later he is still the love of my life. We have been partners in love, in Thymely, in real estate and in life."

Eric Schwartz also took up TM during its heyday in the early 1970s, and it rapidly became far more important to him than traditional academics. The practice shaped his life and his career. As of early 2013, Schwartz's company, Cambridge Investment Research, employed 455 people in a couple of buildings that rise from the cornfields on Pleasant Plain Road a few miles northeast of downtown Fairfield, along with 46 other employees scattered around the country. The company provides investment information, management, and brokerage services to 2,250 independent financial advisors nationwide. With $460 million in revenues in 2012—heading toward a projected $540 million in 2013—Cambridge has become one of the biggest independent firms in the business.

For Schwartz, it all has come as something of a surprise. "I never took a course in anything related to business, finance, law, or accounting," says the Connecticut native, whose family ran a construction business in New York City. It all had to do with meditation, though, he said. Schwartz was studying such subjects as religion and philosophy at Amherst College when he learned to meditate during his first year there. At the end of his second year, he took a TM teacher-training course and soon decided he wanted to be done with school so he could pursue meditation more. To shorten his time as an undergraduate, he transferred to the University of Massachusetts for his third year—his final year as an undergrad—and earned his bachelor's degree in education in 1975. "I was highly interested in the concept of higher consciousness," he recalls. "This was a breakthrough technology and it was making other areas of study obsolete."

He threw himself into the movement with vigor. He spent time in Europe working with Maharishi and the international TM organization. He returned to the United States to earn a master's degree in exercise physiology at the University of Massachusetts in 1979, studying the effects of meditation. He moved to George Washington University to pursue a PhD in physiology but grew intrigued with business because his wife, Jane, whom he met through TM, ran a public relations operation promoting investment firms. Her work stoked an old flame: at age ten, Schwartz had helped his parents make a few thousand dollars on a gambling-related penny stock. Schwartz had picked the company out from the business pages of a New York newspaper because, he said, he had a liking for numbers and its shares seemed to be climbing steadily. The stock's price kept rising, Schwartz recalled, and his parents sold the shares for hefty gains. (Later, Schwartz noted, the Securities and Exchange Commission put the outfit under investigation for illegal manipulation.)

Beyond his youthful stock picking, however, Schwartz had no knowledge of business. What he did have—thanks to TM, he says—was a willingness to try new things. So he and his wife set up a business selling oil and gas tax shelters under the name of Eneric Petroleum Corporation—for energy and Eric. They worked for a time in Washington, D.C., and then in Florida in the early 1980s, until 1985, when Jane developed cancer and died. For a time, Schwartz returned to Washington. During those tough years, he had to restructure his business when the government shut down most tax shelters. He ultimately tried to build up his broker-dealer unit, which served only about twenty advisors in 1992 and logged revenues of about $468,000, a fraction of his earlier revenues.

With his business struggling—"hanging by a thread," Schwartz recalls—he and his second wife decided to get out of D.C. They shopped around, checking out Austin, Texas, and Lawrence, Kansas, before settling on Fairfield. The Iowa town, he felt, would be similar to the small town where he had grown up in northern Westchester County, New York, and he believed he would know a lot of people from the movement. He and his wife still meditated. His only reservation was that advisors he worked with might not warm to the idea. "It took a year for me to get up enough courage to do it," he says of the move. "Perhaps people I worked with might think it strange. Some of those people were highly religious and they might not think TM was a good thing."

Nonetheless, they moved, only to face other challenges. Schwartz's wife didn't care for Fairfield, so they soon divorced and she moved to Boulder, Colorado. In time, he married an employee, Mary Sue Wilcox, who had moved with his company to lead his accounting group. Mary Sue, Schwartz's wife for more than seventeen years now, has left Cambridge to spend her time on such interests as competitive ballroom dancing. She—like Schwartz— still meditates.

Over twenty years, Eneric morphed into Cambridge and bounced back from its troubles. Schwartz rode a wave that reshaped the financial-planning industry, namely, the rise of a fee-based approach among independent planners. Cambridge positioned itself to serve the new needs of such planners, handling brokerage accounts and other transactions for them and their customers. It also built up a unit that provides investment advice that the planners could pass on to their customers, an area that in 2012 accounted for some 55 percent of Cambridge's revenues.

Schwartz credits his involvement with TM for much of his success. Meditating twice a day leaves him "supercharged," he said, giving him energy and "mental clarity" that helped him through school and continues to help him in business. "When I get up in the morning, I'm awake and I'm clear," he says. "I seem to be able to cut through emotional things that make you make wrong decisions. I have an intuition about what will make us money, what will probably work and what won't. I also have come to be known as being somewhat of a visionary—one article used the word 'oracle'—in our industry."

It also brings him a sense of calm that he finds essential in running a business, Schwartz states. He says that in the late 1990s, a colleague slunk into his office to admit to losing $38,000 on a trading error. "Back then, that was about half my salary for a year," Schwartz recalls. "He was expecting some yelling and screaming, even though he knew I wasn't a wild man. Instead, I was extremely calm and said something to the effect of 'have we fixed the error and, two, what are we doing to avoid it in the future?' This doesn't mean it didn't annoy me, but it took 90 percent of the burning that he expected out." The employee rose to become a valued vice president.

Schwartz is careful, however, to keep his company and TM separate. When he built his headquarters, he chose not to build in accord with Maharishi's principles of architecture—except that the main building faces east, which is said by TM to be the most felicitous direction for an entrance. The two buildings—the first built in 2006, the second in 2009—don't sport the rooftop ornaments called kalashes that architecturally correct buildings do, for instance. Using TM-approved architecture would have added substantially to the $10 million the structures cost, he says, and might have sat poorly with some non-meditating executives and employees. Schwartz said he must be sensitive to the concerns of the 80 percent to 85 percent of his employees who do not meditate, including all but five of his eighteen top managers.

Fairfield over the years saw several companies set up by meditators rise and flame out fast, in some cases putting hundreds to work and then quickly casting them out of work. Some of those folks went to work for Cambridge, and Schwartz is wary of doing anything that would give them the idea that his is another "meditator company" bound for quick extinction. "We've gotten from a number of people the fear that we could go out of business because they went out of business quickly," Schwartz says. What's more, he said, he didn't want non-meditators to feel that they were the "odd men out." He's building the company to be inclusive and to last, he says.

But he certainly doesn't discourage meditation. When employees showed interest in the practice, he arranged for the company to pay for meditation training. He is also considering setting aside space in his headquarters for meditation—or prayer, if employees choose.

Outside the office, Schwartz remains a major backer of TM. He sits on the board of trustees of MUM, where he helps focus on long-term planning, and is a generous donor to the school's sustainable living program. Cambridge also counts a dozen MUM graduates among its employees. TM, Schwartz says, "changed the quality of life for me."

Unlike Schwartz, entrepreneur Fred Gratzon sees no problem in the "meditator company" label. "I think being a meditator company is a great honor," he says. "I liked the idea of making Fairfield a strong economic engine, and I wanted to create jobs for people so they could move here and meditate here and support that larger view of creating invincibility for America. I buy into that."

Gratzon's adult life was also shaped by his meditation and activities in the TM Movement. He started meditating in 1968 while earning a fine arts degree at Rutgers University, studied with Maharishi to become a teacher in 1970, and nine years later moved to Fairfield to take advanced meditation courses. That led him into business. He comments that business can be "incredibly stressful" and that TM purges the strains. "It was so valuable to go home at the end of the day and meditate and have all that stress and all that garbage you have to deal with just wash away," he says. "I don't see how a businessman can survive without it, and they don't—they get heart attacks and ulcers and all manner of stress-related ailments."

Certainly, Gratzon had reason for agitation at times in his business life. Both his businesses rocketed to great success—making *Inc.* magazine's list of the five hundred fast-growing companies list—only to collapse in acrimony and lost friendships, including among fellow TM enthusiasts. As Gratzon put it in a blog post, "I've had more than my share of dramatic business ups and downs. I've had breathtaking successes. I've had violent train wrecks. I danced euphorically with friends one day and I've experienced vicious betrayals the next."[2]

Gratzon launched his first business, the Great Midwestern Ice Cream Company, in 1979 because, he says, he needed to support himself and couldn't find decent ice cream in Iowa. At a time when such premium brands as Haagen-Dazs and Ben & Jerry's were building followings, he created an ice cream that seemed to have more going for it than the others. The desserts were judged the best in the land by *People* and *Playboy* magazines, were served in Ronald Reagan's White House (garnering Gratzon a visit with the president), and were the choice of two U.S. Olympic basketball teams. The ice cream rode a tidal wave of media attention through the 1980s.

Gratzon, a lanky, upbeat guy who looks a bit like folksinger James Taylor, certainly proved his knack for marketing. For the Iowa presidential election caucuses of 1988, for instance, he created the Great Midwestern Ice Cream Presidential Poll. He created brands for each candidate, such as George H.

W. Bush's Preppymint, Joseph Biden's Loquacious Peach, and Al Gore's Mint Julep Chip. Alluding to one contender's extramarital affair, he offered Gary Hart's Donna Rice Cream. Others included Pat Schroeder's Run Pat Run Raisin, Pierre "Pete" S. Dupont's Super Rich Fudge and General Alexander Haig's I'm in Charge Chocolate, and Jack Kemp's Quarterback Crunch.

Gratzon's idea, which he put into play in the caucuses run-up in 1987, was that supporters could vote with their taste buds, choosing their candidate's flavor. "The press went wild," Gratzon recalls in his blog. "The evolution of this story over the next six months made the international wire services four times. I was interviewed by the *Wall Street Journal, New York Times Magazine,* NBC Evening News and scores upon scores of others. I appeared on Japanese TV. A friend said he saw my interview when he was vacationing in Italy. A Dutch film crew visited my ice cream factory."

In the end, the ice cream poll turned out to be partly right. Robert Dole (Top Banana) was the choice of dessert lovers and the caucuses, though he ultimately lost the party nomination to Bush, who later captured the White House. On the Democratic side, ice cream poll winner Michael Dukakis (Massachewy Chocolate) was outpaced in the caucuses by Dick Gephardt (St. Louis Bluesberry) and Paul Simon (Bow Tie Brickle), though Dukakis did go on to become his party's nominee. "At the Dukakis presentation in the morning, there were 20 television cameras," Gratzon recalls. A photo of him handing Dukakis his flavor made the front page of the *Washington Post,* reporters warmed to Dole's presentation, and Bryant Gumbel and Jane Pauley interviewed Gratzon on the *Today Show.* Political comedian Mark Russell also interviewed him on *Good Morning America.*

Later in the race, Gratzon's ice cream was served around the country through "The Rolling Polling Station," a promotion sponsored by the Amana appliance manufacturer. (Coincidentally, the famed refrigerator company was born out of the Amana Colonies, the early Iowa Utopian community about seventy-five miles north of Fairfield.) Gratzon's ice cream was served at the Republican National Convention in New Orleans, a major Democratic fundraiser in Washington, D.C., and the White House's annual picnic for members of Congress. Gratzon got to attend the picnic.

Despite all the hoopla, however, the ice cream venture ultimately turned into a heart-wrenching "meltdown" for the founder. The company couldn't turn a profit for years after it expanded outside Iowa, according to *Inc.* magazine.[3] Helped by the ice cream poll, the Great Midwestern Ice Cream Company boosted sales to $2.7 million in 1987, its peak year, but still lost $1.2 million, *Inc.* reported. Gratzon recalled that he and his colleagues refused to pay so-called slotting allowances—payments that big grocery chains require for shelf space—which relegated the ice cream to smaller independent retailers. Distributors, he says, "did miserable jobs," and one cheated the company for more than $100,000.

As the endgame played out, relationships in the small Fairfield company grew strained, despite whatever soothing effects meditation might have had. Gratzon complains that he was traveling the country, exhausting himself with three or four media interviews a day for several days at a time. Then he'd come back to the office for "more and more criticism and resentment from my so-called friends in the office. I overheard one spouse complain, 'My husband does all the work but Fred gets all the credit.'" Life on the job was anything but satisfying for him. "What used to be a place I could not wait to come to in the morning turned into a place I dreaded," he writes. "Each morning I'd go with an awful feeling in my stomach."

It all came a cropper after Gratzon's colleagues decided to retire the company's seemingly potent brand name and produce ice cream under private labels for retailers. "And since PR was no longer needed with such a strategy, I was no longer needed," Gratzon writes. Worse, a deal he made for the company to buy back his stake fell apart, scotched by "a dear friend who desperately wanted to move to my town but could only do so because I gave him a job in the ice cream company." That left Gratzon out in the cold. "I went from following Nancy Reagan through the buffet line to standing on the unemployment line. I had no money, no income, no assets, and having signed a non-compete clause with the most recent investors that said that if I left the business for any reason I could not compete in the ice cream industry."

But unlike the Great Midwestern Ice Cream Company, the resilient Gratzon bounced back, saying his firing by colleagues turned out to be a boon. In 1989, he went on to create Telegroup, a reseller of long-distance phone service that proved to be both a financial and stock-market rocket until it flamed out into bankruptcy after a decade. Brilliant in its simplicity, Telegroup exploited legal mandates on big phone companies that required them to offer discounted rates to bulk buyers of phone time. Telegroup built up a global customer base variously estimated at between 250,000 and 350,000 corporate and individual customers in 180 countries. The outfit pocketed the spread between its charges to customers and the charges levied by the big carriers.

In no time, Telegroup swelled into a major employer, ultimately providing work for eleven hundred people plus twelve hundred independent sales representatives, according to Gratzon. It reported $337.4 million in annual sales in 1997, the year that Gratzon took the company public at $10 a share. "I was living out the dream of entrepreneurs everywhere—taking my company public," Gratzon writes. "During the day, preened investment bankers fawned over me. And at night, visions of sugar plums in 'green shoes' danced in my head, as I price-earnings ratioed myself to sleep."

Along the way, however, the entrepreneur—who styled himself as "a fairly guileless dude"—learned again about the dark side of business, this time in the rarefied air of Wall Street. He met representatives of three investment banks, all in their late twenties to mid-thirties and was dazzled by a pretty banker from a big Wall Street house. "She clearly had game," he writes. "I marveled [at] how she gave no ground and elbowed for rebounds with the best from the other banks. Did I mention she was pretty? It was easy to fall in love with her. And I did."

He wasn't alone. Telegroup's chief operating officer, John P. Lass, a Harvard MBA who had worked for Boston Consulting Group, was similarly smitten, according to Gratzon. Suggesting her for a seat on the company's board of directors, Lass argued that "she's a woman and we're short on women in upper management. She's smart. She knows her stuff and she's well-connected."

But when Gratzon whispered the idea to Telegroup chief financial officer Douglas A. Neish, he got a tart comeuppance. The savvy Canadian with lots of experience in financial circles called the banker a "jackal," counseling Gratzon to envision her "with a patch over her eye, a peg leg, and a parrot on her shoulder." He added, "Fred, these people are not your friends. They're hyenas! The only reason they are being friendly to you is because you are fresh kill. Right now they are fighting over who gets to eat your heart and who gets to eat your head. These people will turn on you and sell you down the river in a wink if it is to their advantage."

Later, Gratzon recalls, the woman's bank became the first to turn against Telegroup, pushing it to sell off assets rather than fix its problems. But that was a ways off. Before that, Gratzon and Company doubled the stock price in less than a year. With his nearly 12 million shares, just over a third of the company, the former ice cream vendor and Salvation Army truck driver had a net worth on paper that, for a short time anyway, topped a quarter of a billion dollars.

Fleeting as the stock valued proved to be, Telegroup turned out to be bountiful for its leaders, including Gratzon. Along with his stock holdings, he took home $600,000 in 1996, plus a $250,000 bonus, and another $600,000 in 1997, according to government filings. Before then, it's not clear what his take-home pay totaled, since the company was privately held. But by his account, it was a rewarding place to work in many ways. As he told *Fortune* magazine in 1993, all but three of his sixty-four employees in those early days were meditators. "This is a very subtle place," Gratzon told the magazine. "There are never any tempers lost, never any anger expressed, and people never criticize each other. I think of TM as a great competitive advantage."[4]

Beneath the placid surface, however, Telegroup barreled toward disaster as the '90s ripened. Competing with such titans as AT&T and MCI, the company grew largely through a bevy of costly acquisitions that thrust it into scores of countries but also weighed it down with debt. It wasn't turning a profit much of the time, either. It reported net annual gains in just two years between 1992 and 1997. Even as revenues soared, the red ink mounted until Telegroup reported a net loss of $46.7 million on revenues of $293.7 million in the nine months ended September 1998. Finally, when the company couldn't turn to the capital markets to help it pay maturing debt, Telegroup plunged into bankruptcy in February 1999 and sold off its assets to another telecommunications outfit.

Gratzon, however, reemerged once again. Now he is enjoying a third career as an author, counseling readers about how to do well in business and, gratifying a personal passion, in sports. In the early 2000s, he marketed his self-published book *The Lazy Way to Success: How to Do Nothing and Accomplish Everything* (2003), in which he maintains that work should be fun. He playfully describes himself as "the most unemployable man on Earth," alluding to being fired as a social worker in New Jersey. "I am lazy and anti-authoritarian. I have a short attention span, a shorter memory, and no intellect. I am devoid of marketable skills and I despise routine," Gratzon writes. "I have never held a job for longer than two months and, in the entire history of the United States government, I am one of five people (at most) to have been fired from a civil service job. . . . Fortunately, these are ideal qualifications for an entrepreneur."

Gratzon teamed up with a friend and athletic coach Steven Yellin to put together a second book, *Instant Athlete Instant Zone*, which he began marketing in 2012 as an e-book. The book, recently renamed *The Mentally Quiet Athlete*, lays out an approach to sports that Gratzon says dramatically improved his tennis and golf games. He offers the book with a money-back guarantee.[5]

Reveling in his antiestablishment persona, Gratzon calls himself "an archetypal tofu-eating, touchy-feely, tree-hugging, organically-nourished, yoga-practicing, New Age, rock-o-phonic Child-of-the-Sixties, author, and entrepreneur." He adds that he remains both an enthusiastic practitioner of TM and "long-suffering, yet ever-hopeful Philadelphia sports fan."

Gratzon also remains a pillar of the TM Movement, serving as a trustee of MUM. He was a founding director of the Maharishi Global Development Fund, which he chaired from 1998 until 2002. The fund is anything but modest in its goals, which it described in one document as being "to inspire the creation of healthy housing, to establish Vedic centers throughout the world, to create world peace and to assist other non-profit organizations with common goals."

Gratzon is no longer involved with the fund, which lately has been taking a battering. The fund, a major repository for the movement's U.S. resources, reported that its net assets fell by more than half between the beginning of 2009 and the end of 2011, a reduction to $88.8 million from $180 million. While fund officials pointed to sliding real estate values for much of the decline, they are also supporting another movement entity based in Maharishi Vedic

City, the Global Country of World Peace. The GCWP houses and provides for a rotating group of about eleven hundred meditators from India—called pandits—who come to the city and "whose daily routine of meditation and Vedic Performances is designed to bring the indomitable influence of Natural Law by helping to create an integrated national consciousness in the United States," the fund's Form 990 financial report says. The fund gave the GCWP $32.3 million in 2011, while giving another $1.08 million to a Fairfield-based foundation that helps the pandits, the Brahmananda Saraswati Foundation.

For the Gratzons, commitment to the movement has been a family affair. Fred's son, Jake, graduated from the Maharishi School of the Age of Enlightenment and went on to study art and business at the University of Iowa. Gratzon's home near Fairfield, built in 1999, is one of the "premier examples of Maharishi Sthapatya Vedic Architecture in the world." The east-facing house includes a shrine-like covered area at the home's center. This Brahmasthan, which TM enthusiasts say supports and nourishes activities in the house, is not to be walked on. Gratzon covers the spot with a table. Sunlight bathes the area from east to west, south to north, and from a skylight above. At the peak of the house is a kalash, or cupola typical of many of the houses meditators have built, which is said to tighten the link between residents and heaven. The property boasts a swimming pool covered by what looks like an ample greenhouse.

"Our garden is a special Sthapatya Vedic design called *Rajadhani*. Rajadhani means *residence of the king*," Gratzon writes in a blog post about his home.

> It is seven concentric squares with each square a specific proportion. Interestingly, the proportions between the squares are also the exact proportions between the seven layers of the brain stem. The brain stem is the part of the brain responsible for consciousness and is considered the "silent ruler" over all the activities of the mind and physiology. The Rajadhani garden has a brahmasthan just like the house. Maharishi Mahesh Yogi has suggested that a Rajadhani garden would be extremely powerful in promoting enlightenment.[6]

Gratzon surrounded the house with a modest fence, also in accordance with the TM architectural principles. This creates a space called a Vastu, which he says defines an individual's relationship to the cosmos.

Certainly, some whom Gratzon have feted in the mansion have had cosmic ambitions. In 2004, for instance, he played host to Dennis J. Kucinich, the former Cleveland mayor and Ohio congressman who made a quixotic run at the Democratic nomination for president. The politician, whose plans to establish a Department of Peace suited the Fairfield ethos, was saluted by former Natural Law Party presidential candidate Hagelin as "a great leader of the country" and a "candidate for all of those who are awake," according to a report in the *Washington Times*.[7]

Getting involved in the movement has helped several entrepreneurs in creative and diverse businesses. One such businessperson is Jim Belilove, whose Creative Edge Master Shop designed and made stunning floors, light installations, and other architectural finishes for such clients as O'Hare International Airport, Monsanto headquarters, World of Coca Cola in Las Vegas, the Astronaut Memorial at the John F. Kennedy Space Center, and Las Vegas casinos. Belilove got involved with the TM Movement starting at age nineteen in 1969. After graduating from the University of California at Santa Barbara, he was part of a group—an "inner circle," he says—that found bankrupt Parsons College in the early 1970s and helped turn it into MUM. He played key roles in the school's public relations office in his early twenties, an experience that helped him get into Harvard Business School, where he earned his MBA in 1977.

Belilove's career took various turns. He stayed in Massachusetts for about ten years, meditating and running a high-tech machine tool operation. In the 1980s he got involved, with some fellow meditators, in a Fairfield start-up called Global Holonetics Corporation, which produced high-speed machine vision inspection systems and was acquired by the DuPont Company. He and a partner, also a meditator, were intrigued in the mid-1980s with the waterjet-cutting technology at a struggling machinery company called Creative Glassworks, so they bought the outfit and turned it into a global business, helping build a staff of artisans. In 2001, Belilove moved into real estate development, helping to build a SunnyBrook Assisted Living facility in Fairfield and laying the ground for several similar facilities in Iowa. Says Belilove, "I'm a hard-core entrepreneur. I keep at it."

Belilove says he continues to practice TM daily. He says he values the ease of the meditation technique, finding it "profoundly restful." In an email, he says that "full integration of the transcendental qualities in this manner is the very definition of Enlightenment, Emancipation, Salvation, sought and treasured by every culture and religious tradition."

Showing a maverick streak, he admits in an interview to reservations about some movement teachings. Further, he says he avoids hiring meditators for factory work in his shop. But, he says, "as for meditators as employees, while we don't make very good factory workers, it would be difficult to find a group that is more dedicated to the pursuit of creativity and visions of interesting ideas."

Backers of the TM Movement insist that the ability of the meditators to focus their minds lets them unleash the creativity that leads to fresh ideas and success. Ken Ross, a serial entrepreneur who was involved with several high-tech start-ups and was active in the Fairfield Entrepreneurs Association, maintains that meditation helps combat stress and "settle the mind." Businesspeople who meditate, he says, can better filter out the "noise" and focus on important questions. "When your mind is more settled, it helps you see the big picture without losing your ability to focus on the details, and this leads to better decision-making," Ross says.

Ross runs Global ID Group, which tests crops and food for the presence of genetically modified organisms and certifies products as free of such organisms. The company also certifies products for meeting social goals. In 2011, the company certified more than three million metric tons of Brazilian soy, for instance, as being produced without child labor or forced labor, using sustainable agricultural practices and protecting the environment in endangered areas such as the Amazon. Global ID operates through offices in the United States, the United Kingdom, Germany, and Brazil.

Of course, Ross—like others—brought a lot of savvy to the table to begin with. Before joining Global ID, he started several companies in the software and consumer services business and worked in information technology jobs at such companies as Irving Trust and Salomon Brothers. With a bachelor's degree from the University of Wisconsin and an MBA in finance and information technology from New York University, he has served on the boards of a string of Fairfield start-ups. Hoping to influence the next generation of meditating businesspeople, he also teaches as an adjunct in the graduate business department at MUM.

Along with the honest business folks, Fairfield's meditating community has also spawned the occasional scoundrel—businesspeople who made money trading on public gullibility. Some attracted national attention. Edward J. Beckley, for instance, became a household name in the 1980s for infomercials hawking a get-rich-quick real estate scheme that earned him mocking mentions by David Letterman, Johnny Carson, and *Saturday Night Live*. He ran afoul first of Iowa state authorities after he failed to make good on promises to pay unconditional refunds to buyers of his home study real estate course, according to then–attorney general Thomas J. Miller. Nearly ten thousand people eventually sought $2.8 million, and the state won a judgment against him, requiring restitution. Beckley took his company into bankruptcy when it was overwhelmed by its debts.

Less than a decade later, Beckley crossed the Feds. He had built another business, Home Business Technologies Inc., which sold do-it-yourself home businesses and, according to the U.S. attorney's office in Des Moines, scammed customers for from $200,000 to $500,000, as reported by the *Des Moines Register*. The business, based in Fairfield, was shut down in December 1996 after state and federal agents raided it. A grand jury indictment later accused Beckley and a partner, Steven Winn, of producing rigged infomercials featuring testimonials from people paid for their endorsements. Seminars held by Beckley's company were bait-and-switch schemes designed to generate more purchases by attendees, the grand jury said. Beckley pleaded guilty to a count of wire fraud and was sentenced to fifteen months in jail. His partner, Winn, pleaded guilty to a count of bankruptcy fraud and got probation after providing "substantial assistance" in the investigation.[8]

Beckley, the author of a handful of books, wrote about his experiences in

Dance of a Rich Yogi: Liberation through Loss (2002). In it, he calls his time in prison "just another stepping stone on a path of spiritual growth."[9]

Some Fairfield entrepreneurs have crossed the line between faith in unusual views and legitimate business. Cliff Rose and David E. Sykes, two other Fairfielders, ran afoul of the Iowa attorney general in 2005 with an outfit that the attorney general in legal papers said sold "the dream of casting off one's glasses—quickly, easily, and without having to undergo worrisome surgery." Between 2000 and 2005, their Vision Improvement Technologies Inc. sold the "See Clearly Method," an assortment of eye exercises based on discredited vision theories, the state's complaint said. For $360 to $380, the visually challenged bought kits with instruction manuals, audiotapes, videotapes, and in some versions of the kit, a nutritional supplement. The state noted that the theories on which the scheme was based suggested that poor vision was a result of "wrong" thoughts. Buyers were urged to "imagine your eyes becoming stronger and healthier." The Iowa District Court for Polk County shut the outfit down in 2006, and the company was ordered to pay $200,000 in consumer restitution and $20,000 to the state's consumer fraud enforcement fund.[10]

Six years earlier, Fairfielder Jerome (Jeru) Harold Hall helped pull off an investment scam that relied on both gullibility and greed. The scheme involved selling certificates of deposit promising interest rates of up to 200 percent a year and used a bank in Grenada in the West Indies called the Sattva Investment Bank (a peculiar name, since Sattva in Vedic philosophy refers to purity and Sattvika individuals work for the good of the world). The scam garnered some $5 million and targeted meditators and others during 1999 and 2000, court records show. Hall and a colleague, Taansen Fairmont Sumeru (also known as David Freeston) of Santa Barbara, California, were convicted of fraud in 2006, but that conviction was overturned on appeal. They were then convicted a second time, in 2008. Friends of Hall in Fairfield's TM community organized a letter-writing campaign through the FairfieldLife group on Yahoo! in a bid to win leniency from a judge and then pressed for gifts to be sent to him in prison. While some Fairfielders argued for sympathy for Hall's defrauded victims instead, others pleaded for support for the convict. One forgiving soul, in 2009, wrote: "People can change—one of the most famous saints in India is Valmiki, who used to be a bandit."

Skeptics, including former Maharishi devotees, say Fairfield is a place where gullibility is not hard to find.

Some of Fairfield's more successful business leaders—those who didn't cross swords with the law—were less forgiving of shortcomings they saw in the movement. Some broke angrily with their guru and their friends after meditating for decades and giving millions of dollars to the movement. They were among the passionate opponents that the TM Movement had bred over the years, along with its supporters.

10

The Disaffected

JUST AS UTOPIAN MOVEMENTS spawn passionate support among their followers, so do they often generate equally fervid opposition from those who grow disenchanted. Some spend years criticizing the movements they had previously treated as their spiritual homes. Others break off to set up competing movements—ignoring their former leaders or, in some cases, paying homage to them even while offering rival products or services, as happened with such prominent meditators as Deepak Chopra. Still others provoke leaders so much that they get kicked out. For various reasons, many devotees have broken with the TM Movement over the past half century.

For instance, David and Earl Kaplan, longtime loyalists and major donors to the TM Movement, split bitterly with it in the late 1990s and early 2000s. Earl, a meditator for thirty-two years at the time, accused his former guru in a widely circulated open letter in April 2004 of ruling "through lies, fear and deceit." David, in a similar note a month later, said, "I and my family have cut all ties with TM, [Maharishi's] movement and his knowledge."

The Kaplans' turn away from the movement was a major blow financially and emotionally, leading to litigation and tumult involving a real estate development project in North Carolina. Earl Kaplan had cut a big figure in Fairfield as the founder, in 1991, of Books Are Fun, a discount books marketing organization that grew to some $220 million in annual sales by 1999, when he sold it to the Reader's Digest Association for $380 million. Kaplan was the principal owner of the company, along with an investment firm controlled by Chicago real estate magnate Sam Zell.

Books Are Fun worked with several Fairfield-area authors to popularize the Chicken Soup for the Soul series of inspirational books, which proved to be a runaway success in the 1990s. About a dozen authors of books in the group live, or at one time lived, in the Fairfield area, as did a designer of book covers used in the series.[1] The Kaplans' company made a national name for itself and the men, who are twins, seemed close to Maharishi.

By turns anguished and angry, Earl Kaplan in his 2004 letter about the TM Movement spelled out charges that stung movement insiders and emboldened critics. He said Maharishi had promised early devotees enlightenment in as few as five years. For thirty years, Kaplan wrote, he "listened and responded and devotedly donated more money to Maharishi's project than anyone ever had." Kaplan's goal, he said, was "to help create a peaceful world" and gain personal enlightenment. In the end, he said, he felt misled.[2]

He accused his former guru of pulling off "the biggest spiritual scam in modern history." Kaplan claimed the Maharishi had accumulated hundreds of millions of dollars, if not billions, in assets for his family in India. And he said followers "are totally brainwashed."

Such charges may have carried a special sting because Kaplan was close enough to the guru to have "an open invitation to come to Vlodrop [Holland, where Maharishi lived in his final years] and sit with the Mahesh when I wanted to." In about 2001, he did so, as the guru talked of using tens of millions of dollars for "building big buildings, buying airlines, etc. etc." When Kaplan suggested that the guru use the money to build a force of ten thousand meditators in India to lead the way to world peace—in much the same way TM Movement honcho John Hagelin later advocated for "invincible defense technology" meditation sessions—the guru was incredulous. "Mahesh looked at me like I was crazy and said 'Earl, if we created the group then we don't know if it would create world peace or not. We would have to have the group and then see what effect it has.'"

Kaplan was shocked by his longtime leader's response, since the guru for years had been raising hundreds of millions of dollars for just such a purpose. But Kaplan also was troubled by the guru's cryptic responses in general, which alluded to movement approaches to practices but didn't offer clear answers.

"When I would ask him spiritual questions he never had answers more than what he offered in the seven steps," Kaplan wrote. "Or he might launch into one of his hour long circular discussions of the Ved and creation or the Ved and human physiology. I finally started to realize, Mahesh doesn't really understand the spiritual process and if I wanted to get enlightened I better take responsibility for the process and seek out people who had been successful in getting others enlightened and who really knew what was going on."

In his anger, Kaplan made claims he himself acknowledges sounded "pretty wild." He wrote that "it is believed" Maharishi had his guru, Guru Dev, poisoned so he could steal a powerful spiritual artifact that gave him control over "certain astral beings." Then, Maharishi created the TM technique that would lead followers to "blank their minds" and be vulnerable to brainwashing by these astral beings.

He also took shots at practitioners. "Why do so many meditators have such a dazed and confused look about them? Why do meditators find it so hard to focus? Why do most people who have been in the movement for thirty years admit that their best experiences in TM were in the seventies and since then meditations have been going downhill?" he asked. "Your physiology is getting weaker. It is because the process of TM is sucking your very life energy out of you."

Followers had "amazing visual experiences and bliss experiences" around the charismatic guru, Kaplan argued. "But I have now come to see they are illusory. They are an occult trick Mahesh uses to brainwash his disciples."

All the then-living guru was really after, Kaplan contended, was power, money, and women. "Why does he live in a big house, own helicopters, airplanes, etc.? Why does he spend most of his time involved in business planning about making money? It is because he is a businessman who has the desires that other wealthy businessmen have. His spiritual front is his scam and the way he gets people to give him their time and money."

Kaplan claimed that the guru, a supposed celibate who honored followers who adopted celibacy, in fact had sex with "a series of girlfriends" in the sixties and early seventies. Since Kaplan wrote this in 2004, the claim has been repeated by others, including author Judith Bourque, who wrote and, in 2010, published a book about her love affair with the guru.[3] The guru also pursued Mia Farrow, Kaplan said, leading some of the Beatles to turn away from Maharishi after initially being smitten by him. (After visiting the guru, John Lennon wrote "Sexy Sadie," with the line, "Sexy Sadie what have you done / you made a fool of everyone." Today, the two surviving Beatles, Paul McCartney and Ringo Starr, continue to support TM, however. They appeared at functions supporting efforts by the David Lynch Foundation to bring meditation to schools and to troubled groups.)

Kaplan also warned about delusions among followers. "The amazing things I have learned over the past three years have helped liberate me from a cult mentality that runs rampant in the TM movement. If you are reading this thinking, 'poor Earl, he is such a deluded soul,' then I feel sorry for you because you are indeed caught in the matrix of delusion that old Mahesh has so successfully spun over the last 30 years."

Kaplan's brother, David, took a more matter-of-fact tone in his May 2004 note. He said he was "kicked out" of the movement in 1999, despite meditating many hours a day for twenty-five years, donating tens of millions of dollars, and working with Maharishi for nearly a decade.[4]

David Kaplan said he took ill in early 1999 and almost died. He gave up celibacy—part of a practice called Purusha for men and Mother Divine for women—and decided in mid-1999 to marry. "For that I was kicked out of the movement," he wrote.

> Thank God I was, for it prompted Earl and me to investigate Maharishi Mahesh Yogi and the TM organization. We have spent a great deal of time, energy and money researching Maharishi and the TM organizations. Due to our findings I can no longer support or be associated with Maharishi Mahesh Yogi, his ideas, his knowledge, or any of his organizations, in any way whatsoever.

The Kaplans' disillusionment reverberated far beyond Fairfield. They had invested in a seven-thousand-acre land development project, the Heavenly Mountain resort, in North Carolina. The development, established in 1996, was intended to create a Shangri-la or Garden of Eden for TM followers. It was to feature single-family homes, condos, and other structures built in accord with TM architectural principles, with dormitories to separately house celibate men and women. Some structures were built and occupied by meditators.[5]

After David Kaplan decided to take the development in a different direction following his rejection of TM, meditators who had bought into the community sued. Nonetheless, the celibate meditators on site were evicted, according to local press reports, moving to Fairfield, among other spots. Some meditators remained. The Kaplans sold off much of the land but planned to develop some of it using green building techniques to create a Center for Sustainability called Heaven's Nest.[6]

The Kaplans, who struck idealistic if bitter chords in writing about TM-related matters, proved to be savvy and tough-minded businessmen. Despite the gains from selling his company, Earl Kaplan missed the business so much that he moved back into it. He helped develop Reader's Choice, a similar company led by a stepson, and in late 2004 teamed up with family members to launch another book marketer, Imagine Nation Books, after a noncompete agreement expired. The Reader's Digest Association, which struggled to make Books Are Fun work as well as Kaplan had, ended up suing Reader's Choice, alleging trade secrets theft, and sought to rope in Kaplan. But four years later, after Reader's Digest took a hefty writedown on the purchase of Books Are Fun, Kaplan regained his brainchild. Imagine Nation agreed to buy Books Are Fun back for $17.5 million, and Kaplan began running it with family members, far from Fairfield, in Louisville, Colorado.

From his home in Colorado, Earl Kaplan appeared in a 2010 documentary, *David Wants to Fly*, in which a filmmaker charts his own disillusionment with TM. In this film, Kaplan was among several disgruntled former adherents who complained of squandered money, deception, and hypocrisy in the highest ranks of the movement, particularly involving Maharishi himself.

Documentarian David Sieveking, in the film, traces his personal journey from seeker of spiritual truth who wanted to make movies like his idol, David Lynch, to someone distressed by the intolerance of dissent within the movement and its apparent unwillingness to brook criticism from the outside. Sieveking, as a meditator who had been initiated into the TM practice, had exceptional access to the movement and, for a while at least, to Lynch.

The young moviemaker chatted with the Hollywood director and with '60s singer Donovan, for instance, on a visit to Fairfield, a town Sieveking referred to as "the middle of nowhere."

The documentarian traveled far for his film. He captured footage of Maharishi's funeral in India and a high-level meeting sometime afterward in Europe, at which a split in the TM leadership seemed to be developing. A critic's microphone was turned off as he spoke at the session, however, and Sieveking was told to stop filming the disagreement. By his account, the young filmmaker's access was largely shut down when movement officials learned that critics of TM would get airtime in the film.

The critics included former Maharishi adherents, like Kaplan, who complains that they gave fortunes to the movement only to see the money squandered. A former loyalist complains that the guru discarded people once they had no more money to give. Others in the film, including writer Bourque, who chronicled her intimate encounters with the guru in her book, claim Maharishi was no celibate, despite his claims to being so. Undercutting Maharishi's standing to build a worldwide movement, Sieveking also showcases an Indian disciple of Maharishi's teacher who suggests that Maharishi, as little more than a secretary to Guru Dev, his teacher, had no right to teach. The filmmaker also features a Western researcher who criticized efforts to recruit young followers, an implicit shot at the drive by Lynch to bring meditation into schools.[7]

For disaffected former adherents, the status of outsider can be tough to handle. Kai Druhl, for instance, made a lot of friends in Fairfield over the fourteen years he taught at MUM. Now, some won't talk to him when he sees them in the street or in restaurants in town. "Some people are open and friendly and some are hard-liners and hate me, but I don't really care about the latter," Druhl, a courtly man whose formal touch and accent betray his roots in Germany, tells me. "I became a Christian and have a good strong community of Christians with whom I share my life. That's more important to me."

Druhl, age sixty-nine in mid-2012, abandoned TM. He sees the TM Movement as espousing a form of Hinduism and says it is incompatible with other faiths, especially the fundamentalist Christianity that he embraced in 2002. More than twenty years earlier, Druhl had adopted TM at a time of personal crisis—the end of a marriage—and he warmed to the way it helped him relax and feel more confident when he needed a boost. Druhl, who earned his PhD in physics at the University of Hamburg and taught for about six years at the University of New Mexico, grew so committed to the practice that he joined the faculty at what was then called Maharishi International University in 1986. He ended up teaching TM and physics, including teaching grad students about the connections between physics and the philosophy of the Maharishi, the Science of Creative Intelligence.

Druhl's initial commitment to the practice was intellectual, emotional, and spiritual. In 1980, a friend seemed to be thriving on TM-style meditation, as Druhl said in a blogpost for the TrueLight.Net website. So Druhl, who felt he needed something to build his inner strength, took up the practice. "I did experience some reduction in tension, and some increase in self-reliance," he says. Over time, he studied the Eastern philosophy that underlay the practice and learned the advanced technique in the TM-Sidhi program, which involves long hours of meditation. He felt he was coming to possess "supreme knowledge," even if not the supernatural powers—such as flying—that the advanced technique promised.[8]

But he grew disenchanted with the university. He felt that intellectual inquiry was not tolerated and interpretation of the spiritual teachings was limited to just a few select professors. Teachers who deviated from "established dogma," he says, were fired. For some, their once high-flying enthusiasm for the TM practices waned as they felt reined in. He says, "You can fully subscribe to the ideology and justify it to maintain the purity of the teaching, or you get disillusioned and disappointed."

He also was troubled by the bad reactions he was having to meditation. He first saw the problems as far back as 1990, when he met Maharishi. "Immediately after the meeting, I noticed signs of demonic oppression. I was no longer able to control my facial expressions during meditation, and my lips would suddenly retreat to expose my clenched teeth," he writes in the TrueLight.Net blog post. "This loss of control eventually even spread into quiet times, outside of meditation."

At first, Druhl chalked up his bad reactions to the release of deep-set stress—the "unstressing" phenomenon that meditators blame for the adverse effects some people have to meditation. TM teachers tell novice meditators that such problems are healthy signs, no matter how uncomfortable. "The official doctrine is there are no negative side-effects to Transcendental Meditation," the former TM teacher says. "If you feel good during meditation, that's good. If you feel bad, it's also good. The release of stress is good."

While TM promises enlightenment, Druhl says he did not experience it. For him, there was "only a counterproductive sense of detachment from outside events." To deal with problems he faced, Druhl says he spent thousands of dollars on purification and herbal therapies—which the movement sells in its Ayurvedic medicines line—and on wearing custom precious stones. Even Vedic sacrifices were offered on his behalf in India. All of it brought "no lasting benefits whatsoever," he says. Instead, he suffered a physical breakdown in the early 1990s. "In the end, I ran out of money to try more programs, and had to leave, to put my life together."

Druhl continued teaching at MUM until the end of 1999. When he left, it was mainly for financial reasons, he says. While living on campus, he was paid just $300 a month to teach, plus room and board—usually, one or two rooms with a shared bathroom and meals in the dining halls. He married and moved off campus and got a bit more pay, but not enough, he says. Concerned about the modest pay scales on campus, officials have been planning to boost stipends, which in recent years began at $700 a month for instructors and $850 for professors, to $1,500 and $2,500 monthly, respectively.

When Druhl left the school, he traded options and commodities for a time but couldn't make a living at it. He ended up teaching physics and earth sciences at Indian Hills Community College in a town not far from Fairfield. Meanwhile, he turned to self-help books and got involved with a church, immersing himself in the Bible. With the help of a church leader and some of his colleagues, he "found deliverance from the demons" that he says were tormenting him. He came to believe that the teachings of Maharishi were deceptive, offering followers "Hinduism in disguise."

He said TM teachers, including himself, offered recruits a Vedic-based form of the religion that is "dressed up in scientific language to suit our western tastes." He accused TM teachers of making "step-wise disclosures," keeping the practice's Hindu nature hidden at first. "You're told it is just a neutral technique and no change in religion and no change in lifestyle is required," he says.

But he came to believe that the philosophy of the movement is incompatible with Christianity, Islam, and other religions. With Christianity, for instance, the core problem is not lack of knowledge, he said, but rebellion against God. Submission to Jesus Christ, he maintained, is the only successful way to deal with the core problem. "No amount of meditation can bring you closer to God," Druhl argues. "In Hinduism, it all depends on how much meditation and good works you do and you get reincarnated."

As a physicist, Druhl taught about invisible particles that form matter and energy. He maintains that there are similarly invisible powers—spirits, he calls them—that TM-style meditation can summon up. Meditators use mantras that he claims were names of Vedic gods—a claim meditators reject, citing Maharishi to say it is based on a misunderstanding of a Sanskrit term commonly used to refer to deities. "I'm very much aware that what we see around us is not all there is to life," Druhl says. "There are spiritual beings which can exercise power and we have the option to give room to them or not. If you meditate using these mantras, you are giving access to your mind to the spirits."

Taking a far different view than he had as a TM teacher, he says meditation is a powerful but not "an innocent technique." He urges people to avoid it. "We have minds so we can think thoughts," Druhl says. "If you let your mind just dangle, there are spiritual beings who can get influence."

Druhl argues there is nothing wrong with listening to soothing music or a voice offering soothing messages to relax. But certain sounds—mantras—may have meanings not even apparent to the meditator and may be potentially harmful, he says. TM teachers, he states, are taught some of the background to mantras, although he adds that even they are kept partly in the dark until they advance through years of Vedic training.

"Deceptions" such as the idea that TM's approach is not religious and that mantras are unrelated to ancient gods, Druhl contends, will ultimately sink the TM Movement. Further, he argues that this movement was the province largely of Baby Boomers and he doesn't see an influx of young followers in anywhere near the same numbers as was the case when he got involved. Even students coming to the university are not drawn by meditation, but rather by such trendy subjects as sustainable living. Foreigners are often wooed to MUM by the prospect of a U.S. education and the chance to settle in the United States, he adds, and sometimes become "upset and shocked" at the meditation-dominated approach at MUM.

Looking forward, Druhl contends that the movement and the university could survive for a decade at the outside, noting that the university now depends heavily on a few generous donors since student payments don't cover the costs. Indeed, the university is aiming to build its endowment dramatically by tapping rich meditators for donations. "I see growing numbers of people disenchanted who still hang onto it because there isn't much alternative," Druhl says. "They've invested a lot and there's a reluctance to really let go. But when a dam breaks, a little trickle suddenly becomes a landslide and it collapses quickly."

Other former meditators have set up websites devoted to criticizing the movement. Mike Doughney, for instance, is among a handful of onetime enthusiasts who chipped in regularly to "TM-Free Blog: Skeptical Views of Transcendental Meditation and Maharishi Mahesh Yogi." Doughney was first intrigued by TM when he attended a lecture about it in high school in Dundalk, Maryland, in 1974. He later began meditating at the University of Maryland in 1977 at the behest of a girlfriend with a few years of experience in the program, and he stuck with it for about a decade. Doughney worked as a volunteer in a TM center in Washington, D.C., helping with publicity. He visited Fairfield and considered moving there to take up advanced meditation studies. But he scrapped the idea of moving, instead launching a career in broadcast engineering that took him to Saudi Arabia, among other spots. Later, in the early 1990s, he set up an early Internet provider, Digex.

Doughney charted the history of the movement in "Thirty Years Later— What Was That All About?," a thirteen-part series he wrote for his blog in 2008 and 2009.[9] Ultimately, he suggested, there is no "there" there in TM, that it is filled with "meaningless sounds, alien rituals in foreign languages, and repetition of elements of the sales pitch for the practice." While it has roots in its dead founder's Hindu background and Indian culture—roots that in recent years have become more apparent—Doughney suggested it is something of a philosophical bastard crafted to appeal to Westerners dissatisfied with their own materialistic culture. While it once sought to develop a broad base of followers through its college and high school recruitment efforts, more recently it pitched itself especially toward wealthy and successful people who see TM as a way to control uncontrollable aspects of their lives and whom the movement sees as donors. Consider Doughney's main points. "It's often been said, often by those who are talking about Transcendental Meditation in a critical light, that TM is some form of Hinduism," Doughney writes in his series.

> But I take a somewhat different view; to me, TM is as American as apple pie, or at least, it is a Western product, reflecting aspects of Western culture. It is as Hindu as Chow Mein is Chinese: the result is something that came from the interaction of two different cultures. From the standpoint of the original cultural context, it becomes something tolerated and even embraced when dealing with tourists, particularly when the tourists are bearing dollars.

Doughney calls the TM program a fusion of Maharishi's first interactions with American suburbia, in Los Angeles in 1959, and his Indian background. He speculates that the guru may have wanted to set up an organization that "would, first and foremost, keep him and his family comfortable for decades if not lifetimes." He suggests Maharishi may have been impressed with the financial success he saw all around him in the United States, a success built partly on clever packaging and marketing. The yogi, who appeared "carrying the most meager of possessions in a bedroll [and] came face-to-face with the material wealth of the middle class," soon developed a way to sell his ideas to Americans. Says Doughney, "From that fusion of cultures came this product, and from that, came the marketing (if the product wasn't itself the marketing), the celebrity endorsements, and the global organization."

The TM regimen was about, among other things, giving practitioners a sense of power over their lives, the blogger suggests. These range from managing personal stress to global effects. "The marketing of the TM program promises yet another level of control over many of those things that aren't particularly controllable," Doughney writes. "The promises stretch from the everyday scale to the global scale: from reducing one's stress level and raising one's happiness to bringing about world peace. It is the consumer product to end all consumer products, giving the buyer (the illusion of) complete control of the uncontrollable."

Even though the movement appealed to Baby Boomers who seemed to be rebelling against the establishment of their day in the 1960s and 1970s, the critic suggests it was tailored more to mid-twentieth-century American life and values. Thus, it wasn't accidental that the students who marched out of buses into Fairfield and onto their new campus at the Maharishi University in 1974 looked as clean-cut as the Iowans who greeted them. "Far from being an example of the counterculture of the late 60's, at its core it was completely tailored to the needy, somewhat conservative suburban American of the early 1960's, so much so that the movement required that former 'hippies' cut their hair, shave and wear a tie before they were allowed to learn how to be TM instructors," Doughney writes.

Still, the movement's appeal rested on the idea that American material wealth falls short of remedying widespread poverty, unhappiness, stress, and other woes. "These are things that often lie in areas where some feel the West has reached a dead end," Doughney suggests. So the "decontextualized pieces of Indian culture presented in the TM movement's programs came into play. The entire movement took on an appearance that was just alien enough to clearly support the assumption that it wasn't from here."

The Ayurvedic medicines available in stores in Fairfield and online, as well as the Maharishi-inspired architecture around town, helped to foster a promising sense of difference that Doughney says the movement markets. "Over the years the TM movement has evolved, and the Indian cultural aspects of the movement have moved from the background to front-and-center," he writes.

A standard photo of the movement's founder is now likewise always present on websites and materials. The movement's products have also evolved from simple meditation to astrology, herbs and architecture, clearly identifying them as being of Indian origin. References to the Vedas, a text generally considered to be of Hindu religious or spiritual origin, are recast as "scientific" in a further decontextualization of their original meaning to be successfully sold to a credulous audience.

"All of these contemporary aspects of the TM movement reflect an underlying strategy: to frame itself as an external source that supposedly addresses the alleged shortcomings of Western life," Doughney argues. "It is designed to exude a level of strangeness that enhances its attractiveness, but not so much strangeness as to be completely irrelevant or repulsive."

But he suggests that the movement is on the wane, relying mostly on a few wealthy donors and on nostalgia for its glory days of the 1970s. Doughney writes, "The fact of the matter is that what the TM organization is doing is collecting a vanishingly small number of people who are willing to spend money and time on what they sell, and who in some cases, participate in the selling. This is an organization that, collectively or through individual people, exerts no actual influence over 'world peace' and very little power over anything else."

Certainly, TM in recent years has lacked the appeal for children of the Baby Boom generation that it had for some of their parents—but even then, its reach was surprisingly modest. According to Stark and Bainbridge's book *The Future of Religion*, the movement taught fewer than 300,000 Americans to meditate during its peak year, 1975. In all, it taught 919,300 Americans TM between the mid-1960s and 1977.[10] But using an advertising tool on Facebook, Doughney in early 2012 calculated that the number of Americans interested in TM had shriveled to about 60,000, even as meditation of various types had gone mainstream in gyms and in smoking-cessation, stress-reduction, and various self-help programs. Doughney based his count on how many Facebook users expressed an interest in TM or related topics, and he then extrapolated that sample to the entire U.S. population.

Accurate numbers are difficult to come by. The David Lynch Foundation pegs the total of people worldwide who have learned TM over the past fifty years at more than 6 million. Bob Roth, the longtime movement spokesman, put the number of Americans who have learned TM at 1.5 million. If the Stark and Bainbridge figure of 919,300 by 1977 is accurate, Roth's tally suggests that the average number of Americans learning the technique dropped to about 16,600 per year between 1977 and 2012, a far cry from the movement's heyday. (Roth questions the authenticity of the Stark and Bainbridge figure. He says 50,000 people each month were learning TM in 1975, which would top the Stark and Bainbridge tally for that year of 292,517. Roth acknowledges that the numbers of new learners declined after that but, without disclosing annual counts, says they have been on an uptick in recent years.) Even as TM waned, however, other meditative techniques apparently took root: the National Center for Complementary and Alternative Medicine at the National Institutes of Health reported that a 2007 survey found that 9.4 percent of a representative sample of Americans had used meditation in the prior twelve months, suggesting that some 20 million Americans meditated. This was up from more than 15 million, or 7.6 percent, in a survey five years before.[11]

Doughney, the critic, has helped sustain the TM-Free blog, which continues to draw posts by Fairfielders and others disenchanted with the TM Movement. Doughney said he helped maintain it for the benefit of people, such as friends or relatives, curious about the movement and its practices, as well as for those exposed to it in school through such promoters as David Lynch's foundation. "Having a body of information, both based on the long-term experiences of those who've been involved, and what the movement actually says about itself (but not necessarily directly to prospective meditators) is of real value," he says. "The blog continues to get hits from all over the globe."

The blog was started by another defector, John M. Knapp, who for a time counseled people leaving cults from a center in Malone, New York. Criticizing TM-style meditation for physical effects that ranged from fatigue, insomnia, and chronic headaches to emotional and mental challenges such as anxiety and difficulty with memory, Knapp argues that "if Transcendental Meditation were a drug, it would long ago [have] been taken off the market."

Knapp gets personal, describing his experience with TM. In one 2008 blog post, he complains of feeling "spaced out" at times in the past, saying there were occasions when he didn't recall car trips at the end of them. "I developed difficulty with speech," he says, after having learned advanced teacher-training techniques involving prolonged meditation. "I would frequently forget what I was saying in the middle of a sentence." The symptoms, he says, largely disappeared within a few years after he quit TM.

Other critics have had different reasons for feeling estranged from the movement. Even some graduates of the Maharishi School of the Age of Enlightenment in Fairfield now look back on their days there with mixed feelings. Children from wealthy families were sometimes coddled. Drug use—marijuana, cocaine, alcohol—was not unheard of. Neither was sex, sometimes between high school girls and older men in the movement.

"There were a lot of people in the movement, a lot of adults, who really avoided adult responsibility," says Erin McCann, who graduated from MSAE's high school in 1992. "Part of the core of the movement were people who joined in the 1960s and 1970s and had been hippies. They just had a different attitude toward youth and never really grew up themselves. Everything was sort of summer of love, and the line between adult and youth was blurred."

It wasn't quite so pleasant, however, for some of the middle-aged women. McCann recalled attending a meditation session in the women's golden dome on the MUM campus and seeing a woman weeping nearby as a friend consoled her. Her husband was leaving her for a nineteen-year-old. "There were a lot of divorces," McCann says.

McCann, who comes from Grand Rapids, Michigan, ended up in Fairfield after her mother took up TM. While McCann was in eighth grade, she and her mother spent a long weekend in Fairfield. Entranced by the boarding-school feel of MSAE—the uniforms that the girls wore and the grown-up way adults treated her—McCann and her mom, then a single parent, decided to move to Fairfield. McCann attended MSAE, and her mom worked as a secretary there. They lived in dormitories on the Maharishi University campus. They had little money, with McCann's mother earning just a few hundred dollars a month plus room and board and the chance to take advanced meditation courses. They took their meals at the university.

From the start, McCann saw a split along economic lines at the high school. Girls whose families were wealthy, she felt, sometimes got favored treatment, including the occasional adjusted grade. "During my first year, I felt like an outsider the whole time," she remembers. "There were the sort of wealthier very cool, very pretty girls. They were very tight-knit, having grown up in the movement together. Coming from the Midwest, I was more like a townie."

Eventually, however, she found her group of friends. She took to hanging out with them in town, sometimes partying with Fairfield public school boys. Drinking on the weekends was not uncommon. "The town girls hated us," McCann recalls. "We were a little more different, and a little more loose."

The movement discourages drinking, and the school has no use for it among underage students, of course. But plenty of students rebelled in the time McCann was at MSAE. Along with drinking, there was occasional use of cocaine, marijuana, and psychedelic mushrooms. A martial-arts school in town, she recalls, became a big hangout, in part because students could find booze and drugs there.

Of course, the abstemious official TM doctrine conflicted with what the students were doing outside of class. Many of them treated the guru's philosophy skeptically and, at least privately, are dismissive of it now, according to McCann.

Studies in the Science of Creative Intelligence, the movement's doctrine, were at best simplistic, says McCann, who in 2012 was working as a human resources executive in Houston. "I personally thought it was bullshit, and all the kids in school treated it that way," recalls McCann. "It was a joke. We knew how to say what we needed to say to get a grade. It doesn't mean we believed it."

McCann, raised with no religion in an extended family of Dutch Christian Reformed Church members, abandoned TM and affiliated with the Church of Jesus Christ of Latter-day Saints, the Mormon church, as an adult. Now, she regards TM as a religion—at least for those who do more than meditate casually. Certainly, she said, it seemed religious to MSAE students who learned Sanskrit, studied religious texts of the ancient Vedic masters, and hewed to notions such as the idea that wearing sapphire stones would improve their lives. "Maharishi lied to people when he said it is not a religion," says McCann. "It was bald-faced lying."

McCann attended Maharishi University for a year but left for financial reasons. She worked in media relations for the movement for a time and earned her undergraduate degree from the University of Iowa in 1999. While she fell away from regular meditation in the mid-1990s, McCann says she stays in touch, via Facebook, with some two hundred MSAE alums. Much like the students at other exclusive private schools, they share a bond that she says she hopes will endure, no matter what the future holds for MSAE. But she is certainly a skeptic, using an email address with the phrase "growingupunenlightened."

Still other adherents, including those in the top ranks, broke with the TM Movement to establish their own followings. Author, physician, and alternative medicine popularizer Deepak Chopra broke with TM and Maharishi, whom he regarded as his guru, after a decade of close involvement. By Chopra's account, published by *The Huffington Post* in early 2008, the men parted company after the guru grew jealous of the physician's growing prominence. Chopra had written scores of books—eventually more than sixty-five—and was a major proponent of Maharishi's Ayurvedic medical approaches. By Maharishi's lights, the disciple was perilously close to eclipsing his teacher.[12] His account reflects a complex and intimate relationship that showed all too clearly how human—and perhaps flawed—the guru was.

Chopra tells of how, in July 1991, he was in Fairfield to take part in a meditation course when the guru failed to make an expected conference call from India. Chopra then meditated and had a vision of his guru in a hospital bed, on a respirator, with intravenous tubes going into his body. He phoned his parents in New Delhi and heard Maharishi was ill and was being treated by Chopra's father, a cardiologist. Chopra headed to India on a plane chartered by a wealthy TM donor, finding the guru just as he had seen him in his vision. The guru had suffered pancreatic inflammation, kidney failure, and a heart attack. Poisoning was suspected.

Chopra and a leader of the movement made arrangements for Maharishi to be admitted to a private hospital in London. Chopra carried the frail guru through London traffic, getting him put on a respirator and hearing of a seemingly miraculous recovery after an attending physician felt Maharishi was clinically dead.

Later, when Maharishi needed a blood transfusion, Chopra proved to be a match. Chopra personally nursed Maharishi and learned advanced meditation techniques from him. Then, Maharishi moved to his home in Vlodrop, Holland, letting Chopra travel the world as one of his main emissaries.

"Ironically, the respect shown to me in his name came to be my undoing. Maharishi started to give me the perception (perhaps that was my own projection) that he felt I was competing with him in a spiritual popularity contest," he adds. "On more than one occasion, he casually mentioned that I was seeking adulation for myself."

The tension came to a head in July 1993, when Chopra and his wife, Rita, went to visit the guru. Maharishi said, "People are telling me that you are competing with me." Far from saintly, the guru seemed to Chopra to be "playing the part of an irascible, jealous old man whose pride had been hurt." The guru then told his student he wanted him to stop traveling, to live at an ashram with him, and to stop writing books, threatening Chopra's livelihood. Chopra in early 1994 bid farewell to his mentor and, despite a contrite phone call the guru soon made to him, decided it was time to leave. "I expressed my immeasurable gratitude to him and told him that I would love him forever," the physician writes. "When we parted, he said, 'Whatever you do will be the right decision for you. I will love you, but I will also be indifferent to you from now on.'"

The movement has also cast out people, including potential movement leaders, that it found objectionable. L. B. Trusty Shriver, a native Fairfielder who died at age sixty-six on May 27, 2013, was one such figure. He certainly had the résumé to be a leader. He claimed to be the first person who was taught TM in Iowa and the first to notify the movement that the Parsons College campus was available. He taught TM, worked on staff for the movement, and graduated from MIU in 1983 with a bachelor's degree in interdisciplinary studies, focusing on art, literature, and the Science of Creative Intelligence. As an undergraduate, he served as student body president from 1981 to 1982. He later earned a master's degree in professional writing at the school.

But by the time he began his graduate studies, Shriver had begun to have reservations about the way the movement was being run. There was, he recalled, a "drift toward dogmatism" at the university. He believed leaders were not attuned to how the movement, then in decline, was seen by the public. Later, between 1992 and 1994, he published a newspaper, *Survival in Paradise*, in which he and several others criticized policies with which they disagreed. Shriver argued against tendencies that he said were causing TM to "morph from a potentially world-impacting movement to an insignificant cult."

Shriver's criticism stung. He warned that TM's appeal would diminish by emphasizing advanced meditation techniques and auxiliary programs instead of the basic twenty-minutes, twice-a-day approach. For example, the TM-Sidhi program purportedly gave practitioners the ability to fly or pass through walls. "A lot of people were just embarrassed about the movement, while others were in denial about how lifeless it had become," he said. Meditators, he said, were also told that they needed to avail themselves of the movement's proprietary health practices and products, Vedic architecture, and Vedic astrology, which many of them could not afford.

"Basically, I just said that the policies and strategies were working against their stated aims," Shriver said. "They were becoming more cultish and they were alienating their own people, all of which appeared to be stunting the growth of the movement. It could be visibly seen to be in decline."

Shriver argued he was publishing dissenting views in the hope they would stimulate debate and discussion. "I had this idea of open discussion in an open society," he said. "I confess I was naive. I thought that if I just forced people to take a hard look at some things, they might reflect on them and maybe change a little bit. I was wrong about that."

In 1994, Shriver was told he was no longer welcome to participate in the movement. He was denied renewal of a badge that permitted him to meditate in the golden domes on campus. "If your badge is taken away, you become a nonperson. You're as good as excommunicated," he said. As a writer in his newspaper put it, "He was brought before the appropriate tribunal at MIU and told he must go—he must stop living and dining on campus, stop participating in group practice in the domes, and stop attending other official events there. Why? Because the ... [newspaper] you are reading was deemed to contain or promote thinking not appropriate for a teacher of TM."[13]

The writer, Thom Krystofiak, called Shriver "a believer in the profound value of TM in his own life and in the lives of most other people who have practiced it." But, Krystofiak wrote, "That was not enough. Other opinions he has expressed differ significantly from the official positions of the TM movement, so much so that it was felt that a dramatic public action must be taken to indicate that L.B. had 'chosen' to separate himself from the body of the movement.

"Many people were encouraged by the fact that L.B. had escaped reprisals for so long. He was, to many, visible evidence of a welcome maturity on the part of the movement, which seemed to have gained an ability to encompass diversity, and to have realized that there is nothing to fear in an individual's questions and opinions," Krystofiak observed. "But now, L.B. stands as a visible example of something different."

Years after his expulsion, Shriver—at the urging of friends who believed movement leaders would forgive and forget—appealed the banishment. He lost—twice. In fact, he was not allowed to set foot on the campus of the school he had graduated from, he says, and could have been arrested for doing so. The university had obtained a restraining order against him and others who he said were barred for "being flaky or irritating or unstable mentally."

His ostracism—something akin to the shunning that occurs in communities such as the Amish—had led to some "social and professional unpleasantness" with a number of former colleagues high up in the TM Movement. But it had an upside for him, too. "It forced me to be on my own and to take responsibility for feelings and behavior to an extent I would not have been able to if I had stayed in the movement," he said. "If I had remained in the fold, my primary loyalties would have been in the movement. My career opportunities would have been in the movement. My whole world would have been in the movement. That's what it is if you are in the fold."

Discussing his fate candidly in a Fairfield café and then in a crowded coffee shop frequented by meditators, Shriver reflected ambivalence about his ouster. Citing the views of some of those involved in the process, he suggested it could be seen as a curse—being cast out of the Garden of Eden—or a blessing—Jonah being expelled from the whale. "It's both," Shriver said.

Shriver worked in Fairfield as a freelance writer until the fall of 2009, when he took a job teaching English at a university in China. In 2012 he returned to Fairfield with a new perspective. He says he felt the movement had matured and was showing a more progressive attitude. "People tell me the same problems still exist here," he said. "I'm sure that's true, but I see real signs of change as well."

He pointed to suggestions he made in his time as a self-styled "radical publisher" that have been put into effect. The dress code for students at MUM has been relaxed, the price of initiation into TM has been trimmed, and meditators who wanted to devote themselves full time in the movement's world peace programs—meditating in the domes—can receive financial support if they need it. He argued that the movement's "persona" had become more attractive and suited to public expectations of a movement that claims to be on the cutting edge of creativity and innovation.

Many individuals previously banned by the movement, he says, have been allowed to return. Shortly after his return to Fairfield, movement insiders contacted Shriver to suggest he would get a favorable hearing in reapplying for a dome badge. He decided to go ahead. "I think when you get older, you begin to lose your taste for contention; harmony becomes more important," Shriver told me at the time. "Your values change. Maybe it's time to bury the hatchet."

His effort toward reconciliation didn't go far, however. Movement officials invited him in to discuss readmission, but Shriver did not repudiate his critical writings, including suggestions that the movement had grown cultish. The officials laid out a plan for him that included attending lectures and getting active in a local TM center—a set of "probationary" activities, he called them, noting that the movement officials wanted to reestablish trust before normalizing his status. He complied, but no one involved would give him an idea of when he would be welcomed back. He came to believe he had "been hosed" and that the movement's inability to act was "just another indication of the sclerosis in the leadership."

Then, in early 2013, Shriver got dreadful news. He had developed terminal liver cancer. Friends sought to have him readmitted to the dome as an act of mercy, but he squelched the effort, rejecting the idea that getting back into the facility was his dying wish. He said he had learned over the years that it's possible to meditate privately, enjoy life and friends, and not be dependent on a group. "Being involved in the movement was a great adventure for me," he said, reflecting on his good days with the TM effort. "It was a fantastic learning experience on many levels and I will always be grateful for it."

But Shriver, saying he felt his job was to be a communicator, writer, and journalist, refused to give up what he called his professional autonomy. Being involved in the movement again, he said, would require him to "serve as something more like a member of a priesthood whose main requirement was obedience." In the end, Shriver opted to follow his own path, saying he had no regrets.

While some loyalists parted company with the movement over the years, still others grew even more passionate about it. Some adherents decided to build their own city, just a few miles outside Fairfield, where they could welcome visitors to a spa and could go even further toward putting Maharishi's vision for an ideal community into practice. Maharishi Vedic City, however, has had its ups and downs.

Maharishi Vedic City

WHEN BOB PALM looked into setting up a hog-feeding operation on his family farm in 2007, he had no clue just how much of a stir he would create. He eventually had to do battle with leaders of the TM Movement, who had set up a most unusual city next door to him—one of the most unusual cities in America—just six years before. The peacefulness and harmony that the movement espouses faded fast in the nasty fight between Palm and officials of Maharishi Vedic City (MVC). The battle also highlights the tension that still lingers, forty years on, between locals—the townies of the Fairfield area—and the followers of the late guru, the "roos."

Palm's family had operated the farm since 1894, when his grandfather and uncle built a sturdy, two-bedroom house on the site where the farmer was born and still lives. He and two brothers call the place "Palms of Dellahome," naming it after the dairy herd that their parents bought in 1942 and long tended on the property. The farm includes 149 acres that border on MVC and another 80 acres on the other side of a nearby road. The dairy operation is gone, but the Palms now raise corn and soybeans there. "All three brothers in our family own it together," says Palm, who was age sixty-three in mid-2012. "That was my folks' wish and it's our wish to pass it on to our kids."

To find a way to bring his son into the farm business in a way that made financial sense, Palm explored the idea of putting in a hog-feeding operation. His plan called for a pair of buildings that would each house twenty-four hundred pigs at a time. The hogs would be fattened in the so-called concentrated animal feeding operation (CAFO) and then sent off to a slaughterhouse some fifty miles away. While lucrative for farmers, such hog-confinement operations have generated a stink in Iowa and beyond over issues ranging from the humane treatment of animals to odor and pollution. Palm insisted his facilities would have toed the mark on state regulations, including such features as underground concrete pits with ten-inch-thick walls to keep waste from leaching into groundwater and carbon filters to minimize odor. He planned to plant trees to shield the site. "I wasn't going to do anything where I wasn't exposing myself twice as much," he says. His house, he suggests, would be just a sniff away from the buildings.

But when the officials of MVC caught wind of Palm's plan, they leapt into action. To them, the hog operation seemed like an existential threat, jeopardizing the health-promoting, resort-like community they were creating. Residents and visitors alike would be revolted by the hog-fattening operation. They also feared it would make life unbearable for hundreds of young scholars—pandits—whom they were bringing in periodically from India to live in barracks-like facilities less than a mile from Palm's farm. "Since campuses and other development in the city would have been directly downwind from the CAFO, this was a major concern to residents and other members of the surrounding community," Maureen Wynne, a councilwoman in the city and former city attorney, told me. Wynne, who is also the wife of Mayor Robert G. Wynne, compared the move to building a landfill next door.[1]

Indeed, given the sensibilities of the residents and backers of MVC, it would have been far worse than any landfill. Chartered in July 2001 as the first new city set up in Iowa in nearly twenty years, MVC was created by TM adherents to showcase the movement's principles for living and building in accord with what the movement calls Natural Law. All land in the city is USDA-certified organic. All products sold there, particularly food, must be organic, and synthetic pesticides and fertilizers are big no-nos. Conceived of first as the Maharishi Center for Health and World Peace, the city has its own constitution—called the Constitution of the Universe and drawn from ancient Vedic literature—and adopted Sanskrit as its "ideal language." Nearly all thirteen hundred residents, as of mid-2012, are meditators, according to Kent Boyum, the city's director of government relations and of economic development. The population includes a group of eight hundred to eleven hundred Indian scholars, or pandits, who each come for stays of from two to three years.

Many of the meditators live far different lives than those of Iowa farmers. For one thing, they live in buildings fashioned in accord with the architectural principles of Maharishi Sthapatya Veda, a style that a movement webpage says reflects "Nature's own timeless laws of structuring or building which maintain every particle in creation in perfect harmony with everything else." The architecture of all the buildings in MVC—265 structures as of mid-2012, according to Boyum—thus "takes into account the influences of sun, moon, stars and planets with reference to north and south poles and the equator." As the webpage says, the buildings "connect individual life with Cosmic Life, individual intelligence with Cosmic Intelligence, optimizing both the close and distant positive environmental influences on the individual." The structures all face east and adhere to certain proportions and layouts. They are topped by kalashes that sometimes are covered in gold and are said to connect heaven and earth.[2]

Visitors to the city, especially those seeking health treatments, are also cut from different cloth than many Iowa farmers. At The Raj, a luxurious spa in MVC that could double as a French country chalet, wealthy guests undergo assessments to determine their "unique Ayurvedic constitution and state of imbalance." They get dietary and lifestyle recommendations, as well as suggestions for herbal supplements. They might take an anti-stress massage or undergo Maharishi Light Therapy with Gems, a technique where patients are bathed in light shone through precious stones ("promotes higher states of consciousness," says the promotional literature). Programs at the spa address health concerns "ranging from chronic disorders and weight-loss to anti-aging and rejuvenation." Individualized programs serve sufferers of fibromyalgia, arthritis, chronic fatigue, and other ailments.[3] Geoff Gilpin, in *The Maharishi Effect: A Personal Journey through the Movement That Transformed American Spirituality*, a 2006 memoir about his times in Fairfield, describes The Raj well: "Nice place—peach carpets, creamy upholstery, lots of gold and marble. If Jay Gatsby wanted to purify his nervous system, this is where he'd come."[4]

The pampering doesn't come cheap. It could set visitors back as much as $660.80 a day, with ten-day, eleven-night packages costing about $6,800 as of mid-2012. Of course, one could pay in Raam Mudra, the currency of the Global Country of World Peace, based nearby. One Raam costs ten dollars under a fixed exchange rate. Back in 2002, local officials started distributing Raam, adopting it as "the ideal local currency to support economic development."

For Palm, dealing with the MVC representatives got ugly fast. He didn't feel good about them to begin with because, he said, TM Movement people had tried to pressure his mother into selling the family farm years before as they amassed land for the city. "'What part of 'not for sale' do you guys not understand?,'" he had asked them then. "I had to throw them out of her house and say, 'Don't come back.'" So when MVC representatives got an appraisal on his farm in 2007 and tried again to buy it, he countered with a figure that Wynne says was several times the appraisal figure. As he recalls it, the appraisal was too low and he ultimately balked. "This farm has never been on the market since my granddad bought it back in 1894," Palm says. "Everybody wants to keep it in the family."

Blocked from buying the land, the MVC officials shifted ground. They raised the possibility of exercising the legal right of eminent domain to condemn the property and seize it, ostensibly for the public good. Other cities around the country were taking such steps in highly publicized—if controversial—cases. They would turn Palms of Dellahome into a park, complete with windmills, soccer fields, a swimming pool, and a place to charge electric cars.[5]

Then, relations grew uglier. Palm had to hire a lawyer, costing him $36,000 over time, to fight to keep his land. For their part, MVC officials seemed to be losing an embarrassing public relations battle. Bloggers nationwide—often politically conservative folks or TM critics—railed against the possible land grab. "We say go whole hog on those hogs, boys, just to spite them uppity, ass-bouncing losers," fulminated one blogger. "They'll all be gone in 10 years anyway, after their loony leader, the Maharishi Mahesh Yogi, gives up his ghost, freeing the world of one of the most grandiose gurus to hit the scene in the last 100 years."[6] Another argued, "This is a bunch of idiots who chose to build their city next to a farm that's been in operation for 115 years. They have NO right . . . none whatsoever as far as I'm concerned to tell that farmer and his family what to do with that land."[7]

One lyrical critic, Tony Arnold, even wrote a song about the flap called the "The Maharishi Vedic City Blues."[8] Among the verses:

The cult that came to Iowa
Bought a school, and then the town.
They tried to take a family's farm
So they could tear it down.
But not a single one had worn
A pair of working shoes . . .
It's food for thought, those
Maharishi Vedic City Blues.

There's too much history, too much at stake:
The farmer needs a living, the farmer needs a break.
There's no consideration, no common sense:
Just too much fiber, too much incense.

Then–city attorney Wynne hosted a public meeting in a tent outside her home in June 2007 to let people air their feelings. It drew about two hundred people, most opposed to the proposed seizure, according to Dick Reed, vice chairman of the Jefferson County Board of Supervisors at the time. "It's a little shady," Reed said, according to a news report. "When you have a local government talking about doing condemnation on a farm when they [the local government] have excess land themselves is ludicrous. Being able to own land is one of the rights in this country."[9]

The *Ottumwa Courier*, a local newspaper based about thirty miles away, minced no words in an editorial about the battle. "Vedic City officials seem to have forgotten that they are smack dab in the center of farm country," thundered the paper. "Odor, dust, pesticides—it's the price we pay for quality Iowa produce—the best in the world. This IS farm country and bullying tactics by Vedic City officials send the wrong message. If Vedic City officials are unwilling to accept the reality of living in Iowa, then they can build a community somewhere else."[10]

MVC officials at one point tried a softer approach, Palm said, offering financing to help him turn his operation back into a dairy farm—an organic one. But he declined, saying that tending dairy animals is an all-consuming job. "I don't want to be tied down 24/7 with a dairy operation," he says.

But the MVC officials won in the end. Palm shelved the idea for a hog operation. The city, for its part, backed down on pursuing eminent domain to grab his land—at least as long as Palm doesn't try to put in the hog houses. Palm's son stepped back from the farm, buying a seed dealership instead. Palm says his lawyer advised that fighting MVC would bleed him dry. "They seem to have bottomless pockets," Palm says of his meditating neighbors. "It's more money than I can buck against."

Years after he lost the fight but got to keep his farm, Palm's distaste for his neighbors has not abated a whit. Life near MVC, he says, remains challenging. He says, for instance, that he legally can spray herbicides on his crops only before 6 a.m. or after 8 p.m. because meditator neighbors registered their property as a bee farm. One day, he says, a friend strolled by the place, only to find there was "not a bee in the hive." Even so, he says, he has to live by the restriction. Making life difficult for farmers who balk at MVC's preferences "is the whole plan," he says. "And it's not only me—everybody with a farm in the area is up against it."

He doesn't know what the future holds for Palms of Dellahome. He's not sure whether he wants his son to have to struggle with the neighbors. But he's adamant about not selling to them, either. Says Palm, "That will never happen as long as I've got a breath to draw."

It's not clear what the future holds for MVC either, but the city does have ambitious plans. Six of ten neighborhoods laid out in a city plan remained undeveloped as of mid-2012, according to Boyum, the government relations director. "Is there room to grow and are there plans to grow? Definitely, that is the case," Boyum says, as we chat in a plush, well-lighted sitting area in The Raj. "We've done pretty well in ten years."

Called a model for "ideal city life," MVC functions almost as a bedroom community for Fairfield. The city has no retail shops, no operating schools (though it has a charter for a university devoted to Vedic knowledge that might open someday), no manufacturers, and no police force. It has a couple of hotels, including The Raj, along with a few small residential developments and a greenhouse business associated with the TM Movement. It contracts with Jefferson County for police services. The city is also home to offices of a handful of outfits associated with the movement, such as the Global Country of World Peace, which owns the area that houses the meditators from India and develops properties around the world. The GCWP, in fact, owns much of the land throughout the eighteen-hundred-acre city and proudly flies its own flag on properties here—a yellow sunburst surrounded by a ring of red on a field of yellow and white.

Still mostly green spaces, MVC is a work in progress. Aside from the pandits, residents live in condos and small housing developments in areas called mandalas. The condos range upward from 450-square-foot units that cost about $65,000 to 900-square-foot units that fetch about $120,000, according to Boyum. In the small developments, houses go for between $200,000 and $400,000, carrying a stiff premium over ordinary homes in nearby Fairfield that weren't built in accord with the movement's architectural principles. Boyum says some homes in MVC are worth as much as $1 million.

Officials of The Raj encourage visitors to drive around town to see the houses, as well as the handful of other places put up to showcase the Vedic science of consciousness. The Maharishi Vedic Observatory, for instance, displays "in one compact form the whole structure of the universe along with all the movements of the sun, the planets, and the stars," according to a self-guided tour sheet distributed by The Raj. "The collection of large, outdoor masonry instruments, based on the principle of the sun-dial, makes it possible to observe the intelligence of the universe as it is displayed throughout the universe." The observatory, a collection of spare and eroding white structures arrayed in a circle that visitors can walk through and around, "has been developed as a result of travel in inner space-unbounded awareness," a guide from the TM Movement explains.

Another spot on the self-guided tour is the Capital of the Global Country of World Peace. Visitors are told the GCWP is a "country without borders created to establish world peace by unifying all nations in happiness, prosperity, invincibility, and perfect health, while supporting the rich diversity of our world family." According to the articles of incorporation the GCWP filed with the Iowa secretary of state in 2002, the organization's goals are lofty indeed. One aim is "to establish Heaven on Earth by raising the quality of life of every individual to complete fulfillment and affluence in enlightenment." Another is to "promote throughout the world the knowledge that life is the everlasting evolving expression of Natural Law, which administers the universe with perfect order, and thereby bring an end to all problems and suffering." The organization's capitol building makes for an excellent photo opportunity, visitors are told, but they are discouraged from entering because the building is also a private residence.

The GCWP can also hold gifts and bequests, and it does in fact handle a fair amount of money—though its fortunes have been shrinking. It took in $16 million in contributions and grants in the fiscal year accounted for in its 2010 Form 990 filing, a document that tax-exempt organizations file with the IRS. This was down from $21.5 million in the prior year and from $31.7 million in the year before that. The GCWP reported total assets at the end of the 2010 reporting year of $91.4 million, down from $115.3 million in the prior year and from $126.6 million the year before.

Developers have a lot to say about how MVC has grown and will in the future. Three of the city's five city council members in early 2013 were developers, including Rogers Badgett, a founding council member who owns and operates The Raj (together with his wife, Candace, who also served as a founding council member). Another council member, Tim Fitz-Randolph, headed Mandala One Village, a residential development in town. A third councilman, Chris Johnson, headed the Rukmapura Park Hotel and Resort, the city's other big hotel (his wife, Dee, too, worked in his development operations and she, too, was a founding council member). A fourth council member, William Goldstein, serves as general counsel for MUM and the David Lynch Foundation.

Goldstein, a fan of golf, has championed a plan for a golf course to dominate much of the city's land in a revamped city plan, according to Boyum. The course could prove a big draw for relaxation-seeking visitors, the economic development chief said. Tentatively to be called Constitution of the Universe Golf and Learning Center, the course will "provide knowledge, experience, and entertainment to enliven the health, intellect, and mind/

body coordination of the golfer," according to the city's website. A pavilion at each tee box will feature an interactive model of a golfer illustrating "the expression of a specific theme of Natural Law in the golfer." Each pavilion will also incorporate aromas, refreshments, and knowledge displays.[11]

Though elected, the city's leaders are all tightly tied to the TM Movement. MVC's founding mayor, Robert G. Wynne, is a leader in the GCWP, for instance, and served as a dean at MUM. He boasts a bachelor's degree from Stanford University, a master's degree from MIT's Sloan School of Management, and doctorates from the Maharishi European Research University and MUM. Maureen Wynne chairs and serves as secretary of the GCWP.

The former city attorney has made headlines beyond the Palm farm flap. When TM Movement members laid cornerstones in 2004 for the dwellings that now house the visiting meditating pandits, for instance, Wynne was quoted in the *Fairfield Daily Ledger* happily saying the date, April 22, was Akshaya Tritiya. "It's a day in the Vedic calendar where, if you do things, they have a lasting achievement," she said.[12]

Visitors are discouraged from bothering the pandits. A gate sprawling across the dusty entrance to their compound warns visitors to stop. Each day, the hundreds of pandits step out of their one-story, barracks-like dwellings. The men gather in halls nearby where they sit for hours. At times, they are silent. At times, they chant. They are Brahmans, members of the high caste in India, and they rarely leave the compound. Their all-consuming job is to meditate for world peace. "When I go to work," says Boyum, "they go to chant."

Just how long the chanting will go on may turn on whether there is a future for MVC and for the TM Movement. Many Utopian communities have faded or slipped into discord after the death of a charismatic founder. Some have adapted, making room for new blood in the leadership, and gone on to thrive. The TM Movement's greatest test, its ability to see and create its future, now lies before it.

12

Does TM Have a Tomorrow?

FOR THE TM MOVEMENT, people such as Jonathan Clifford should be the face of the future. He is a son of meditators who got the TM bug during the movement's heyday in the 1970s and who refreshed themselves with courses in meditation in Fairfield. Inspired by family visits to the tiny town a world apart from his high-stress Long Island junior high school in New York, he decided to attend the movement's high school in Fairfield. After graduating from the Maharishi School of the Age of Enlightenment in 2006, Clifford joined friends from the school in enrolling at MUM, just across the parking lot. He graduated from there in 2009 with a major in sustainable living, worked for a time for a website-development company in Fairfield that serves green-friendly companies, and then moved to Boulder, Colorado, to work for a web-based marketing firm. He was trained in TM's twice-daily twenty-minute meditation technique and moved on to learn an advanced technique, in the TM-Sidhi program, which can involve meditating for several hours a day.

By pedigree and training, Clifford seems a natural leader for the TM Movement. But he has no interest in such a role, and indeed he bridles at being associated with the movement. "I'm not committed at all," Clifford says. "Maharishi's main teaching that I loved is to be self-sufficient, to be self-referral. I learned TM as a twenty-minute technique. And then I learned the TM-Sidhi's program. And that's all I need. I can be completely self-sufficient with that. I don't need to be part of the movement. I don't need to do any of their other things you can do."

As the leaders of the movement gray, few people seem to be coming along to take their place. The movement's putative global leader—former neuroscientist and physician Tony Nader, also known as the Maharaja Adhiraj Raja Raam, is little known outside TM's inner circles and has not filled the spiritual shoes of the deceased guru. More troubling for the movement, few second-generation TMers have come forward to take leading roles in the TM organizations or have been allowed to assume such roles. While Maharishi installed a leadership group to take his place, this group has not spelled out a succession plan for themselves or for the national leaders around the world who were installed by the deceased leader. Such national or regional leaders, or rajas as they are called, were appointed to their positions less for their governance abilities than because they contributed hefty sums of money. Essentially, these leaders—some of whom wear gold crowns at movement events—bought their titles with million-dollar donations.

For folks such as Clifford, money is a big part of the problem with TM. While he doesn't fault Maharishi's teachings and feels he got a lot of value from his education at MUM and, earlier, at the movement's high school, Clifford is troubled by the movement's lack of disclosure to its adherents about financial matters. "I don't think the movement is honest. I think their main interest is money," he says. "I don't think they're transparent at all. A large percentage of my money that I gave to the university was sent to other programs that they wanted to fund all over the place, teaching people TM, putting it in India. They take a certain percentage of money and they send it to other places. . . . First comes first. You take care of your students at the university."

Clifford and a group of other MUM students and young people reared by TMers discussed their feelings about the movement's future at a café in Fairfield. All admitted to falling short on the practices with which they were raised, saying they either never meditate anymore or rarely keep up with the twice-a-day basic regimen, much less the prolonged-meditation regimen under the TM-Sidhi program. Some did say they try to meditate once a day or say they could come back to a more regular regimen as they get older. One, saying he'd like to be a TM teacher someday, admitted he would have to ratchet up his meditation practices by then.

Despite their personal lapses—perhaps not uncommon among people in their late teens and early twenties raised in various cultural or religious traditions—the students all find value in the movement's teachings and some of its outreach efforts. Most praised programs by the David Lynch Foundation for Consciousness-Based Education and World Peace to reach out to homeless veterans, impoverished Indians, and children in tough inner-city schools, for instance.[1] The practice of meditation, they argue, can be enormously helpful. "I love it. I feel like it changes people's lives," says one young man who took his first steps in meditation at age five in a TM technique urged on him by his parents.

Still, much as they believe in it and want to help perpetuate the movement, they planned to make their careers elsewhere. One young man, a staunch supporter of TM, did not see his life unfolding in the movement's offices in Fairfield. That could be a big loss to the movement in which his family has played a big part. The young man's father did important research for the movement, showing the beneficial effects of meditation on various populations with special needs. He helped bring in millions of dollars from the National Institutes of Health and other groups for his work and that of colleagues. The young man's mother also played an important role at MUM.

"Everyone who is running the movement now is going to die. That's just gonna happen. And they're going to stop working way before they die. And people our age are going to be the ones who take over," says the young adherent, who asks not to be named.

But even as he admits he feels an obligation to perpetuate his family's legacy, taking a leading role in the organization is just not something he would prefer for himself. He expects never to "turn his back" on the movement because doing so, he says, would be like turning "my back on my mom." But he won't be running it. "Whatever I would be doing, I would be perpetuating the idea of TM being taught to people. The only reason I wouldn't want to be involved in a leader position is that my interests are more in film and music. If I was successful in any field I was in, I would definitely attribute a lot of my success to the fact that I was taught TM when I was young," he says. Still, he adds, "My interests are not to be a leader in an organization. I want to do other things."

With its emphasis on personal development and freedom to be creative, the movement paradoxically may be fostering its own leadership shortfalls. The students say they have been encouraged to develop their personal and professional lives as they would like, even if that's outside the movement. While some complain of being pressed at MUM to meditate more often— pointing to teachers who suggested they would be "less evolved" than others if they didn't practice TM often—they say they were never pushed to gear themselves up for top movement roles.

Because the TM Movement has been a top-down organization—an autocracy long led by one man, the deceased guru—leadership and succession are touchy topics. Veterans of the movement, speaking anonymously because they still serve at high levels, say there is much debate about how best to handle governance going forward. Many of today's movement leaders were thrust into top roles while still in their twenties—the founding president of MUM, Robert Keith Wallace, was in his mid-twenties when he took up leadership of the school, for instance. Now, however, the aging Baby Boomers at the helm show little inclination to cede authority to people half their age or younger. "They look at the twenty-five-year-olds and say, 'that person is not as committed as I was at twenty-five. They never met Maharishi,'" says a current leader of a U.S. arm of the movement, a Baby Boomer who is pressing to make room for younger people. "This is an issue going on at the highest levels of the organization."

Indeed, TM organization leaders are well aware of the challenge. Bob Roth, who holds the title of national director of expansion at the Global Country of World Peace and the Maharishi Foundation–USA, points to a few trustees at movement organizations such as the Maharishi School of the Age of Enlightenment who are younger than thirty. He admits that the top leaders in most arms of the organization are in their fifties and sixties. A scan of the board of MUM, as of 2012, turns up none among the thirty-six who appear to be younger than thirty (and only seven women in the group overall). At Lynch's foundation—which dates back just to 2005—Roth said seven of the forty-one members of the board of directors and board of advisors are younger than thirty (and twenty-five are women). "Five years ago, there wasn't a focus on this," Roth says, adding that top management ranks of Lynch's foundation do include younger people and mostly women. "Now, not only is the focus on to open up more leadership roles to young people, but the desire among young people to do it." With so many at the top in their sixties, he adds, change is bound to come, and soon. Predicted Roth in 2012, "Within two to three years, you are going to see 30 percent or more of the leadership in their late twenties or thirties."

Maybe so. But the history of most groups built around charismatic individuals suggests a less rosy future. Geoff Gilpin's 2006 book *The Maharishi Effect*, about his time in the TM Movement, suggested the movement at that point was at an "isolation stage" common in the trajectories of gurus. This was a time, he writes, when demands for money and obedience increase and the guru's pronouncements become "increasingly grandiose and apocalyptic." That could lead to death of the movement either in a "bang or a whimper," with something dramatic like mass suicide, "or the group just fizzles out and everybody gets on with their lives."

"There's also talk of a schism," Gilpin writes. Once the guru passed, he speculates, "the truly faithful [could] rally from the shadows and restore the Movement to its pristine glory. No more inflated prices, no more dubious products and services, no more delusions of grandeur. Just sincere individuals teaching Transcendental Meditation to a spiritually hungry world. Just like old times."[2]

Now, as memories of the guru fade, schism seems to hold sway. The top ranks of the movement globally are split between strict preservationists committed to upholding the letter of the law, as dictated by the late guru, and so-called progressives who press for the movement to adapt, according to a prominent movement veteran and supporter who believes the TM organization needs to plan better for succession. Much like leaders of the Catholic Church or the rabbinic leaders of Judaism, the factions debate over keeping the knowledge and practices "pure" versus adapting to changed circumstances. It's not clear how much change in Maharishi's dictates is acceptable.

It is also not clear whether the movement can successfully separate veneration for a dead leader and propagation of his basic meditation technique. Is TM just a simple technique, an almost mechanical approach, practiced twenty minutes in the morning and twenty minutes in the evening? And can that technique be stripped out of the full package of Maharishi's ideas and taught for its own benefits, as David Lynch's foundation and organizations it backs seem to be doing? Or should potential followers be urged to plunge into the broad collection of teachings, available in print or extensive video and audio records of the guru? Should the technique be separated from the dogma?

Indeed, it's an open question, even among young people raised in the movement, of whether the guru, especially now, would have much traction with people in their twenties or thereabouts. The idea of following a guru "is dangerous in this day and age," says a twentysomething whose parents are longtime meditators in Fairfield. "It's taking orders from one person and putting all of your personal intuitions and feelings behind and devoting it to this one person, who is no longer living," says the young critic, who preferred to remain unnamed for fear that her criticisms would mistakenly be seen as "antimovement."[3]

This second-generation meditator is another person who, on paper, would seem an ideal candidate for leadership in the TM Movement. Educated from preschool through grade twelve at MSAE in Fairfield, she went on to a distinguished college and has worked at MUM. But the MSAE grad has little interest in taking a leadership role in the TM Movement and holds views that might trouble movement leaders. She values meditation—practicing forty minutes in the morning and forty minutes more each evening—but contends that a one-size-fits-all approach to meditation may not be the best for everyone. "Offering it [meditation] as something that is valuable to you is great," she says. "I think the movement is attuned to pushing it and deciding that it's the best thing. That puts you in a bad spot because nothing is the best thing for everyone."

This critic also finds the movement's approach to seeking scientific validation for meditation's benefits ill-suited to the times. Under the guidance of Maharishi, who was schooled as a physicist, the movement produced hundreds of studies aimed at proving to a science-oriented Western audience that TM offered a broad array of health and social benefits, including even reducing crime rates.[4] When Americans and others were unfamiliar with meditation, the approach may have been necessary, but the critic maintained that it's not a winning style nowadays for much of TM's prospective market. "I don't think that is what draws in young people anymore," she argues.

The raft of studies that the TM Movement produced—and continues to produce—doesn't carry much weight, moreover, with some outside scientists. To critical experts, the research seems self-serving and, too often, is not validated by experts outside the movement. "In general, the scientific community does not look very favorably on the TM Movement's research," says Richard J. Davidson, a professor of psychology and psychiatry at the University of Wisconsin, head of the school's Laboratory for Affective Neuroscience, and a regular practitioner of Tibetan-style meditation. "The claims made on the basis of the extant research are way beyond what the research really supports. The research is typically conducted within the envelope of a kind of religious zeal that I think can obscure the ability to see clearly and be dispassionate about the findings and also to report negative findings. I've never seen a paper from the TM Movement reporting a nonfinding."

Certainly, TMers point to plenty of studies to back up claims about the meditative practice's benefits. Dr. Norman E. Rosenthal, in his book *Transcendence*, points to 340 peer-reviewed articles published on TM, many that he says appear in highly respected journals. He details some of the research to make his case for TM. Sharing his own reaction to a few years of practicing the technique, Rosenthal says, "I cannot remember a time when I have felt happier or more at peace with myself and my surroundings." Further, he says it offers great therapeutic benefits for people in mental or spiritual anguish. The psychiatrist writes, "The potential clinical power of this technique is amazing. It offers the promise to transform the lives of millions who suffer."[5]

But others in the scientific world take issue with some of the broader claims about the power of TM-style meditation. Consider the question of whether TM can make someone smarter, specifically that the meditation improves cognitive function and increases intelligence. A pair of researchers in the United Kingdom, Peter H. Canter and Edzard Ernst of the Peninsula College of Medicine and Dentistry at the Universities of Exeter and Plymouth, in 2003 published a review article in *Wiener Klinische Wochenschrift* (*Middle European Journal of Medicine*) in which they skewered much of the research published about TM, much of it conducted by devotees.

Canter and Ernst examined 107 published articles reporting the effects of TM on cognitive function, tossing out all but 10 because of such flaws as not using controls—non-meditators—along with the meditating subjects in the research or failing to randomize the subjects appropriately. Four of the surviving scientific trials involved reported TM's positive effects on cognitive function, four others were completely negative, and two were largely negative, they reported. But the pair trashed even the positive trials, saying they used subjects favorably predisposed toward TM; Canter and Ernst dismissed the results as a product of the subjects' expectations. Their damning conclusion stated that "the claim that TM has a specific and cumulative effect on cognitive function is not supported by the evidence from randomized controlled trials."[6]

Beyond finding the pursuit of scientific validation pointless, the second-generation meditator in Fairfield suggests MUM has seemed split in its mission, and she faulted its marketing. On the one hand, she says, the university appeals to "superspiritual" students interested in meditation and the Science of Creative Intelligence, the movement's intellectual underpinnings. On the other hand, it appeals to students interested in practical fields such as sustainable living systems. In its marketing, the twentysomething says, the university has seemed to play down requirements for meditation and SCI instruction, not telling students that they need to put in a certain amount of meditation to graduate, for instance. "What they were promoting was only half of what they were," she says. "They needed to say they were part ashram."

She does feel good about the work of Lynch's foundation. The group's work in teaching TM to communities in need, such as impoverished Native Americans and children in hard-pressed schools, seems to echo the early days of the movement. The foundation, the critic says, is "getting back to the roots of wanting to help people." It seemed reminiscent of the days when the grad's parents were learning TM and it was "fun, young, and cool." Nowadays, she says, "the movement has gotten old and it's not in the phase of fun, young, and cool and let's do something. It's older."

Driven largely by David Lynch's foundation, some of the movement's marketing efforts have changed, and TM proponents have found new venues for the technique. Roth, who also serves as executive director of the foundation, points to moves by the Veterans Administration to offer TM as an additional therapy for soldiers struggling with depression and post-traumatic stress. Some companies, he adds, now offer to pay for the meditation training as a wellness benefit, while schools offer it as "learning-readiness" program. The numbers of people learning TM may not be as high as in 1975 when as many as fifty thousand Americans a month learned it, Roth says, but he believes it could have more staying power now. "It's less important how many people are learning and more important where they are learning," Roth contends. "In the '70s and '60s it was a fad, and fads come and go."

TM is in transition and undergoing a "natural evolution," Roth contends. But he argues that the problems it helps people deal with—particularly stress—are more daunting than ever. And he said that "conventional approaches to handling stress, whether it's medication or talk therapy or even exercise, are limited." Further, Roth contends, meditation has gone mainstream, along with such practices as yoga, making TM more acceptable. He points to Trinity College in Hartford, Connecticut, where squash players use TM to help improve their performance and the school's chaplaincy offers yoga, t'ai chi, aikido, karate, Zen meditation, mindfulness meditation, and TM, with credit available.[7] Norwich University, a private military college in Vermont, has also found that TM helps its cadets.[8]

Roth also plans to reinvigorate the ranks of TM teachers in the United States, and he tries to persuade people when he visits college campuses that they can make a career out of teaching the meditation technique. There are about ten thousand TM teachers, but only about five hundred now teach the technique, he says. He wants to add two thousand new teachers over the coming five years.

But while meditation may seem nearly as ordinary in the United States now as jogging—thanks largely to Maharishi's inroads decades ago—it is not clear that the TM version of the practice will prevail. To appeal to potential adherents, the TM organization has cut the cost of its programs from $2,500 a person to $1,500 for a working adult. (Family rates permit a partner to learn for an additional $750 and a child to pick up the skill for $375 more. There's also a $750 military rate.) Still, far less costly meditation programs are available in gyms all across the country. (For people in need, the David

Lynch Foundation does provide scholarships and claims it has provided such support to more than 250,000 people since 2005.)

But while the simplicity of its meditation instruction and technique is a major drawing card, some rival systems are even simpler. Blue Mountain Center of Meditation, a group in Tomales, California, teaches people how to meditate—for free—by way of an online course. Rather than being given a mantra by a teacher, meditators pick their own—some Christians choose "Jesus," while Jews sometimes pick a favorite short Hebrew prayer. The center sells books and other materials by its founder, the late Eknath Easwaran, an English professor who came to the United States from India in 1959, like Maharishi, and later taught meditation at the University of California at Berkeley.[9] Easwaran's "passage meditation" approach involves meditating on a spiritual or religious text passage.

Similarly, former Buddhist monk Andy Puddicombe is using the Internet to teach a type of "mindfulness meditation" that blends calming and insight meditation in ten-minute-a-day sessions. His website, headspace.com, provides daily messages, including guided audio meditations, online or by way of smartphones. The site pointedly says sitting cross-legged on the floor is not required and neither are robes, incense, or getting involved "in any of that stuff which could all too easily look like mumbo-jumbo." Customers can buy his book, Get Some Headspace (2011), attend events (for a fee), and subscribe to his online program, the Headspace Journey, for charges ranging from $5.74 a month up to a flat fee of $399.95 (which gives the buyer all Headspace content for life).

Puddicombe, age forty in early 2013, may be the Internet era's answer to TM—much as Maharishi used celebrities and the technology of the 1960s and 1970s to pitch his brand of meditation, so the bald, hip-looking native of Bristol, England, uses the Internet and other modern means to market his practice. Indeed, he makes TM look "oh so yesterday" with his ingenious marketing. For example, he has a deal with Virgin Atlantic to provide a channel with guided meditation, via headsets, to passengers in flight. He has done promotions with Britain's Selfridges department store where shoppers plop themselves under Headspace pods and hear his guided meditations on food, love, and fragrance, depending on the department they are in.[10] His fall 2012 talk about the practice, titled "All It Takes Is 10 Mindful Minutes," attracted more than 1 million views on the TED Talks academic conference website in just the first three months of 2013.[11]

Puddicombe owes some of his success to TM. He learned meditation first at a TM center as a child in about 1982, when his mom took him there. He abandoned the practice at age thirteen or fourteen, when it seemed hopelessly uncool. "There's no question that it was put forward in quite a hippie context for me," Puddicombe told me. "The whole incense, cross-legged, long-haired kind of thing didn't connect in terms of my social group." Subsequently, he discovered Buddhism in his late teens and early twenties after losing his stepsister in a bicycle accident and then seeing two people killed and others hurt when a car crashed into him and a group of friends standing on a sidewalk. While searching for solace, he opted against TM because "the language used and the whole mysticism around it didn't work for me." Instead, he studied Buddhism in India and Nepal, was ordained as a monk, and tossed off his robes after about ten years when he returned to England in 2004.

Indeed, Puddicombe and his colleagues at Headspace studied TM's outreach approaches—but not in a way that would gladden TM leaders. He points to the high cost of TM courses and the practice's mystical bent as turnoffs for a lot of people. "We used TM as a learning process and I don't mean that as a way how to sell meditation. I'd say it's almost how not to do it," he says. "We owe TM a lot. We looked at it to see how we can do this so we don't fall into some of the same traps they have." The result: he claims some six hundred thousand people use the Headspace website or its mobile app, many of them using some of the services for no charge. His company is based in London and, as of early 2013, Venice, California.

Meditation clearly has broad appeal. The Veterans Administration and the Department of Defense are sponsoring research into meditation as a technique for veterans to deal with post-traumatic stress disorder (PTSD). Rather than favoring one approach over others, the agencies are spreading their markers around, funding multiple efforts to study TM, the Easwaran-inspired Mantram Repetition Program (MRP), and Jon Kabat-Zinn's Mindfulness Based Stress Reduction (MBSR), as well as other approaches, such as "compassion meditation," a Buddhist form that fosters empathy. The agencies are spending more than $5 million to determine which methods work best for veterans and active-duty military personnel.

Researchers from Fairfield, including MUM professor Sanford Nidich, are using a $2.4 million grant from the Department of Defense to compare TM with a treatment approach commonly used in the VA system called prolonged-exposure treatment. The study, undertaken in a partnership with the San Diego Veterans Administration Medical Center, will follow 210 people and take four years to wrap up. Separately, the VA is running three big trials on the MBSR and MRP approaches, as well as a demonstration project using various types of meditation at eight spots around the country.

Not all forms of meditation are the same, says Jill Bormann, a research nurse scientist leading VA-sponsored efforts in San Diego and an enthusiast for the Easwaran mantram approach (a mantram in the MRP approach is similar to TM's repeated mantra). While most forms of meditation share the idea of focusing one's attention, the similarity can end there. Some practices involve focusing on images, others on words or activity. Some can be done walking and others require sitting. The goal of the MRP approach, she suggests, is not for a person to "transcend," or to enter a twilight state, but rather to interrupt negative thoughts or behaviors and refocus to generate relaxation. "You choose your own mantrams," she says. "You don't have to pay anybody to assign one to you." Sitting twenty minutes twice a day, she adds, takes a commitment that many cannot fulfill, and so she believes that MRP "is more sustainable and more quickly doable by more people."

Bormann is also careful not to oversell the usefulness of any meditation technique in curing PTSD. Meditation can help, as can intensive desensitization therapy programs that the VA uses—programs in which vets relive their traumas until they can better manage their feelings. But for many, problems can linger. "I am not sure that there is truly a cure, frankly," says Bormann, who has a PhD and who has studied scores of veterans. In one study, 24 percent of those in a group that used mantrams for only six weeks no longer met the diagnostic criteria for PTSD, compared with 12 percent who received only case management.

"It is not a silver bullet. It is another tool we can use to help manage depression, anxiety, and the adverse effects of post-traumatic stress disorder," says

Tim Bahr, a retired Marine, now in his late fifties, who teaches MRP to other vets in a VA clinic in Rhinelander, Wisconsin. Bahr, who served during the Vietnam War, the Desert Storm and Desert Shield operations in Iraq, and later in Iraq again on a recall, advocates the MRP approach where veterans pick a mantram and repeat it to calm themselves when stressed. The idea is to focus on a calming phrase to break a cycle of ugly thoughts or feelings, Bahr says. He suggests that the mantrams that participants pick should be words that bring peaceful thoughts. "My first mantram was 'Allahu Akbar'—God is Great. But, having served in Iraq, it invoked pictures of suicide bombers," Bahr says. "That didn't work."

Bahr, who remembers that in the late 1960s and early 1970s, returning Vietnam vets faced a counterculture that was often hostile to the soldiers, isn't keen on TM and doesn't think many of his fellow fiftyish and sixty-ish veterans would be. "I make sure when I work with a group of veterans to let them know that this is not Transcendental Meditation, this is rapid relaxation," he says. For many, he adds, "when you say 'mantra' or 'TM,' they picture communes and flower power and people calling you 'baby killer' because you did what your country wanted you to do."

Outside of VA and Department of Defense circles, competition from rival meditation approaches appears to be worrying the TM organization enough for it to resort to the courts. Maharishi Foundation–USA brought a trademark-infringement lawsuit in 2011 against The Meditation House LLC, a life-coaching operation based in Ankeny, Iowa. The TM group accuses its rival of lying about the benefits of Vedic meditation and of confusing the public.[12]

Jules Green, who runs The Meditation House and conducts workshops around the country, bristles at the suit. "It seems they believe that no one other than the Foundation or its licensees has knowledge of this meditation tradition, or can claim to teach according to it," Green says on her website. "In my opinion, the Foundation does not have, nor should have, a monopoly on teaching this ancient Vedic type of meditation, which predates the Foundation by thousands of years. There are many persons in India and elsewhere who are knowledgeable about this meditation tradition, other than the Maharishi Foundation and its licensees."[13]

Indeed, she seems offended that the TM organization, an outfit with such lofty goals, should stoop to litigation. "Even though I am the sole employee of a very small business, I plan to defend the case to the best of my ability," Green says. "I think it is incorrect, and contrary to the principles of the Vedic tradition, and does not seem to me to be the sort of thing a not-for-profit organization with spiritual goals should be doing."[14]

Whether maturity will mean decline for TM is an open question. The movement now has financial backers, some of whom have practiced TM for decades, who can contribute large amounts to sustain MUM or its other arms. The school is mounting an ambitious endowment campaign. Further, thanks to the support of some wealthy believers in the Maharishi Effect, the movement brings hundreds of meditators to Fairfield from India on a regular basis. Such resources may keep movement institutions afloat for many years. But it's not clear whether the movement can reignite the appeal that drew hundreds of thousands into the meditating ranks in years past.

For Fairfield, the issue is more complicated. Even if TM endures, that doesn't mean adherents will flock to the little Iowa town as they did in answer to the guru's call in 1979. Already, the town's population is shrinking, albeit modestly: since rising 12 percent, to 9,768, between the censuses of 1970 and 1990, the population has slipped about 3 percent in the past two decades to an estimated 9,476 in 2012. As the Baby Boomers move away or die, it's not clear how many others, if any, will sweep in to take their places. Simple attrition could shrink the community over the coming decade. So far, judging by the dwindled enrollments at the MSAE, there's not much growth beyond a handful of second-generation meditators returning from schools or work experiences elsewhere to live with or near their parents. Without a guru with the charisma to inspire adherents anew, Fairfield's allure for meditators has declined.

Still, the question of TM's future is crucial for the town. Even if the local population of meditators shrinks, the campus could endure. But if TM fades away with the Baby Boom generation, as some skeptics expect, residents of Fairfield will be stuck with a campus filled with architecturally unique buildings for which local leaders will have to find new uses. Hundreds of homes and some office complexes, built in accord with TM's architectural dictates, may not appeal to non-meditating buyers (or may plunge sharply in price to meet the budgets of local non-meditators). For Fairfield, such changes would lead to another sea change in the town's commercial, cultural, and political life. The shift might be anything but heavenly.

Should TM fade away, Fairfield in some respects might come to resemble the Amana Colonies or other intentional communities whose days in the sun proved fleeting. Parts of the town—or of neighboring Maharishi Vedic City—could turn into tourist sites for future generations curious about the group that once thrived there. But whether TM finds a way to endure or becomes a footnote in the history of Utopian communities in America, the movement that reshaped Fairfield and that cast its influence far from Iowa won't soon be forgotten in this tiny corner of the state.

ACKNOWLEDGMENTS

○   ○   ○

MANY PEOPLE made this book possible. First, I must acknowledge my wife, Donna, who offered consistent encouragement, put up with my frequent travels to Fairfield, and offered invaluable pointers on my text. Thanks, too, to Will Norton, former dean of the College of Journalism and Mass Communications at the University of Nebraska–Lincoln, who provided the time and funding the project required. And thanks to Prem S. Paul, vice chancellor for research and economic development at the University of Nebraska–Lincoln, and to Jerry and Karla Huse. Their financial support has made my post possible at the university.

Past or current residents of Fairfield and others connected to the town gave of their time, some generously over three years, and shared their ideas. Among them were Richard Beall, Jim Belilove, Marc Berkowitz, Laura Bordow, Connie Boyer, Robert Boyer, Kent Boyum, Reverend Mark Brase, Larry E. Fells, Damian Finol, Fred Gratzon, Gregory Guthrie, Mark Hagist, Police Chief Julie Harvey, Doug Hamilton, Jennifer Hamilton, Cody Heyn, Judy Heyn, Michael Heyn, Jody Hollingsworth, Michael H. Jackson, Earl Kaplan, Jim Karpen, Suzan Kessel, Cindy Lowe, Mayor Ed Malloy, Erin McCann, Sheriff Gregg Morton, Craig Pearson, Reverend Joseph Phipps, Robert Palm, Teresa Palm, former mayor Robert Rasmussen, Kenneth Ross, Bob Roth, Tom Rowe, Shuvender Sem, Patrik Siljestam, Becky Schmitz, Eric Schwartz, L. B. Shriver, Pamela K. Slowick, Michael Spivak, Mahesh Subrahmanyam, Francis Thicke, Fred Travis, parishioners of St. Gabriel and All Angels, congregants of Beth Shalom, and several individuals who chose to remain unnamed.

Others helped in various ways. These included Tony W. Arnold, Tim Bahr, Jill Bormann, Dean R. Broyles, Miles T. Bryant, Angela Burnett, Evelyn Butler, Jimmy Caplan, Richard J. Davidson, Mike Doughney, Steven R. Eckley, Susan Jensen, Jason Kaplan, John M. Knapp, Charles Knoles, David Nanberg, Kenneth Price, Andy Puddicombe, Jeff Rice, Jim Rothblatt, Jan Ryan, Larry Scalise, Linda Shipley, Lee Shriever, Andrew Skolnick, Rodney Stark, Steve St. Clair, Julie Totten, Howard Wolinsky, John R. Wunder, and Joeth Zucco.

My thanks, too, to talented and patient copy editor Michael L. Levine and to William Friedricks, who edits the Iowa and the Midwest Experience series for the University of Iowa Press. Special thanks go to my editor at the University of Iowa Press, Catherine C. Cocks. She saw the project's potential and championed it. I am in her debt.

While the contributions of all these folks were crucial, the responsibility for any errors and omissions lies with me.

∘ ∘ ∘

Transcendental Meditation, TM, TM-Sidhi, Yogic Flying, Consciousness-Based Education, Maharishi Vedic Science, Maharishi International University, Maharishi School of the Age of Enlightenment, Science of Creative Intelligence, Maharishi Vedic Science and Technology, Maharishi Ayurveda, Vedic Science, and Maharishi European Research University are protected trademarks.

The lyrics of "The Maharishi Vedic City Blues" are reproduced by permission of the songwriter and copyright holder, Tony W. Arnold, and are used by permission of Gray Mortuary Recordings.

NOTES

○   ○   ○

Please note that links to webpages, current at the time of this writing, may break over time. Material on those webpages may also change.

Unless otherwise noted, quotations throughout this book were drawn from interviews conducted by the author. In some cases, generally noted, quotes come from blogposts, emails, or cited sources. In a few cases, speakers declined to be named, and I respected their wishes.

WHO CARES ABOUT FAIRFIELD, ANYWAY?

1. For information about Shirley MacLaine, see "Shirley MacLaine: Having Fun 'Just Being Me,' *USA Today*, April 11, 2011, available at http://usatoday30.usa today.com/life/people/2011-04-11-shirleymaclaine12_CV_N.htm. This article is the source of the quotation in the epigraph.

2. For information about the National Center for Complementary and Alternative Medicine and its work on meditation, see http://nccam.nih.gov/health/medi tation/overview.htm/.

3. For information about the Amana Colonies, see http://amanacolonies.com/.

CHAPTER 1

1. See http://cityoffairfieldiowa.com/.

2. See http://barbarabrennan.com/welcome/healing_science.html.

3. For more information on Maharishi Vedic City from the point of view of city boosters, see http://www.vediccity.net/.

4. See http://www.farmfoundation.org/projects/documents/Report8Fair field.pdf.

5. See http://www.oprah.com/own-oprahs-next-chapter/Rush-Hour-in-Fair field-Iowa-Video.

6. For richly detailed accounts of Utopian communities, see Donald E. Pitzer, ed., *America's Communal Utopias* (Chapel Hill: University of North Carolina Press, 1997).

7. Judith Bourque, *Robes of Silk, Feet of Clay: The True Story of a Love Affair with Maharishi Mahesh Yogi, the Indian Guru Followed by the Beatles and Mia Farrow*, self-published, 2010. See http://robesofsilkfeetofclay.com/.

8. See National Center for Education Statistics, available at http://nces.ed.gov /ipeds/datacenter/.

9. For more detail about the Maharishi School of the Age of Enlightenment, see http://www.maharishischooliowa.org/.

10. For recent Form 990 filings, required of tax-exempt organizations, see http:// www.guidestar.org/ or http://foundationcenter.org/findfunders/990finder/. Assets, liabilities, salary information, and other financial details are spelled out in such filings. The $168.4 million net asset figure includes assets held by the Maharishi Global Development Fund, the Global Country of World Peace, and Maharishi University of Management, as well as smaller organizations, including Maharishi Global Administration through Natural Law, Maharishi Foundation USA, Maharishi Purusha Program, Brahmananda Saraswati Foundation, and the David Lynch Foundation for Consciousness-Based Education and World Peace. For the organizations as a group, net assets declined from at least the end of 2008, the year the guru died, through the most recent periods for which reports were available in mid-2013. Declines were reported by the Maharishi Global Development Fund, the Global Country of World Peace, and the Maharishi Purusha Program, while increases were reported by the others. Michael Spivak, treasurer of the university, notes that MUM's assets—worth $37.75 million as of mid-2012—had risen more than $8 million over the prior ten years and that the school had acquired or built more $26 million worth of land, buildings, and equipment in renovating its campus during that period. Further, he said the university is independent of other organizations in its governance and its financial arrangements.

11. See "Yogi's Disciples Contort His Legacy," *India Today*, June 23, 2012, available at http://indiatoday.intoday.in/story/maharishi-mahesh-yogi-rs-60000-crore-for tune/1/201925.html.

12. See Susan Spano, "The 20 Best Small Towns to Visit in 2013," *Smithsonian*, April 2013, available at http://www.smithsonianmag.com/travel/The-20-Best-Small-Towns -to-Visit-in-2013-196855051.html?c=y&page=8&navigation=previous#IMAGES.

CHAPTER 2

1. Philip Goldberg, *American Veda* (New York: Harmony Books, 2010), 67–86.
2. Goldberg, *American Veda*, 87–100.

3. Goldberg, *American Veda*, 82–83.

4. Goldberg, *American Veda*, 81.

5. See http://www.yogananda-srf.org/Default.aspx.

6. Goldberg, *American Veda*, 119.

7. Goldberg, *American Veda*, 155.

8. Goldberg, *American Veda*, 156.

9. Rodney Stark and William Sims Bainbridge, *The Future of Religion: Secularization, Revival, and Cult Formation* (Berkeley: University of California Press, 1985), 292.

10. Goldberg, *American Veda*, 157.

11. Goldberg, *American Veda*, 157–158.

12. Stark and Bainbridge, *The Future of Religion*, 292.

13. Thomas A. Forsthoefel and Cynthia Ann Humes, eds., *Gurus in America* (Albany: State University of New York Press, 2005), 62–65.

14. Goldberg, *American Veda*, 164.

15. Goldberg, *American Veda*, 166–168.

16. Forsthoefel and Humes, *Gurus in America*, 65.

17. Stark and Bainbridge, *The Future of Religion*, 301–302.

18. Stark and Bainbridge, *The Future of Religion*, 299.

19. Goldberg, *American Veda*, 170.

20. Goldberg, *American Veda*, 170.

21. Stark and Bainbridge, *The Future of Religion*, 299.

CHAPTER 3

1. See http://stgabe.org/stgabe-origin.

2. See http://minet.org/www.trancenet.net/secrets/puja/oath.shtml.

3. See http://www.maharishiyagya.org/jyotish/, http://www.vediccity planning.com/architecture-and-urban-design-in-harmony-with-nature/, and http://www.mapi.com/ayurveda_health_care/self_care/blissfuljoy.html.

4. *Malnak v. Yogi* Civ. A. No. 76-341. 440 F. Supp. 1284 (1977), United States District Court, D. New Jersey. October 20, 1977. http://www.leagle.com/decision /19771724440FSupp1284_11529.

5. See Cynthia Ann Humes, "Maharishi Mahesh Yogi: Beyond the TM Technique," in Forsthoefel and Humes, *Gurus in America*, 55–79.

6. Humes, "Maharishi Mahesh Yogi," 55–79.

7. Humes, "Maharishi Mahesh Yogi," 55–79.

8. Evan Finkelstein of MUM argues that TM mantras do not use the names of Hindu gods in "The Mantras Used in TM Are Some of the Most Fundamental Vibrations of Natural Law," a commentary found at http://www.truthabouttm.org /truth/IndividualEffects/IsTMaReligion/TMMantras/index.cfm. For a counterargument, see "Trancenet: What's Your Mantra Mean?" available at http://minet .org/www.trancenet.net/secrets/mantras.shtml.

9. See Stark and Bainbridge, *The Future of Religion*, 24–26.

10. Stark and Bainbridge, *The Future of Religion*. See chap. 13, "The Rise and Decline of Transcendental Meditation," with Daniel H. Jackson, 284–303. The chapter was originally published in Bryan Wilson, ed., *The Social Impact of New Religious Movements* (New York: Rose of Sharon Press, 1981), 135–158.

11. For a full discussion of Noyes and the Oneida Community, see Lawrence Foster, "Free Love and Community: John Humphrey Noyes and the Oneida Perfectionists," in Pitzer, ed., *America's Communal Utopias*, 253–278.

12. See Dean L. May, "One Heart and Mind: Communal Life and Values among the Mormons," in Pitzer, ed., *America's Communal Utopias*, 135–158.

13. Karl J. R. Arndt, "George Rapp's Harmony Society," in Pitzer, ed., *America's Communal Utopias*, 57–87.

14. See "TM Comes to the Heartland of the Midwest," available at http://www.religion-online.org/showarticle.asp?title=1863.

15. "David Lynch Is Back . . . as a Guru of Transcendental Meditation," *New York Times Magazine*, February 22, 2013, available at http://www.nytimes.com/2013/02/24/magazine/david-lynch-transcendental-meditation.html?pagewanted=all&_r=0.

16. See http://bethshalomfairfield.com/about-us/.

17. See http://www.smallsynagogues.com/fairfield_io.htm.

18. See Denise Denniston, *The TM Book: How to Enjoy the Rest of Your Life* (Fairfield, IA: Fairfield Press, 1991), 56.

19. See http://stgabe.org/content/easter-sermons-2011.

20. See http://www.divinemotheronline.net/about/about-the-founder-connie-huebner/.

CHAPTER 4

1. See http://factfinder2.census.gov/faces/nav/jsf/pages/index.xhtml.

2. See Bob Saar, "Worth a Trip to Iowa, Sondheim Theater," *The Hawk Eye*, November 15, 2009, available at http://www.thehawkeye.com/story/McCartney-review-111509.

3. See Irina Alexsander, "Look Who's Meditating Now," *New York Times*, March 18, 2011, available at http://www.nytimes.com/2011/03/20/fashion/20TM.html?pagewanted=all.

4. See Alexsander, "Look Who's Meditating Now."

5. See http://www.davidlynchfoundation.org/.

6. See http://www.tm.org/blog/people/howard-stern-and-david-letterman-discuss-tm/.

7. A youthful Stern interviewed the guru in 1985. See http://www.youtube.com/watch?v=GJQweEsgupM.

8. See http://www.youtube.com/watch?v=7sUv2kQjyXI.

9. See Ben Smith, "Obama Wows Iowa Meditators," Politico.com, July 5, 2007, available at http://www.politico.com/news/stories/0707/4797.html.

CHAPTER 5

1. See Scott Canon, "Maharishi's Followers Have Integrated into Small Iowa Town," *Kansas City Star*, September 27, 1999, or at http://www.rickross.com/reference/tm/tm5.html.

2. See http://fairfieldsafemeters.com/.

3. See http://www.natural-law.org/news/press_articles/2000_08_30.html.

4. See Neil King Jr., "Meditators Back Paul for Peace," *Wall Street Journal*, January 3, 2012, available at http://online.wsj.com/article/SB10001424052970204368104577136890939606290.html.

CHAPTER 6

1. The TM-Sidhi program, which includes Yogic Flying, also drew legal action. Four individuals sued parts of the movement, including the university, in part over the technique. The movement lost a 1985 case in trial court but won on appeal, on certain grounds, and settled for undisclosed terms rather than face retrial on other grounds. In a case that was dismissed, the Court of Appeals for the District of Columbia Circuit held that claims were time-barred under the discovery rule because "the defendants made representations which any reasonable person would recognize as being contrary to common human experience and, indeed, to the laws of physics. If, as Ms. Hendel alleges, she was told that meditators would slowly rise in the air, and that some of them were 'flying over Lake Lucern' or 'walking through walls, hovering, and becoming invisible,' and that her failure to go to bed on time could bring about World War III, then a reasonable person would surely have noticed, at some time prior to September 1, 1986, that some of these representations might not be true." See *Hendel v. World Plan Executive Council and Maharishi International University*, Appellees, No. 96-CV-105, available at http://caselaw.findlaw.com/dc-court-of-appeals/1316965.html.

2. Consciousness-Based Books, an imprint of the Maharishi University of Management Press, published a twelve-volume set of books in 2011 under the series title Consciousness-Based Education: A Foundation for Teaching and Learning in the Academic Disciplines. They address Maharishi Vedic Science, physiology and health, mathematics, art, government, sustainable living, education, physics, literature, management, computer science, and world peace. A note at the close of every book explains that "each volume includes a paper introducing the

Consciousness-Based understanding of the discipline and a Unified Field Chart that conceptually maps all branches of the discipline, illustrating how the discipline emerges from the field of pure consciousness, the Self of every individual. These charts connect the 'parts' of knowledge to the 'wholeness' of knowledge and the wholeness of knowledge to the Self of the student." See Keith Levi and Paul Corazza, eds., *Consciousness-Based Education and Computer Science* (Fairfield, IA: Maharishi University of Management Press, 2011), 107–150.

3. For the full interview, see http://master-degree-online.com/interview-maharishi-university-of-management/.

4. See Terrance Fairchild, ed., *Consciousness-Based Education and Literature* (Fairfield, IA: Maharishi University of Management Press, 2011), 223–278.

5. Fairchild, ed., *Consciousness-Based Education and Literature*, 283–346.

6. Fairchild, ed., *Consciousness-Based Education and Literature*, 171–197.

7. See Susan Fulton Welty, *A Fair Field*, Bicentennial ed. (Detroit: Harlo Press, 1975).

8. See http://www.mum.edu/about/history.html.

9. See Welty, *A Fair Field*.

10. See http://www.mum.edu/about/history.html.

11. *Maharishi University of Management, Education for Enlightenment: The Story of Consciousness-Based Education* (Fairfield, Iowa: Maharishi University of Management Press, 2011), a booklet distributed by the university.

12. *Maharishi University of Management, Education for Enlightenment*, 9.

13. *Maharishi University of Management, Education for Enlightenment*, 9.

14. *Maharishi University of Management, Education for Enlightenment*, 16.

15. See http://master-degree-online.com/interview-maharishi-university-of-management/.

16. See http://www.collegetimes.tv/maharishi-university-of-management/#reviews.

17. For full-time beginning undergraduates, the average net price of the school, calculated after financial aid, was $16,261 in the latest reporting period, 2010–11. Before aid, all costs, including on-campus living costs, for undergrads totaled $35,230 in 2011–12.

18. Total fall enrollment at MUM, tracked by the National Center for Education Statistics, peaked at 3,231 in 1989, with the numbers dipping to 631 in 1993, then climbing to 1,422 in 1997. The enrollment then trended downward to 695 in 2004 and rebounded to 1,206 in 2008. It then dipped to 1,199 in 2009, to 1,180 in 2010, and to 1,134 in the fall of 2011. Undergraduates in 2011 accounted for 350 of the 1,134 total enrollment. Readers may build tables with the annual data at http://nces.ed.gov/ipeds/datacenter/Trend.aspx?hfSelectedIds=23355|10|||.

19. See http://nces.ed.gov/collegenavigator/?q=Maharishi+University+of+Management&s=IA&id=153861.

20. See http://www.act.org/research/policymakers/pdf/retain_2010.pdf.

21. The university in 2013 published revised projections on its website, at http://www.mum.edu/RelId/636786/ISvars/default/Financial_Projections.htm. Its earlier projections are available at http://www.mum.edu/Customized/Uploads/ByDate/2012/November_2012/November_11th_2012/2011%20Strategic%20Plan%20sgl%20pg22737.pdf.

22. See http://www.mum.edu/Customized/Uploads/ByDate/2012/November_2012/November_11th_2012/2011%20Strategic%20Plan%20sgl%20pg22737.pdf.

23. See "Towns Meditate on Fate of Peace Palace Project," Associated Press, September 19, 2008, at http://www.rickross.com/reference/tm/tm178.html.

24. See http://www.maharishicentraluniversity.org/.

25. See Mike Corn, "TM Project in Smith County on Hold," *Hays Daily News*, April 7, 2010.

CHAPTER 7

1. See http://www.myspace.com/levibutler.

2. See http://www.myspace.com/levibutler.

3. For more information about the Desert Sands Student Assistance Program, see http://www.dsusd.us/DSUSD/EducationalServices/StudentAP/.

4. *Estate of Levi Andelin Butler v. Maharishi University*, U.S. District Court for the Southern District of Iowa, Central Division, Case 4:06-cv-00072-JEG, First Amended and Substituted Complaint and Jury Demand.

5. See http://www.truthabouttm.org/truth/IndividualEffects/Researchon MentalHealth/index.cfm.

6. See Denniston, *The TM Book*, 203. Further, on page 101 she says "psychological stability—maintenance of mental and emotional balance—increases" with TM, as indicated by "increased emotional stability, decreased anxiety, reduced depression, reduced neuroticism, stronger intellect, stability of attention, increased inner control, increased self-confidence, stabilization of organized memory, increased individuality, increased self-actualization, increased self-esteem." She adds, "Psychological stability develops automatically when the mind repeatedly gains and becomes habituated to its most stable status—pure consciousness—through the regular practice of the TRANSCENDENTAL MEDITATION technique."

7. See http://pieceofsite.seniorbrown.com/LeviReport.txt.

8. See *Fairfield Ledger*, March 4, 2004, and http://www.religionnewsblog.com/6331/mum-officials-suspect-was-calm-after-first-assault.

9. See Judge Gritzner's order of December 11, 2008, available at http://www.leagle.com/xmlResult.aspx?xmldoc=20081739589dcfsupp2d1150_11633.xml&docbase=CSLWAR3-2007-CURR.

10. See http://www.guardian.co.uk/world/2004/may/02/usa.theobserver.

11. See Judge Gritzner's order of December 11, 2008.

12. See http://nces.ed.gov/collegenavigator/?id=153861.

13. See http://nces.ed.gov/collegenavigator/?q=University+of+Iowa&s=all &id=153658.

14. See http://www.fbi.gov/about-us/cjis/ucr/crime-in-the-u.s/2010/crime -in-the-u.s.-2010/tables/table-8/10tbl08ia.xls.

15. See http://www.guardian.co.uk/world/2004/may/02/usa.theobserver.

16. See http://www.familyaware.org/.

17. See http://www.youtube.com/watch?v=mqYTEShW3cA.

18. See http://ww2.gazette.net/stories/10072008/poolnew192824_32476.shtml.

19. See http://ww2.gazette.net/stories/10072008/poolnew192824_32476.shtml.

20. Norman E. Rosenthal, *Transcendence: Healing and Transformation through Transcendental Meditation* (New York: Jeremy P. Tarcher/Penguin, 2012), 151–152.

CHAPTER 8

1. To see how MSAE presents its program to applicants, see the school's web-site at http://www.maharishischooliowa.org/.

2. See "Introduction to Invincibility Schools: Total Knowledge for Every Student, Invincibility for the Nation," 2007, available online at http://www.maharishi school.ch/files/Inv_School_Intro_070505_EN.pdf.

3. See the Dillbecks' paper at http://old.mum.edu/pdf_msvs/v01/dillbeck.pdf.

4. See http://www.maharishischooliowa.org/.

5. See http://www.maharishischooliowa.org/.

6. See http://www.maharishischooliowa.org/.

7. See http://www.maharishischooliowa.org/.

CHAPTER 9

1. See http://www.absolutelythepurest.com/retailer/store_templates/shell _id_1.asp?storeID=58FA72C67A3D4A83BA7FCE7BF4843E8D.

2. Gratzon offered career counsel in *The Lazy Way to Success: How to Do Nothing and Accomplish Everything* (Fairfield, IA: Soma Press, 2003). See http://lazyway .blogs.com/lazy_way/page/11/.

3. For a detailed discussion of the travails of the Great Midwestern Ice Cream Company, see Paul B. Brown, "When Quality Isn't Everything," *Inc.*, June 1, 1989, available at http://www.inc.com/magazine/19890601/5691.html.

4. See Rick Tetzeli, "Getting an MBA the Maharishi Way," *Fortune*, January 25, 1993, available at http://money.cnn.com/magazines/fortune/fortunearchive/1993 /01/25/77422/index.htm.

5. For information about the book, see http://www.instantathlete.com/.

6. See http://gratzon.com/fred/garden.htm for a full description of the Gratzon home.

7. See "Kucinich's Own Crusade," *Washington Times*, January 14, 2004, available at http://www.washingtontimes.com/news/2004/jan/14/20040114-113844-3797r /?page=all.

8. See Frank Santiago, "Infomercial Guru Pleads Guilty Right before Trial," *Des Moines Register*, July 1, 1998. The case, filed in U.S. District Court in the Southern District of Iowa, was case no. 4-97-cr-54.

9. See Ed Beckley, *Dance of a Rich Yogi: Liberation through Loss* (n.p.: 1st Books Library, 2002).

10. See *State of Iowa v. Vision Improvement Technologies*, Iowa District Court for Polk County, case no. CE51687.

CHAPTER 10

1. For a detailed discussion of the book series and its ties to Fairfield, see Burt Chojnowski, "Open-Source Rural Entrepreneurial Development," *Rural Research Report*, Illinois Institute for Rural Affairs, 17, issue 2 (Spring 2006).

2. Earl Kaplan confirmed this account. The full text of his open letter is available at http://tmfree.blogspot.com/2008/04/earl-kaplans-letter.html.

3. Judith Bourque, *Robes of Silk, Feet of Clay*. See http://robesofsilkfeetofclay .com/.

4. David Kaplan's letter is available at http://www.mail-archive.com/fairfield life@yahoogroups.com/msg06623.html.

5. For details, see Sally Treadwell, "What's Going on at Heavenly Mountain?," *High Country Press*, March 2, 2006, available at http://highcountrypress.com /weekly/2006/03-02-06/n_heavenly.htm.

6. See Monte Mitchell, "Heavenly Way Complex Up for Sale," *Winston-Salem Journal*, September 13, 2011, available at http://www2.journalnow.com/news/2011 /sep/13/wsmet01-complex-up-for-sale-ar-1383933/. Also see Ben Wofford, "The Past, Present and Future of Heavenly Mountain: Boone's Hidden Wonder Finally Finds Restoration and Respect," *High Country Magazine*, June 2012, available at http://www.hcpress.com/news/his-holiness-sri-sri-ravi-shankar-to-inaugurate -world-class-international-center-for-peace-and-well-being.html.

7. See http://www.davidwantstofly.com/.

8. See http://www.thetruelight.net/personalstories/kaidruhl.htm.

9. See http://tmfree.blogspot.com/2008/05/thirty-years-later-what-was-all -that.html.

10. See Stark and Bainbridge, *The Future of Religion*, 284–303.

11. See http://nccam.nih.gov/health/meditation/overview.htm.

12. This account is drawn from Deepak Chopra, "The Maharishi Years—The Untold Story: Recollections of a Former Disciple," *The Huffington Post*, February 13,

2008, available at http://www.huffingtonpost.com/deepak-chopra/the-maharishi
-years-the-u_b_86412.html.

13. See http://www.krystofiak.com/jupiter.html.

CHAPTER 11

1. See "Vedic City Considers Eminent Domain to Seize Farmer's Land," Associated Press, June 26, 2007, available at http://www.rickross.com/reference/tm/
tm157.html.

2. For a discussion of the architecture, see http://www.vastu-vidya.org/en
/index.php?page=VEDIC_ARCHITECTURE&f=1&i=VEDIC_ARCHITEC
TURE.

3. See http://www.theraj.com/.

4. Gilpin, *The Maharishi Effect*, 136.

5. See "Vedic City Considers Eminent Domain to Seize Farmer's Land."

6. See http://guruphiliac.blogspot.com/2007/06/senile-old-man-hates-hogs
.html.

7. See http://kindwordand2x4.blogspot.com/2011/11/0707-stupid-people.html.

8. Lyrics quoted by permission of Tony Arnold. See http://musaphonic.band
camp.com/album/shadowbox.

9. See "Vedic City Considers Eminent Domain to Seize Farmer's Land."

10. See "Century Farm Should Stay," *Ottumwa Courier*, June 29, 2007, available at
http://ottumwacourier.com/opinion/x519417447/Century-farm-should-stay.

11. For more details on the planned golf course, see http://www.maharishive
diccity-iowa.gov/amenities/golf.html.

12. See "Vedic City to Break Ground on Housing for 500," Erik Gable, *Fairfield
Daily Ledger*, April 22, 2004, available at http://www.rickross.com/reference/tm
/tm87.html.

CHAPTER 12

1. For background on Lynch's foundation, see http://www.davidlynchfounda-
tion.org/.

2. Gilpin, *The Maharishi Effect*, 203–204.

3. The TM Movement has punished critics. The late L. B. Trusty Shriver, a former student body president at MUM, for instance, was denied privileges to meditate in the dome because he published a newspaper criticizing movement practices.
The MSAE grad quoted here fears jeopardizing a relationship with a movement
organization.

4. For the TM Movement's view of its research, see http://www.tm.org/
research-on-meditation/.

5. Rosenthal, *Transcendence*, 8–14.

6. Peter H. Canter and Edzard Ernst, "The Cumulative Effects of Transcendental Meditation on Cognitive Function—A Systematic Review of Randomised Controlled Trials," *Wiener Klinische Wochenschrift* 115, nos. 21–22 (2003): 758–766, available at http://link.springer.com/article/10.1007%2FBF03040500.

7. For details about Trinity College's meditation instruction, available through its chaplaincy program, see http://www.trincoll.edu/StudentLife/SpiritualReligiousLife/communities/Pages/The.aspx.

8. See http://www.politico.com/news/stories/0512/75872.html.

9. See http://www.easwaran.org/eknath-easwaran.html.

10. See http://www.alist.vanityfair.co.uk/a-list/2013–01/what-to-do.

11. See http://www.ted.com/talks/andy_puddicombe_all_it_takes_is_10 _mindful_minutes.html.

12. See http://blogs.desmoinesregister.com/dmr/index.php/2011/11/29/maharishi-foundation-to-competitor-meditate-on-this-lawsuit/.

13. See http://themeditationhouse.com/2011/12/01/response/.

14. See http://themeditationhouse.com/2011/12/01/response/.

SELECTED BIBLIOGRAPHY

○   ○   ○

Bourque, Judith. *Robes of Silk, Feet of Clay.* Self-published, 2010.
 Bourque provides an insider's account of the early days of the TM Movement, with autobiographical reflections on her romantic encounters with the guru.

Denniston, Denise. *The TM Book: How to Enjoy the Rest of Your Life.* Fairfield, IA: Fairfield Press, 1991.
 This guide to TM offers a movement supporter's descriptions and views of meditation and its values.

Forsthoefel, Thomas A., and Cynthia Ann Humes, eds. *Gurus in America.* Albany: State University of New York Press, 2005.
 This volume discusses important gurus who have brought their teachings to the West.

Gilpin, Geoff. *The Maharishi Effect: A Personal Journey through the Movement That Transformed American Spirituality.* New York: Jeremy P. Tarcher/Penguin, 2006.
 This affecting memoir recounts a devotee's return to Fairfield after years away.

Goldberg, Philip. *American Veda: From Emerson and the Beatles to Yoga and Meditation—How Indian Spirituality Changed the West.* New York: Harmony Books, 2010.
 The author traces the rich history of Indian gurus who brought their traditions to the United States. He argues that their influence has been pervasive.

Gratzon, Fred. *The Lazy Way to Success: How to Do Nothing and Accomplish Everything.* Fairfield, IA: Soma Press, 2003.
 Advice from a successful entrepreneur.

Levi, Keith, and Paul Corazza, eds. *Consciousness-Based Education and Computer Science*. Fairfield, IA: Maharishi University Press, 2011.

This text links the canons of the TM Movement with computer science. It is part of a twelve-volume set published under the series title Consciousness-Based Education: A Foundation for Teaching and Learning in the Academic Disciplines. The texts address Maharishi Vedic Science, physiology and health, mathematics, art, government, sustainable living, education, physics, literature, management, computer science, and world peace.

Pitzer, Donald E., ed. *America's Communal Utopias*. Chapel Hill: University of North Carolina Press, 1997.

This is a richly detailed and thorough history of intentional communities that have risen and fallen in the United States over time.

Rosenthal, Norman E. *Transcendence: Healing and Transformation through Transcendental Meditation*. New York: Jeremy P. Tarcher/Penguin, 2012.

Rosenthal, a psychiatrist at Georgetown Medical School, details stories of people whose lives, including his own, were changed by meditating. He taps clinical research on the practice to support claims about its health effects.

Stark, Rodney, and William Sims Bainbridge. *The Future of Religion: Secularization, Revival, and Cult Formation*. Berkeley: University of California Press, 1985.

This scholarly work provides a comprehensive survey of religions in the modern world, including emerging faiths.

Yogananda, Paramahansa. *Autobiography of a Yogi*. Los Angeles: Self-Realization Fellowship, 1946.

An influential work, it paved the way for modern Indian gurus in the United States.

INTERVIEWEES

Tim Bahr
Richard Beall
Jim Belilove
Marc Berkowitz
Laura Bordow
Jill Bormann
Connie Boyer
Robert Boyer
Kent Boyum
Mark Brase

Dean R. Broyles
Miles T. Bryant
Jimmy Caplan
Richard J. Davidson
Mike Doughney
Larry E. Fells
Damian Finol
Fred Gratzon
Mark Hagist
Doug Hamilton

Julie Harvey
Cody Heyn
Judy Heyn
Michael Heyn
Michael H. Jackson
Jason Kaplan
Jim Karpen
Suzan Kessel
John M. Knapp
Charles Knoles
Mayor Ed Malloy
Erin McCann
Gregg Morton
Robert Palm
Craig Pearson
Joseph Phipps
Andy Puddicombe
Robert Rasmussen
Jeff Rice

Kenneth Ross
Bob Roth
Jim Rothblatt
Tom Rowe
Jan Ryan
Becky Schmitz
Eric Schwartz
Shuvender Sem
L. B. Trusty Shriver
Patrik Siljestam
Andrew Skolnick
Pamela K. Slowick
Rodney Stark
Mahesh Subrahmanyam
Francis Thicke
Julie Totten
Fred Travis
Howard Wolinsky

INDEX

○   ○   ○

jobs, 26, 82, 83
John F. Kennedy Space Center, 140
Johnson, Chris, 174
Johnson, Dee, 174
Jones, Ellen, 63
Jones, Sonia Tudor, 32
Jung, C. G., 74
Jyotish, 29, 119

Kabbalah, 42
kalashes, 132, 139, 169
Kansas City Star, 63
Kaplan, David, 145–49
Kaplan, Earl, 145–50
Karan, Donna, 58
Karpen, Jim, 84
Karunamayi, 47
Karunamayi, Amma Sri, 52
Kemp, Jack, 134
Kennedy, John F., 91
Kessel, Suzan, 53
Killian, John, 93–95, 98, 100
Knapp, John M., 158–59
Knight, Gladys, 54
Knoles, Charles
Knoles, Thom, 98
Krystofiak, Thom, 163–64
Kucinich, Dennis J., 140

Lass, John P., 136
Leadership (publication), 31
Lee, Mother Ann, 6
Lennon, John, 148
Leno, Jay, 58
Letterman, David, 58, 142
libertarians, 69
Life magazine, 74–75
livestock, 67, 167–68, 170–72
lodging, 60, 62, 126, 172–74
Look magazine, 11, fig. 1
Love, Mike, 54
Lubavitchers, 5. *See also* Chabad
     Lubavitch rabbis

Lutheran church, 38, 61, 62
Lynch, David, 12, 30, 41, 54–56, 67,
     149–50
Lynch Foundation. *See* David Lynch
     Foundation

Mackey, Douglas A., 74
MacLaine, Shirley, 1
MAD magazine, 11, fig. 2
Maharaja Adhiraj Raja Raam. *See*
     Nader, Tony
Maharishi Ayurveda, 29
Maharishi Center for Health and World
     Peace, 168. *See also* Maharishi Vedic
     City (MVC)
Maharishi Central University, 87–88
Maharishi Effect, 22–24, 68, 82, 87,
     89–90, 99–101, 189
Maharishi European Research Univer-
     sity, 62, 175
Maharishi Foundation–USA, 56, 98,
     179, 188–89, 194n10
Maharishi Global Administration
     through Natural Law, 194n10
Maharishi Global Construction, 64
Maharishi Global Development Fund,
     138–39, 194n10
Maharishi International University, 22,
     39–40, 43, 46, 75–77, 151, 156, 162–63
Maharishi Light Therapy with Gems,
     169
Maharishi Mahesh Yogi: in American
     culture, 1–2, 19–20; on architecture,
     16, 71, 77; on business, 126, 127; and
     Butler murder, 102–4; celibacy of, 13,
     35, 147–48, 150; changes in dictates,
     180–81; death of, 11, 88, 150; devotees
     in Fairfield, 9, 10, 128–29; dishon-
     esty of, 148, 149, 152; and education,
     24–26, 71–73, 78, 82, 111–18, 120, 122; at
     European TM organization, 130; Fred
     Gratzon with, 133; fundraising by,
     14; and future of TM, 11; on Hindu

conversion, 19; as "His Holiness," 29–30, 56; illness of, 161–62; influence in Fairfield politics, 63; and Kaplans, 145–47; legacy of, 3, 5, 6, 18; loyalty to, 46–47; marketing by, 19–22, 34–35, 155–57; on ministers as meditators, 40; popularity of, 11, 17, 19–22; on radiation, 66, 81, 109; science of, 75, 181–82; on self-sufficiency, 176; Thom Knoles with, 98; use of celebrities, 57–58, 185; videos of, 14, 93

Maharishi Purusha Program, 194n10

Maharishi Research Institute, 56

Maharishi School of the Age of Enlightenment: city council members at, 63; Claire Hoffman at, 41; competition at, 117–18; cost of, 117; criticism of, 159–61; curriculum at, 110–22, 160; enrollment at, 13, 119–22, 124, 189; funding of, 56, 124; future leaders from, 181; future of, 11; goals of, 109–11; Jake Gratzon at, 139; Jonathan Clifford at, 176, 177; leadership of, 10, 123–24, 179, fig. 14; Pamela Slowick's children to, 128–29; Richard Wolfson at, 66; Trusty Shriver at, 202n3

Maharishi University of Management: assets of, 194n10; avoidance of, 38; board of trustees of, 132, 138; buildings of, fig. 10, fig. 11, fig. 12; business owners at, 129, 142; chapel at, 54–55; city council members at, 63; commencement ceremonies at, 58–59; cost of, 82–83, 198n17; criticism and appeal of, 81–84, 96; curriculum at, 71–75, 77–79, 82, 84, 197n2; enrollment at, 13, 71, 84–87, 90, 154, 198n18; faculty and staff compensation at, 86–87, 105, 152, 165; founding of, 42, 75–76, 140, 156; funding of, 56, 86, 154, 189; future leaders from, 181; future of, 11, 15, 154; goals of, 26, 76–77, 79–80, 85, 87, 88, 183–84;

Internet connections at, 109; John Hagelin at, 57; Jonathan Clifford at, 176, 177; Kai Druhl at, 150; Levi Bulter at, 89–98; litigation against, 71, 197n1; McCanns at, 159, 161; meditation frequency at, 179; meditation in domes at, 9, 10, 40, 46–49, 71, 77, 80, 84, 99–100, 159, 163–65, fig. 10; meditators' conflict with, 4; MSAE graduates to, 117; MSAE leadership at, 123; political representation for, 61; research at, 187; Richard Beall at, 110; Richard Wolfson at, 66; Robert Boyer at, 62; Robert Wynne at, 175; safety at, 88, 94–100, 102–4, 108; success of, 3; suicides at, 105; support of Ed Malloy at, 64; Trusty Shriver at, 202n3; William Goldstein at, 174; Yogic Flying at, 23

Maharishi University of Management Press, 72, 73, 197n2

Maharishi Vedic City (MVC), 3–4, 9, 29–30, 115, 126, 138–39, 167–75, 190, fig. 17, fig. 18, fig. 19

Maharishi Vedic Observatory, 173

Maharishi Vedic Science, 10, 21, 29, 30, 34, 41, 56, 71–74, 77–78, 98, 114–15, 173, 197n2

Maharishi Word of Wisdom, 110

Malloy, Ed, 63–66, fig. 6

Malnak v. Yogi (1977), 30, 33, 56

Mandala One Village, 174

mandalas, 173

mantra meditation, 2, 17, 18, 30, 31, 44–45, 185–88

mantras, 9, 21, 31, 35, 37, 71, 153, 195n8

marketing, 14, 19–22, 34–35, 90, 98, 99, 120–22, 133–34, 145–46, 149, 155–57, 183–86

marriage, 12, 36, 46, 148, 150–51

Maryland, 106–7, 127–28

Massachusetts, 12, 18, 24, 47, 104, 127, 140

Massachusetts Institute of Technology, 18, 83, 110, 175

math, 119, 197n2

McCann, Erin, 159–61

McCartney, James, 54

McCartney, Paul, 12, 54, 148

media, 15, 17, 23, 68, 134

medication, 51, 92, 95, 96, 101–2, 106–8

meditation: attitudes toward, 1, 6, 186–87; benefits of, 21–22, 33, 40, 55, 92, 104, 106, 108, 113, 131–32, 141, 155–56, 181–83, 188–89, 199n6; in business, 125–33, 137, 140, 141; at Carolina International School, 123–24; dangers of, 96–97, 101–2, 107–8, 151–53, 158–59; Deepak Chopra's study of, 161–62; denial of badges for, 46, 163; education in, 12, 55–57, 148, 183–84; effect of Butler murder on, 89–90; in Fairfield, 9–10, 36–38; history of, 2; Levi Butler on, 91; in mainstream American culture, 1–3, 184; at MSAE, 110, 117–19, 121; practice by modern followers, 177–78, 181; routine at MUM, 80–81, 83–84; statistics on teaching of, 157–58; techniques of, 2, 4–5, 16–20, 30, 32, 41, 49, 93, 98, 147, 158, 163, 180–82, 185–88. *See also* mantra meditation; meditators; TM-Sidhi program; Transcendental Meditation (TM); Vedic Meditation

The Meditation House LLC, 188–89

meditators: and arts center, 52–54; aspirations of, 177–79; attitudes toward in Fairfield, 5, 14–15, 36–42, 51, 59, 65, 132–33; attitudes toward in Smith County, 88; attraction to Fairfield, 9–10, 189; college credit for, 84; decline in number, 147; at Global Country of World Peace, 139; at Heavenly Mountain resort, 149; to India for world peace, 146; in investment scam, 143; irresponsibility of,

159; at MSAE, 120, 121; in MVC, 168–69; payment of, 85, 100, 165; in politics, 60–70; suicides of, 106; worship by, 28–29, 41–46. *See also* pandits

mental illness, 92, 93, 95–97, 99, 101, 104–8

mental well-being, 17, 32, 33, 41, 50, 56, 76, 77, 92, 96–97, 104, 105, 126, 131–32, 141, 158–59, 173, 199n6

military, 50, 57, 64, 68, 103–4. *See also* veterans

military colleges, 56, 184

Miller, Thomas J., 142

mind reading, 23

mindfulness meditation, 184–87

Minnesota, 67

minyan, 43

Missouri Synod, 38

Moby, 54

money, 17, 170, 180

Monsanto, 68, 140

Moore, James, 15

Moore, Mary Tyler, 22, 58

Mormons, 5, 14, 29, 33–34, 36, 160

Morris, Bevan, 77–78, 99, 100, 103

Morton, Gregg, 101

Mother Divine, 148

MUM. *See* Maharishi University of Management

Muslims, 28

MVC. *See* Maharishi Vedic City

mysticism, 21, 41, 42, 45, 186

Nader, Tony, 115–16, 177

National Center for Complementary and Alternative Medicine, 2, 158

National Center for Education Statistics, 84, 86, 100, 198n18

National Center for Law and Policy of Escondido, California, 32

National Center for Small Communities, 126

National Institutes of Health, 2, 158, 178

spirituality, 5, 17, 18, 21, 41, 44, 76, 80, 121, 123, 127, 151, 153, 157

Spivak, Michael, 194n10

sports, 117–18, 138, 174–75, 184

St. Gabriel and All Angels Church, 28–29, 43–46

Stanford University, 75, 110, 175

Stanley, Tom, 63

Stark, Rodney, 33–35, 157–58

Starr, Ringo, 12, 54, 148

Stephanopoulos, George, 11, 12, 34, 58

Stern, Howard, 12, 34, 57–58

Steven Sondheim Center for the Performing Arts, 51, 52, 54

Strategic Planning Council, 64

stress, 1–2, 4, 21, 32, 55, 56, 58, 79–80, 84, 87, 93, 104, 110, 113, 118, 122, 133, 141, 151–52, 155–57, 169, 184, 188

Students' International Meditation Society, 20

Stump, Robert, 69

substance abuse, 54, 56, 76, 85, 100, 104, 122, 159, 160

Sufis, 5, 41, 45

suicides, 90, 104–8

sun, 119, 169, 173

SunnyBrook Assisted Living facility, 141

Sunpoint meditation, 49

Super Radiance Dairy, 67

Super Radiancy, 82

Survival in Paradise (newspaper), 163–64

sustainable living systems, 26, 66–68, 71, 84, 121, 132, 141, 149, 154, 183–84. *See also* environmental concerns

Swami Brahmananda Saraswati Jagadguru. *See* Guru Dev

Swami Nikhilananda, 19

Swami Prabhavananda, 19

Sykes, David E., 143

Taansen Fairmont Sumeru. *See* Freeston, David

t'ai chi, 184

Taize services, 37

teachers of TM: business owners as, 128, 129, 133, 142; dispatch of, 14, 24–25; dissent of, 16–17, 26, 151–53; first in Iowa, 162; harassment by, 98; mantras from, 71; at MIU, 76–77; at MSAE, 111–13, 115–18; MSAE leadership as, 122–23; at MUM, 71, 75, 78, 81, 86–87, 101–2; oath of, 29; in public schools, 31; shunning of, 47–48

technology, 31, 57, 68, 116, 126, 129–30, 141–42, 146, 185; wireless, 66, 81, 109–10

TED Talks academic conference website, 186

Telegroup, 135–37

television commercials, 14

television networks, 68, 134. *See also* individual network names

tennis, 117–18, 138

Texas, 25, 130

Thicke, Francis, 66–68

Thoreau, Henry David, 2

Thymely Solutions, 8, 11, 38, 125, 128, 129, fig. 8

Tibetan-style meditation, 182

Time magazine, 11, 23

TM-Sidhi program, 23, 71, 74, 87, 115, 151, 163, 176, 197n1

Today Show, 134

Totten, Julie, 105–6

Totten, Mark A., 104–5

tourism, 12, 64, 190

trademarks, 4, 188–89

Transcendental Meditation (TM): in American culture, 2–3, 12; attitudes toward in Smith County, 88; critics of, 4, 13, 18, 22–26, 29, 30, 32–33, 37, 82, 96–99, 141, 145–66, 170–71, 181–83, 186, 202n3; decline of, 18, 23, 25–26, 35–36, 157, 163; devotees in Fairfield, 9; future of, 4–5, 11–16, 27, 154, 157–58, 165,

Winfrey, Oprah, 11, 12
Winn, Steven, 142
Wolfson, Richard, 66
World Plan, 22, 76–77
World's Parliament of Religions, 18
Wynne, Maureen, 168, 171, 175
Wynne, Robert G., 168, 175
Wysong, Joel, 94, 95, 103

Yagyas, 50
Yale University, 75, 113

Yellin, Steven, 138
yoga, 2, 23, 32–33, 119, 121, 184
Yogananda, Paramahansa, 19
Yogic Flying, 10, 13, 17, 23, 25–26, 41, 57, 71, 151, 163, 197n1. *See also* yoga
Young, Brigham, 33–34

Zell, Sam, 145
Zimbabwe, 24
Zimbalist, Efrem, Jr., 20
Zinn, John-Kabat, 186